SULTAN

SULTAN

A MEMOIR

WASIM AKRAM

with GIDEON HAIGH

Hardie Grant

BOOKS

Published in 2022 by Hardie Grant Books, an imprint of Hardie Grant Publishing

Hardie Grant Books (Melbourne)
Wurundjeri Country
Building 1, 658 Church Street
Richmond, Victoria 3121

Hardie Grant Books (London)
5th & 6th Floors
52–54 Southwark Street
London SE1 1UN

hardiegrant.com/au/books

 A catalogue record for this book is available from the National Library of Australia

Sultan: A Memoir
ISBN 978 1 74379 869 0

10 9 8 7 6 5 4 3 2 1

Publisher: Pam Brewster
Cover design by Luke Causby/Blue Cork
Typeset in ITC New Baskerville by Kirby Jones
Printed and bound in Great Britain by Clays Ltd, Elcograf S.p.A.

Hardie Grant acknowledges the Traditional Owners of the country on which we work, the Wurundjeri people of the Kulin nation and the Gadigal people of the Eora nation, and recognises their continuing connection to the land, waters and culture. We pay our respects to their Elders past and present.

To my children Tahmoor, Akbar and Aiyla, so you'll always have my story.

CONTENTS

Homing instinct: back where I came from in 2014.

INTRODUCTION

At the beginning of June 2014, I took a trip back in time.

It wasn't planned. It wasn't for a particular purpose. My father had died six weeks earlier. I had returned to Lahore for the first time since his funeral after seeing Kolkata Knight Riders, whom I was coaching, chase 200 to win the Indian Premier League. The campaign had been exhausting. Now I had a chance to pause, to visit my father's grave in Model Town, to share the news with family that my wife Shaniera was expecting our child, and to act on a vague homing instinct I had felt for a while – a desire to return to the area in which I'd grown up, where I'd played my first cricket in the street with a tape ball and an old bat. The place of my childhood. The place whose imprint is still on me.

I have been known to do things suddenly. Shaniera likes reminding me that I gave her two hours' notice of getting married – more on that later. But a spontaneous decision was the only way to make this trip. Had word got out in advance, the frenzy would have rendered it impossible. So I put on a blue T-shirt, tugged on a cap, and a friend's driver dropped us on Mozang Road, Mozang's main thoroughfare, near Ahmed Pura – bright, busy, crowded, alive. We turned into my old gali, barely a couple of metres from side to side and cast in shadow by three-storey frontages – something of a relief from the day's heat.

Having not been back for so long, I first of all noticed some changes. Paving had replaced the old red bricks. The open sewering had been covered. Otherwise it was all exactly as I remembered. The tandoor from which I had bought my rotis; the stall that sold what we thought were the best chickpeas in Lahore; the paan shop on the corner supplying the bitter leaf we Pakistanis chew; the mosque where we prayed; the schoolyard where my friends and I sometimes played after hours, except when we were chased away by a Pathan guard with a huge moustache: they were all there. I could have found my way blindfolded.

I started seeing faces I recognised. Where I had bought milk was now run by the former owner's offspring; people reappeared who I had played tape ball cricket against, now adults with children, to greet me as though I had never been away. The front of our tiny old house was also unchanged, save that the old green wooden door had been replaced with iron. We knocked and a tiny figure, an elderly mother, answered. 'I know you,' she said with a smile. 'You used to live here.'

I was welcomed warmly, and Shaniera with something like amazement – a pale-faced, fair-haired *gauri* (white woman) was in this gali a rare sight indeed. And the memories continued flooding back, of years here with my mother, her parents and my sister on the ground floor, while my uncle, his wife and their children lived upstairs. To the left was still the tiny kitchen with its simple stove;

on the right was where we had slept on our wood-framed, woven charpai, except for my grandfather because he rose early to sell vegetables near Mochi Darwaza, one of the old city gates. There even remained the interior door on which I had been allowed to stick posters of Imran Khan, Javed Miandad and Zaheer Abbas – the cricket gods who would improbably become my colleagues. Shaniera stood back a little, taking it all in, including the inch of water on the floor. Me, I could hardly wipe the smile off my face. Although I had an urban childhood, my friends jokingly call me a *pendu* – a villager, with the tastes and the world view of the village. I like simple things, straightforward people, common courtesies.

That makes me unusual. Patronage has always mattered in Pakistani cricket. The Pakistan Cricket Board chairman is a political appointee; there is a lineage of generals, judges and senior civil servants in the role. From the Mohammads to the Niazis, our game is pervaded by dynasties. Names recur: Ahmeds and Akmals; Rajas and Ranas. In the current team, Babar Azam, Abdullah Shafique, Imam ul Haq, Usman Qadir and Azam Khan are all sons, cousins or nephews of former players.

I have no such background. I picked cricket up from watching others. The approaching sprint, the fast arms, the back foot pointing to the sightscreen – they just came naturally. I went from the streets to the Test team in a couple of years despite having no link to the top and no cricket in my blood. I was still sleeping alongside my beloved, doting grandmother when I was selected, aged eighteen, to represent my country. 'I was praying for you my whole life,' she confided. 'Now you will be fine.' Almost forty years later, she has been proved right.

It has never, of course, been easy. Bowling fast extracts a lot from you, and I did it for twenty years. I ended up delivering more than 80,000 balls in first-class and List A cricket, and at least as many again at training. Yet cricket was never the problem. In some ways, challenging as it often was, it was the simplest part of my life. Bowling to Viv Richards, Sachin Tendulkar and Brian Lara or batting against Shane Warne, Malcolm Marshall or Muttiah Muralitharan was child's play compared to handling the expectations of my nation, the turmoil of my team and the machinations of my administration.

In Pakistan, nothing is as big as the country's XI. Cricket was the first thing my countrymen did to a global standard, what we have been best at for longest, what has most reliably united us – while also, on occasion, bitterly dividing us. Above all, it reflects us. People complain that the Pakistan team is not consistent. But the country itself is not consistent. Nothing in Pakistan happens the same way twice. On no institution can you entirely rely, and that goes right to the top: in three-quarters of a century, no Pakistani prime minister has served a full term. I played for thirteen different captains, most serving multiple terms; I had four spells in the job myself. I was under the supervision of ten national coaches and nine PCB chairmen. I recoiled from politics. But you know what they say: you might not be interested in politics, but politics is interested in you. It had a way of finding, frustrating and tormenting me; finally, as it expressed itself in the match-fixing controversies of the last decade of my career, it tainted me, and still does.

We did not have long that day in Mozang. I noticed the telltale signs of gathering commotion – for a well-known person in Pakistan, twenty minutes is about as long as you can spend anywhere in public – and we retraced our steps to the car. But I was ecstatic at having had my faith in my memory confirmed. It was all just as I remembered. And having seen the past light me up so, Shaniera started encouraging me to tell my story, of how the Ahmed Pura *pendu* had become the so-called Sultan of Swing. In all the chaos and controversies I had been part of, you see, I had kept my own counsel. I had never been sure what to do, what to say, where to begin. Suing for defamation in Pakistan is almost entirely pointless. And to head off every inaccurate story about you, particularly in the age of social media, would consume your whole life. But wasn't there a case, Shaniera said, for setting the record straight?

I had reservations. I could not claim only to be a victim. I have made some terrible mistakes. I harbour some deep regrets. And if I could not be completely frank, then there was no point, was there? So while I rush into some things, I brood on others. I got on with my life, which involved, among other things, being a good husband, and a better father to the sons, Tahmoor and Akbar, I had had with my first wife Huma, who died in 2009. Aiyla arrived at the end of 2014. She has been nothing but a joy. Now, at fifty-six, while I still suffer the diabetes that afflicted me in the second half of my career, I feel strong, secure and content.

There was, then, no particular moment or specific incident that made me change my mind, made me decide to write *Sultan*. I just gradually realised that I was ready. Most cricket autobiographies are written either during your career, when you can see nothing but the game, or immediately afterwards, when you have barely taken off your pads for the last time and are working out who you are now that you are no longer a cricketer. But dividing my time between my new home city of Karachi, Shaniera's old home city of Melbourne and my adopted city of Manchester has given me a fresh perspective on my cricket, my country and my life. Will it upset some people? Sure. But I have already seen the worst they have to offer, and they hardly matter compared to the true people of Pakistan, from whose ranks I came, and in some respects have never left.

CHAPTER 1

THE BOY FROM THE BRITISH GOVERNMENT

I grew up watching videos of Wasim swinging the ball both ways, bamboozling batters all over the world. Perhaps even more impressive to me was seeing him just recently still able to do it in the nets on cue. I was lucky to have Wasim as a bowling coach at Kolkata Knight Riders for two years. For a young fast bowler just starting out on my career, I found his insights as entertaining as they were helpful. His love for pace bowling is infectious and he is a giant of our game.

Pat Cummins

There is nothing like sitting down to tell your story to make you realise how much you don't know.

My father Chaudhry Mohammad Akram was born in Chawinda Devi, a village outside the Indian city of Amritsar. After partition, the family settled in Kamoke, 50 kilometres north of Lahore, where my father would later move to work. He had two brothers and five sisters. I am not sure I met any of them. Apparently he had a first wife, and maybe children with her. I do not know. But that was typical of his self-containment. He was a quiet, reliable, patient man who said very little, and nothing about himself. He was my first hero.

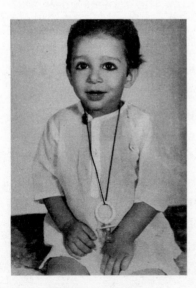

Baby face: one-year-old, with two older brothers set to pull me into line.

My father's first job was as a court proofreader. For many years he ran an automotive spare parts business. My parents' marriage was arranged. My mother Begum was very beautiful, more emotional than my father, and significantly younger: she was only fifteen on her wedding day, and bore her first child nine months later. I'm the third of four, born on 14 June 1966. My brothers Naeem and Nadeem are six and four years older respectively. My sister Sofia is three years my junior. Another child was lost. My early years were spent in Model Town, a comfortable residential suburb south of central Lahore founded as a cooperative along the lines of England's 'garden city' movement.

Every day my father put on a jacket and tie and went to work; and every Sunday evening he would pour himself a single Scotch, which was his sole indulgence. Perhaps the only exotic thing about him was that for a time he ran a single-screen cinema, the Niagara, in Ferozpur Road. He advertised coming attractions by means of a donkey and a cart with billboards on the side, which my brothers and I would ride, preparatory to watching the movies ourselves, from both Bollywood and its Lahore counterpart Lollywood. I loved Amitabh Bachchan and Zeenat Aman. Everyone did. I loved Sultan Rahi and Mustafa Qureshi, particularly locked in their great rivalry in *Maula Jatt*. Many years later, I would perform in a spoof re-enactment of that movie's climax with Shoaib Akhtar. It came completely naturally.

When I was born, Pakistan was divided west and east, and ruled by a military dictatorship. I was four when the first multi-party elections were held, securing power for the Pakistan People's Party (PPP) in the west; I was five when India sided with insurrectionaries in the east, leading to the breakaway of what became Bangladesh. A strong imprint of colonialism also remained and, because my parents had some ambition for me, I started at Lahore's Cathedral School, riding there each morning on our donkey cart. At home, we spoke Punjabi. Now every class save Urdu was in English; every male teacher was addressed as 'Sir', every female teacher as 'Miss' – Sir Lawrence, Miss Sonia and so forth.

My first preferred sport, as it was for Naeem, was probably table tennis, which was huge in Pakistan at the time: thanks to the feats of Saiyid Mohammad Sibtain in the Asian Table Tennis Championships, it eclipsed even hockey. But cricket loomed large, mainly for a single reason: Imran Khan had attended Cathedral School before going to the elite Aitchison College. His name was on the honour boards; his face, at the time, seemed to be everywhere in Pakistan. I read about him in *Akbari e Watan*, an Urdu cricket magazine; I cherished a Wills cigarette card bearing his image. There was a particular television advertisement at the time for Laurensphur Clothing Company featuring Imran's action in slow motion. I loved that advertisement. When it came on the screen, I would stop whatever I was doing to look. It was so spectacular, so beautiful. How did you get to be like him? I got a taste one day when I made 100 opening the batting at school. Everyone the next day knew who I was. I liked that feeling; I wanted it again.

• • •

In Pakistan, the ground beneath you is seldom solid. I was ten when the military, under General Zia ul-Haq, ousted the PPP. More significantly for me, my family crumbled.

My parents' separation was tense, sudden and unexplained. I remember raised voices, muffled conferences, and moving.

Boys club: I'm the smallest, with Naeem and Nadeem in their matching chequered shirts, and my cousins Khalid, Pervaiz and Tariq.

My mother took Sofia and me to live with her parents in Mozang, 10 kilometres north. For reasons never entirely clear, although apparently to do with income tax problems, my father went to England for a year, while Nadeem and Naeem were left to fend for themselves in Model Town. I would visit them at weekends.

It was a strange, disorienting time. Mozang was a comedown. There were no parks and gardens there, just very narrow streets, very near neighbours, and always frenetic activity. Money was scarce, and we were often hungry. To this day I don't like to see plates pushed away with food still on them. The idea of waste upsets me. I was also an active boy. Because space was at a premium at home, a lot of life was spent outdoors, in the streets and on our rooftops: in summer, I would even sleep under a mosquito net on the roof, to slightly ease the relentless heat. Everyone knew everyone else. You could knock on any door, play with anyone. Cricket, of the six-a-side variety with a tape ball, became my great outlet. Day and night, there was always a game somewhere, occasionally interrupted by rickshaws and motorbikes, regularly collecting a little crowd. I formed a team with five other local boys: we called ourselves 'The British Government'. What was I saying about that imprint of colonialism? We thought it sounded powerful, impressive. And – who knows? – maybe it worked on some opponents because we won a lot, in games in Ahmed Pura and in tournaments at the Waris Road ground.

I had other hobbies too. Left-handedness is not all I have in common with the Australian Bill Lawry. I was a teenage pigeon fancier and erected a coop on top of our house for the birds I would buy for a few rupees from Lytton Markets. But my grandmother could see that it was cricket I lived for. I shared my charpai with her, and was her favourite. 'You're so innocent,' she would say. 'How are you going to live?' She was always ushering me out to play, even as my mother looked on severely. I played a lot with Nadeem in the garage at Model Town when I visited my father at weekends, and I went to my first big cricket matches, which included seeing Imran for the first time in the flesh, playing for Pakistan International Airways at Gaddafi Stadium; when I queued for his autograph, I was almost speechless. In the first Test I saw, at Gaddafi Stadium in November 1980, he made his maiden Test 100.

There were notable cricketers in my area too: cousins Ameer and Sajjad Akbar, who between them played more than 300 games for Lahore, hailed from the next gali. And that world was nearer than I imagined. One day, in the hiatus between school and college, I was playing in the streets with my friends when a man in his early thirties on a bicycle stopped and called us over. 'Why don't you play with a proper cricket ball?' he asked us.

'Please uncle, we can't afford the fifty rupees,' I replied.

'Well, if you come to my club, you can play with a real cricket ball,' he said. 'How would you like that?' He looked at me: 'You've got something. You could be a cricketer.'

I was surprised. I had not thought of myself as standing out, except for my left-handedness, and maybe being a little taller than average. I was hardly even aware there were such things as cricket clubs. But the offer sounded enticing.

The man's name was Khalid Mahmood. He was a medium-pacer who had played four matches for Pakistan Customs, and who was now a member of Ludhiana Gymkhana CC, one of the city's stronger clubs. When I accepted his offer, he started picking me up every day at 2.30 pm for the forty-minute cycle to their ground, New Chauburji Park, where there were fifteen practice pitches, half turf, half concrete. As an habitually early arriver, it became my job to help water the surfaces and erect the nets. Then, as other players began to appear, I would bowl, and bowl, and bowl – basically until there was nobody left to bowl to, which might be four hours. Nobody was monitoring my 'loads'; nobody was telling me to vary my activity. I simply bowled as fast as I could. I seldom got a bat, and the hard, bare ground at Ludhiana made it inadvisable to practise fielding.

There were, nonetheless, eyes watching. There was Saood Khan, a long-haired left-armer. There was Sadiq Khan, a former Test umpire. They offered encouragement in the form of new balls, paid for from their own pockets, which I learnt to swing in, at increasing speeds. In Pakistan, you must swing the ball. The pitches offer nothing for someone simply hitting the seam and nibbling the ball round. There is no alternative.

Having returned from his year in the UK, my father bought me a motorcycle, a Kawasaki GTO. The weekend would find me zipping through the narrow streets, already in my whites, spikes over my handlebars, on the way to games. Eventually, inevitably, I came off it. The gash on my right arm was so deep that you can still see the mark left by the many crude stitches. I played the next day anyway with one arm. Nothing was going to stop me.

Ludhiana Gymkhana is gone now; Waris Road no longer hosts cricket; vanished also is the University Ground, where I would climb over the railing and play with my friends Zulfiquar, Shahid and Shahbaz on the days I wasn't at Ludhiana. Urban sprawl and the elimination of precious green space has more or less annihilated sporting clubs in big cities like Lahore; it is a key reason for their decline relative to regional cities as cradles for cricket talent. But in the early 1980s there was fierce competition for the Gymkhana Cup, a two-day, 150-over tournament. I started to play well. I started to get noticed. I could feel my progress. One day I was bowling to Nadeem; I would have been fifteen or sixteen, which means he was nineteen or twenty. At the time he was my idol, my benchmark – proud, a fighter. Suddenly, I hit him, in the head, in the midriff. I was too quick for him. It was an important moment. He decided he would bowl to me also, so I got my first chance to work on my batting. I began to allow myself fantasies. Around this age, I bought a pair of white pants from Lambda Bazaar and had my grandmother sew on a Pepsi logo – the dream of my first sponsor.

Constant competition benefited my cricket. I applied successfully for admission to Islamia College, a ten-minute ride from Mozang, on essentially a sporting scholarship – they were so keen to have me that they did not even return my examination papers. Actually, I was not best pleased. I had wanted to attend the co-educational Government College across the road from Islamia; accustomed to my mother, grandmother and sister, I found it hard adjusting to Islamia's all-male teaching staff. Nor, at first, were there the cricket opportunities I sought. The captain of the first XI, Zahid Khan, was himself a left-arm pace bowler, and resentful of a rival, he kept me twelfth man for an entire season. I was a poor student too. Nominally, I was studying fine arts, a course carefully chosen for involving the least work; mostly, despite my parents' strictures, I was truant, because the playing fields of Lahore were my real school, my cricket school. Lahore Gymkhana's home in Bagh-e-Jinnah, for instance, was the Subcontinent's second-oldest cricket ground. Before partition, it had been an Indian Test venue. It was the club of Imran Khan, and of Nawaz Sharif: Imran would later accuse Sharif of insisting on his own umpires so as to ensure he got a reasonable knock. The ground had a beautiful, rambling pavilion, formerly a British colonial club; the outfield was a grass carpet of a thickness seldom seen in Lahore. This was the place to succeed, and one day, aged seventeen, I did, taking three prize wickets in a spell: Intikhab Alam, the Test all-rounder; Ramiz Raja, younger brother of Test player Wasim; and Ahmad Raza, Imran's uncle and a former national selector.

Pakistani cricket had its eyes peeled for speed. Sarfraz Nawaz had just retired. Others, like Saleem Altaf and Sikander Bakht, were fading. This was also during the period when chronic injury was keeping Imran out of Test cricket, leaving Zaheer Abbas in charge. When I went to Gaddafi

Stadium for the Test against England in March 1984, the toast was Abdul Qadir, who took ten wickets. But soon after, the Board of Control for Cricket in Pakistan foreshadowed a training camp for the best hundred teenage players in Lahore – and thanks to Sadiq and Saood at Ludhiana, I was invited. The night before, in my shared bedroom in Mozang, I could hardly sleep for excitement. I would be treading the same turf as the cricketers whose posters I gazed on at home.

At first, it did not go well. I arrived tired from lack of sleep, and for three days I was too intimidated by the company to go near a ball. There was Ramiz, who at the time was regarded as the city's brightest batting talent; there was Shoaib Mohammad, son of the great Hanif; there was Mohsin Kamal, who had just earned his first Test caps; there was Ejaz Ahmed, about to earn his. On the third evening I returned to my club and complained to Saood that there was no point my going back. I would never get a go. 'We'll sort it out,' he said patiently. Saood must have rung the camp commandant, Agha Saadat, because the next day he threw me first an old ball then a new one, which I began to swing, sharply. Again I bowled Ramiz; I got Ejaz; I troubled everyone.

When Agha and his colleagues chose those players who would go on to a second under-nineteen camp in Karachi, I was one of them. Our family was overwhelmed. My father had always been strict: education came before cricket, business before pleasure. Now he relented somewhat. He would not let me travel to Karachi by train, insisting instead on buying a plane ticket. I had never travelled by air before. When I met my fellow colts Ramiz, Mohsin and Azmat Rana, they had to show me how to buckle my seatbelt. When the food came round, they had to assure me it was free.

The coaching centre at National Stadium was part of a precinct containing hockey pitches, table tennis courts, a gymnasium and an athletic track – now, alas, like Ludhiana, long gone. We stayed in a dormitory but it seemed palatial – I slept in a bed rather than on a charpai. Again, there was no thought of anything but learning by doing. The sixty of us practised in the morning and the evening, which for me just meant bowling, as I hardly conceived of batting beyond a token slog, while fielding was something others did. Still, the little coaching I received was priceless. I was introduced to the great Khan Mohammad, then fifty-six, who had delivered Pakistan's first ball in Test cricket. To that point, my action had been completely untutored. I ran twenty-five paces for no other reason than that it felt right. Mohammad pressed me to reach up higher with my right arm and to uncoil my left from a cocked position. He described the act of bowling as a kind of 'cartwheel' – an expression I had never heard and that needed to be explained to me. But he was right. The longer I stayed side-on, I discovered, the later the ball would swing.

Just as I was enjoying this revelation, there was a commotion on the other side of the ground. Javed Miandad, Pakistan's premier batsman, had arrived. Like Imran, he had also been troubled by injury; he had come along for a convalescent session in the nets. When I was asked if I wanted to bowl to him, I could not say yes fast enough. With some other youngsters we ran in at him for two hours. Of course, I had never bowled at someone so good, but I forced him to study my swing, and every now and again was sharp enough to hurry him.

That spell probably changed my life. I stayed in Karachi a few weeks after the camp, lodging at the YMCA while being paid 600 rupees a month to play for PACO Shaheen, the

Pakistan Automobile Corporation under-nineteen team. We reached the Quaid-e-Azam Trophy semi-final, finally losing to Lahore City Blues. I gained my first mention in *Pakistan Cricketer*, which called me 'Wasim Ashraf'. Then one day my father opened a newspaper and there was my name, correctly spelled, in a fourteen-man squad for the BCCP Patron's XI to play the touring New Zealanders. My father, usually so phlegmatic, could not hide the excitement in his voice as he told me: 'You're going to Pindi!'

Javed was the reason, of course. He was an avid talent spotter. Four years earlier he'd faced Tauseef Ahmed in the nets before a Test at National Stadium, and cajoled the selectors into picking him: Tauseef had taken seven Australian wickets, none of whose names he knew. I was a bit the same. Bar Martin Crowe, I had no idea who any of the New Zealanders were, although that didn't seem to matter because I was sure I wouldn't play. I was barely eighteen, skinny and wild; and Tahir Naqqash, who had opened Pakistan's bowling with Imran, was in the squad. I was wrong. The night before the match, Javed told me that I had been chosen ahead of Tahir. I returned to the room I was sharing with Hafeez-ur-Rehman at Rawalpindi's Flashman Hotel reflecting on the chances involved in my being about to play first-class cricket: first being spotted in the street, then being singled out in the nets. I've had those same thoughts many times since.

The first over the next day was delivered by Asif Faridi, a local quick; I was thrown the new ball for the second. I was in my fourth over when John Wright, New Zealand's captain, nicked to Ramiz at second slip. For all his batting skill, Ramiz was at slip for reasons of rank, because his father was a commissioner and because he'd attended Aitchison

College – he dropped more than he caught, frankly. Fortunately, Saleem Malik grabbed the ball as it bounced from Ramiz's hands, and I had my maiden wicket. Crowe, in the first of many battles, added 100 with Bruce Edgar, but in my third spell I had Edgar caught at the wicket, trapped John Reid and Ian Smith, then went through the tail. My seven for 50 seemed so magical, so providential, that my brothers back in Lahore donated seven bags of rice to the poor in thanks.

I hardly knew what I was doing; I was just running in and bowling. I did not expect to continue my advance. As Pakistan's captain, Zaheer already had the services of an excellent left-arm pace bowler, Azeem Hafeez, and in the home Tests against New Zealand chose as many as three spinners. Nor did I really feel ready. When I was chosen for my first one-day international, in Faisalabad on 23 November, Zaheer gave me the ball for the final over with the New Zealanders needing 24 to win. I bowled four consecutive short balls, each of which Jeremy Coney pulled for four – by the end of the over, our victory margin had been reduced to an uncomfortable five runs. Zaheer was telling me to bowl a yorker, but I had never heard the word, and nobody explained it later. I was as flat afterwards as I had been buoyant in Pindi. When you're young, every setback feels like the end. Maybe Pakistan Automobile would give me a job because cricket was obviously over for me.

In fact, I was shortly to be chosen for my first tour, to New Zealand. Again, I had Javed, now restored to the captaincy, to thank. I was immediately anxious. I could not drive. I had neither money of my own nor even a bank account. I rang Javed and asked him how much it would cost me to go on the tour; he replied deadpan: '100,000 rupees.'

My heart sank. 'Javed *bhai*, my dad would never give me that amount of money,' I said gloomily. 'I'm sorry. I won't be able to come.'

Javed burst out laughing. 'You idiot!' he said. 'You don't have to pay; you *get* paid.'

I couldn't believe it. 'I get *paid*?' I said. 'To play for Pakistan? Unbelievable!'

Perhaps because he could see what a naif I was, Javed took me under his wing. He sat next to me on the plane, gave me his food. When we landed in Christchurch, I immediately went for a jog, then asked where I might find a curry. Curry? Javed told me there was no point looking. He introduced me to steak and chips. Like most Pakistanis, I ate with my hands; suddenly I had to learn how to handle a knife and fork.

It was fascinating getting acquainted with these players who not long before I had known only as names. But I had a tough time with my roommate, Saleem Malik. Though only twenty-one, he was an established player, with five hundreds in twenty Tests, and keen I should know my junior status. He was negative, selfish, treated me like a servant. He demanded I massage him; he ordered me to clean his clothes and boots. I was pleased when some of the younger team members in Ramiz, Tahir, Mohsin, Shoaib Mohammad and Anil Dalpat invited me to a 'nightclub', even though I had no idea what they were talking about and was amazed when they explained. 'Do you mean girls dance as well?' I asked. Not only that, I was told. Indeed, no sooner had I arrived than a girl introduced herself. I could see the others fuming: he's arrived last night, he doesn't even know what a nightclub is, and already he's chatting a girl up. To their further consternation, she took me for a drive, and after parking on a hill we snogged all night. It went no further.

When she rang the next day, and I asked Saleem if I could have the room on my own for a bit, he sneered at me: 'You met a girl? That's not nice, and it's against your religion. So forget it.' That, as I learnt, was Saleem: wonderful player, miserable teammate.

Team manager Yawar Saeed, by contrast, was a lovely man: organised, soft-spoken, a veteran of county cricket in the 1950s. Zaheer was always the perfect gentleman. Mudassar Nazar was the epitome of the team player: calm, dependable, reassuring, and, married to an English woman, worldly. He also introduced me to Western customs – little niceties like holding a door open for people, waiting for passengers in a lift to get out before you got in. I needed encouragement for the first few weeks. I went wicketless in the three-day warm-up match against Canterbury because I could not get the Kookaburra to swing, and was then picked for neither the one-day internationals nor the First Test. By then, I could not see how that would change, so it was a shock when Javed came to me in Auckland on the night of 24 January 1985 and said I would be making my Test debut the next day. I was not sure I was ready; the experience suggested I was right.

The pitch was green. So was I. We were sent in against a classic New Zealand attack of Richard Hadlee, Ewen Chatfield and Lance Cairns, who knew exactly the lengths to bowl and the fields to set. When I came in, Hadlee hit me hard on the knee. I was wearing an old pair of pads that Javed had given me, in addition to the new spikes he had helped me find, and unfortunately they afforded little protection. I could hardly move, was caught soon after, and limped painfully through my first Test spell. I finally got a wicket in my second spell – again John Wright, again caught by Saleem. But my figures of two for 105 in a heavy defeat left me convinced, again, that it was all over for me. When Javed confirmed the night before the Third Test at Dunedin that I had been left out, I rang my father from a payphone, crying down the line as I tipped in coin after miserable coin.

Pakistan on tour, however, is never predictable. Our leg spinner Abdul Qadir was a genius, albeit a volatile one, especially in the absence of his great supporter Imran. He was sensitive about his nickname Baoodata ('Big Balls'), which related to his having one oversized testicle. When Zaheer used the nickname at the wrong moment in the dressing room at Wellington, the result had been an altercation and Qadir's ticket home. When New Zealand rolled out another green top on the morning of the Third Test and packed their team with seamers, Pakistan decided to do the same: Azeem, Tahir, Qadir's replacement Rashid Khan, and me.

It proved to be a classic Test match, under cold, dark skies, with nothing between the teams. Sent in, we wasted a solid start by losing our last five wickets for 10, mainly to Hadlee. New Zealand had reduced their arrears to less than 200 with nine wickets in hand when I bowled my first successful Test spell: in a crowded half-hour I bowled Geoff Howarth off an inside edge and John Reid behind his legs, then trapped Jeff Crowe well back on his stumps. Jeff's brother Martin held us out with Coney for a while, but I came back to have him and Lance Cairns caught in the cordon, ending with five for 56 in twenty-six overs – in a game I had never expected to play.

Before tea on the third day, we were 126 ahead with nine wickets in hand. But their seamers kept winkling us out and it needed me as last man to hang round for an hour in a last-wicket partnership of 42 with Rashid Khan to set the home team 278 to win. New Zealand looked a lost cause when I had Reid caught down the leg side, Howarth skewering to slip, and this time pinned Jeff Crowe first ball. The last day opened with the hosts needing 164 and us needing six wickets. Martin Crowe took a lot of shifting, but when he fell to Tahir just before lunch, we were able to work around Coney.

I was confused when Cairns came out without a helmet. He could bat; he used to hit big sixes. 'Should I bounce him, Javed *bhai*?' I asked my captain. He said yes, but, when I did, umpire Fred Goodall warned me for intimidatory bowling – a statute I'd never heard of and had to ask Javed to explain.

'It means you're not allowed to bowl him another bouncer,' said Javed. 'But don't worry about it. Bowl a bouncer anyway. I will sort it out.'

The bouncer hit Cairns in his unprotected temple as he turned away, and he sank to the turf. I'd never minded hitting batters. I once hit five in a club match and, I have to admit, I loved it. But this bothered me. Everybody knew that Lance was a top guy, and the injury looked serious – his legs were twitching as the St John Ambulance men came running, and the rumour was that he'd suffered a fractured skull. In fact, when number eleven Ewen Chatfield came out to join Coney with New Zealand needing 50, Lance sat groggily with his pads on in the tunnel in case he was needed. These days he'd have been instantly subbed out.

The last pair played well. We grew frustrated. Chatfield was one of those tailenders who play forward to everything, so we bowled short. When I hit him in the helmet, Goodall again told us off. 'If he continues to do it, I can take him off and by God I will,' he said to Javed as I stood to one side. The last ball before tea, with Javed's encouragement, I bowled another bouncer. Goodall wagged his finger at me, then gestured angrily at Javed that I had been given an official warning.

Funnily enough, in his autobiography, Chatfield said that he sympathised with Javed and 'felt' for me: 'Akram must have been put off when Fred Goodall warned him for bouncing a few at me. I was fair game … It was not the bowler's fault I couldn't handle his bowling.' We felt the same, and were in disarray when play resumed with New Zealand needing 25. Dalpat immediately dropped Coney at the wicket, and so fixated were we on Chatfield that we let them take singles with impunity: no fewer than 43 in what turned out to be a matchwinning partnership. So we had thrown away a Test we had the winning of.

With ten wickets for 128, nonetheless, I had had my first international impact. After the game, Glenn Turner made me man of the match and I gave my first tongue-tied television interview. When we landed in Sydney, I was even more overwhelmed. Waiting in the airport lounge, having just finished a season regaining his fitness with New South Wales, was Imran. The closest I had been to him before was getting his autograph as a boy; now he was coming up to me.

'*Salim aleikum* Imran,' I said haltingly.

'*Wale cum salaam*, Wasim,' he replied in that deep, resonant voice. 'You really bowled well in New Zealand.'

I don't remember any more, but with Imran you don't always, so overwhelming is his presence, his beauty. In 1985, he looked like a god: the face, the hair, the physique. I simply couldn't take my eyes off him. And for a young fast bowler, this was a very good thing.

CHAPTER 2

THE GURU

I first watched Wasim Akram in 1985, and I could tell
straight away he was going to be a serious problem
for all batsmen. He could bowl everything from
every angle, had the best yorker in the business, a
skiddy bouncer because he ran through the crease,
fast arms that made the ball hard to pick up – he
was such a freak, in fact, that there was no way
you could practise playing against him. In my time,
only Malcolm Marshall was his equal for reading a
batsman and setting him up. He was also a far better
batsman than his figures suggest, and a remarkably
disciplined athlete with an amazing fitness record.

Ravi Shastri

We were in Australia for two weeks early in 1985 to play the World Championship of Cricket, a mini World Cup being staged for the sesquicentenary of the state of Victoria. It was an introduction to fifty-over cricket Australian style, which was then way ahead of the world, thanks to the impact of the Packer revolution. Cricket with a white ball and players in coloured clothing under floodlights – it was dazzling. I might have found it overwhelming but for Imran's stern, explicit direction. To this point in my career, I had been largely driving myself; even the national team had neither coach nor physiotherapist. Now, acting as my guru, almost as my messiah, was Imran. Having rebuilt his body after a period on the sidelines, he had grown obsessed with fitness. 'We must work on your fast bowling muscles,' he said. When I asked him which these were, he said: 'From the top of your head to the tips of your toes.'

Strangely, Imran was always dismissive of his talent, did not see himself as gifted. He believed in hard work – a gospel he drummed into me. I had looked up to Nadeem as my older brother, then surpassed him; now, in Imran, I had an older brother I could never beat, even if I wanted to, which I didn't. We trained together every day, starting with a five-lap jog and a succession of sprints before our bowling, fielding and batting. When we went on the field, he was never far away, usually at mid-off or mid-on when I bowled. He was there the day we played Australia, in my first appearance at the Melbourne Cricket Ground, counselling me as I walked back. 'Full,' he would say. Then: 'Length ball.' And: 'Yorker.' I finally knew what this was, and I bowled Robbie Kerr, Kepler Wessels and Dean Jones in quick succession.

At first I was scared to bowl bouncers in one-day cricket, as umpires were quick to penalise them. When Kim Hughes came in, I knew his reputation for cross-bat shots. 'Bowl him a bouncer,' Imran said curtly.

I was confused: 'But Imran *bhai*, the umpire will call it a no ball.'

Imran shook his head: 'It doesn't matter. Bowl it short, across him, just outside off. He won't be able to resist.'

Imran was right: Hughes was a compulsive hooker and top-edged to mid-on, Imran himself took the catch, and the umpire let it go. I took five for 21 in our victory that day, but they were all his. Imran was also good at reassuring me when things did not go so well. I would grow frustrated, for example, when the ball did not swing, as it did not when we played England and Allan Lamb drove me repeatedly; Imran told me to be patient, talked me through other variations such as changes of pace and grip. There were other ways to have an impact too. I'm not sure I ever took a better catch than the one I did that day, in the circle at fine leg, to end Lamb's innings, off Azeem.

Not that I was as yet a particularly good fielder, which was reinforced the day before we met India in the final. In the absence of a coach, Wasim Raja was leading training that day, and I took one of his skyscraping hits on the left forefinger; without a physio to advise otherwise, I did not ice it. When I came to bowl, I could not grip the ball, and had to tell Javed I could not play. 'But you have to!' he barked. 'It is just a little bit of pain.' But the cost to my control was too great, and I was finally left out of a game we lost.

In those days, of course, there seemed to be a one-day international around every corner, and the team was next scheduled to play a four-match quadrilateral involving India, Australia and England in Sharjah, a burgeoning city in the United Arab Emirates whose cricket stadium had begun hosting international matches the year before. Javed had been one of the first cricketers to enjoy the largesse of the Cricketers' Benefit Fund Series established by the businessman Abdul Rahman Bukhatir, and everyone in the city seemed to know him. When we went shopping together, people would drape us in gold medals and jewellery, offer us free food and goods. Parties at the Sharjah Continental Hotel were thronged with celebrities and, having grown up on Bollywood movies, I was agog at the faces. Occasionally, an exotic touch – we would hear rumours of the presence of 'the D-man', the crime boss Dawood Ibrahim, whose daughter would later marry Javed's son.

Strangest of all was adjusting to being a celebrity too. We finished third in the Rothmans Trophy, but the occasion was as heady as the result. Likewise my arrival home after three months abroad. The whole of Mozang came out to welcome me – friends, neighbours, old teammates and rivals all gathered outside my grandmother's tiny home in Ahmed Pura. I spent some of my 70,000 rupee tour fee on a light-golden 1974 Toyota Corolla. When I parked, all I had to do was tell the shopkeepers to keep an eye out – nobody dared touch it. Pepsi became my sponsor, as I had once fantasised, and I was featured on the cover of the magazines I had once pored over. 'Courage and charisma,' it said next to my picture on the front of *Pakistan Cricketer*. What?

It was time to move up a little in the world. My father built a new storey on top of his house in Model Town for me to share with my sister; later he built a house across the road for my mother. But at nineteen I was still very junior, and much too young to be aware of the tensions that characterised the relationship between Javed and Imran. I revered both of them; each, in their own ways, had treated me with immense kindness. Over the captaincy, nonetheless, they were always quietly jostling. In February 1982, Imran had been one of nine colleagues who had declined to play under Javed's leadership. I was unaware of any undercurrents when we hosted Sri Lanka for three largely uneventful Tests in late 1985, but at the end of the series Javed stood aside from the leadership in favour of Imran: he says he 'decided never to captain Pakistan if Imran was also playing'. It probably suited me. Where I admired Javed, I idolised Imran, and hung on his every word. His first act as captain in the Rothmans Three Nations Trophy in Sharjah in November was to throw me the new ball against the West Indies. Imagine that moment. Pakistan's greatest fast bowler ceding you the first over. As I prepared to bowl to Desmond Haynes, Mudassar chipped in. 'Pitch it up to Haynes,' he said. 'He plays across it early.' My fourth ball bowled him.

Sometimes you meet a hero and it is disappointing. I had met mine, and he wasn't. Just to spend time with him was a privilege. He was so poised, so magnetic, always with a book in his hand, addressing you in that calm, bass voice and Oxford accent. To my bowling he gave his complete attention. When he was at home, in Zaman Park near the other Niazis, he was always seeking me out. I was his project.

I had never given any thought to how I bowled. I had never seen myself do it, had never explored any other way. Why did my back foot point to the sightscreen in my delivery stride? I had no idea. You watch footage of me in the World Championship of Cricket: I am all shoulder, a boy on a man's mission. Imran changed all that. He got me to accentuate my pivot as I hit the crease, so that my shoulder really snapped. He got me locking my wrist and securing the ball with my third and fourth fingers, so that the seam came out stable. He refined my run-up; he worked on my variations; he taught me to bowl at the death in one-day internationals. In one such match at Kandy, Sri Lankan tailender Ashantha de Mel took four fours off my final over as I pitched short. The next day Imran grabbed a bag of old balls and dragged me into the nets to bowl at a set of stumps, aiming at the base; the next day I went back and did it with new balls. The bouncer, he explained, was an easy ball; the yorker had always to be bowled flat out. I was an apt pupil. Three of my four wickets the next time I bowled were yorkers.

Imran was a great watcher of the game, and he liked others to do so as well – he would ask questions afterwards about what we had observed. But his chief insistence was on bowling. In the nets, we bowled and bowled. We bowled until we were tired, then we kept on bowling, precisely because we knew we would often have to bowl when we were tired. There was no point tapering off. You had to be as fast in the last over as in your first. It is a kind of practice very out of style now. Young bowlers come to me now and say: 'Wasim, how do I get faster?' I say: 'It's simple. You bowl.'

How do they expect to get faster when their strength and conditioning coaches are restricting them to two or three overs a day? Work builds speed. Work also builds skill. Most of all, Imran tutored me in reverse swing – the swing an old ball develops towards the shiny side rather than away.

We called it *sibar* – 'the opposite way'. The principle was the same as for conventional swing – getting the ball to move by sharpening the difference in the condition of each side. But with reverse swing, which usually emerged around the 35–50-over mark, you entered this bizarro world of opposites: you pointed the seam towards the slips and it swung back in; you pointed the seam towards fine leg and it swung away. Polishing was still important, Imran explained, but the key was keeping the unpolished side as dry and rough as possible. Imran told me how to prepare a ball, how to cant my wrist, how to disguise my hand, and how optimally to deliver it – fast and full. In some ways it was easier than the orthodox variety. If you tried too hard with the new ball, swing could desert you; with the old ball, the quicker the better.

The technique is usually thought to be synonymous with the Subcontinent, where abrasion scuffs balls naturally, but Imran says he first encountered it in a Test in Australia, on a pebbly pitch in Melbourne in 1977, then refined it while playing for Sussex in ensuing years. Accelerating the deterioration of one side of the ball would come to be regarded as a dark art – in a fabled match at Eastbourne, Imran later confessed to using a bottle top. Mostly, however, despite the obsession with 'ball tampering', nothing much more was needed than natural abrasion. A ball hit as hard as is standard in international cricket will deteriorate fast if you do nothing to repair or shine it. Back in those days, too, boundary ropes and cushions were almost unheard of. Balls hit fences and boundary hoardings. Balls rolled in concrete gutters and bounced on bitumen concourses. Balls bowled cross-seam scuffed up readily. Keep the damaged side dry by holding it in your fingers rather than your palm and the effect was even more pronounced. It was also better to ballast the ball with sweat, this being oilier than saliva.

Imran's ethos was to attack relentlessly, to try everything, to aim for completeness. 'The whole point of bowling is to sow doubt in the batsman's mind,' he would say. 'Hold it across the seam. Use the crease. When you come over the wicket, bowl your inducker from wider to exaggerate the swing. When you come round the wicket, start your run from behind the umpire so you're close to the stumps and appear at the last minute.' I liked this. It reminded me of the tricks of playing in the street in Mozang. But it wasn't just play. I learnt to hate giving runs away, even singles. T20 has changed that, of course. The game is so boundary-centric now that merely giving away a single feels like a win. But I could not bear singles, could not bear to let a batter off strike. I wanted to pin him down, isolate him, intimidate him. Twenty overs in a day? I would budget to concede no more than 40 runs.

Imran was also, at the time, all-powerful. At the end of November 1985, we hosted the West Indies in a five-match Wills Series. They were at their absolute peak: Viv Richards could call on Malcolm Marshall, Michael Holding, Courtney Walsh, Joel Garner and Tony Gray. There were no spinners, no part-timers – no respite. I prayed to Allah before that series: I prayed that we would be competitive, because our batting was susceptible to pace, and our fielding was fifteen years behind the rest of the world. Imran was more proactive. Figuring that the West Indies's natural length was shorter than ours, he instructed the groundsmen preparing pitches to roll only the 8 metres at each end. We won in Lahore and Rawalpindi – the first time we had beaten West Indies in one-day internationals at home.

Paradoxically, Imran had also become the most powerful advocate for third-country umpires, first in Sharjah. People have forgotten what an issue this was. Almost every big series of the time was disrupted by arguments about the bias of home officials. Pakistan took its share of criticism, although it was no more difficult to get Javed lbw in Pakistan than it was to get Viv lbw in the West Indies or Arjuna Ranatunga lbw in Sri Lanka – Imran, in fact, loathed Ranatunga for the way he intimidated umpires on a tour we made there in February 1986. It was after that ill-tempered series, where Javed at one point waded angrily into the crowd after being given out, that the Asia Cup and the subsequent John Player Tournament in Colombo made use of England's Dickie Bird and David Shepherd. In the Austral-Asia Cup in Sharjah involving Pakistan, Australia, India, Sri Lanka and New Zealand, two West Indian umpires then stood – although it's not surprising that this has been forgotten given what happened in the final.

I still get goosebumps even thinking about that game on 18 April 1986. It was like the distilled essence of cricket at Sharjah: us challenging India, the World Cup holder; a big, passionate crowd roughly divided between expatriate Pakistanis and Indians; two powerful teams with outsized personalities led by great all-rounders in Imran and Kapil Dev. Off the field, in fact, the teams got on famously. Imran and Sunil Gavaskar were very close. I made a pal in Ravi Shastri, a Gemini like me, and great company. On the field, of course, that meant nothing. At one for 216, India were all over us that day. Then Imran bowled his friend Sunny, I bowled my friend Ravi, and claimed three wickets with the yorkers my captain had taught me.

Cricket in Sharjah was always tough. There were no lights. Every match was played in the heat of the day. Big occasions made for raw emotions. For the time, too, India's seven for 245 was a huge total, especially when we slipped to four for 110. Still, we had Javed in the kind of scenario for which he was born. His style was to start very slowly. You might want three an over to win, but Javed seemed always to let it blow out to five or six, because he felt you could catch up, although maybe he also liked the drama of such situations knowing that his own will and nerve were so strong. I remember as the asking rate rose in that match there were players crying in the dressing room, from the tension, from the growing hopelessness. I kept telling them to quiet down, but I understood their distress. When Imran was out we needed eight an over; from the last thirty balls we needed 51.

Somehow Javed kept us in touch. I came to the crease when Ravi caught Manzoor Elahi off a skier from the first ball of the forty-eighth over; the batters had crossed, so Javed, on 90, was on strike. The bowler was Chetan Sharma, a serviceable medium-pacer who had earlier dismissed Mudassar. Javed hit him for six over long-on, then took a two and a one. After scrambling a leg bye, I ran a hard two to backward point to bring Javed his century. We took seven off the penultimate over from Kapil Dev, leaving us needing eleven from the last six deliveries.

I can say, tongue in cheek, that I played my part. When we communed mid-pitch, Javed decided he needed a longer blade, and the only such bat available in the dressing room was one of mine. When he then tugged the first ball of the final over from Sharma to long-on, I sacrificed myself coming back for a second to keep him on strike, and he hit the next ball for four. Of course, everyone remembers the last ball. Sharma took the obvious option – a yorker. But he had not had a teacher as good as mine. The ball came out as a full toss, which Javed, standing out of his ground and leaning back, hit out of the ground. I saw an interview with Sharma a few years ago where he talked about there still being days when he's recognised by strangers who tell him: 'You're the guy who got hit for six!'

In Sharjah, the scenes were all jubilation, and our bus journey back to the Sharjah Continental seemed to take hours. In Pakistan, where even federal cabinet had adjourned to watch the game, the reaction was still more overwhelming. Beating our nearest rival united politicians and celebrities with rickshaw wallahs and bus drivers. Security being almost unheard of at the time, there must have been 500 people on the tarmac alone when we landed in Lahore. It felt like we were soldiers returning from a war. Ramadan intensified the sense of thanksgiving, and Javed performed the first umrah of his life in Mecca, although the flow of gratitude ran mostly the opposite way. Javed was feted everywhere, showered with honours, plied with gifts, including a famous luxury Mercedes. I never did get the bat back. He must have auctioned it ten times!

But fair enough. That unbeaten 116 off 114 balls was an epochal innings. To that point, India had had a slight edge over Pakistan in ODI cricket, having won eight times to our seven. Afterwards, we seemed to have a huge psychological advantage. Over the rest of my career, our record against

India in Sharjah was sixteen wins and only four defeats. Pakistanis called the venue *Har Shahar*, which means 'lose'. Nowadays sixes are nothing special, the standard currency of T20. But that six could genuinely claim to have been, like that of the New York Giants's Bob Thomson, a shot heard round the world.

• • •

Imran continued taking responsibility for my cricket education. A couple of weeks after that amazing finish in the desert, I arrived in London for the first time. It was mid-afternoon; I was wearing my leather jacket and sunglasses; it was pitch-dark, freezing cold, and I had a welcoming committee of one: Imran's friend Masood Chishty. Chishty, a well-connected lawyer from Lahore now based in Birmingham, had organised for me to play a season with a little club in Durham, Burnopfield CC, best known as the home of Ollie Milburn, if not much else.

Imran said he wanted me to 'learn English conditions'; he was probably just as intent on my learning about life. After all, I still lived at home in Lahore. Now I would be earning £50 a week and looking after myself in a one-room flat in Newcastle's Hillgate Quay. On Saturdays and Sundays, I did learn some lessons about cricket in England, notably about playing in the freezing cold, and the importance of warming up properly and then changing your shirt, vest and jockstrap after your first spell to prevent lower back stiffness. I got a century, helped by our home ground's 30-metre boundaries; I took an eight-for, including a hat-trick. But the more significant experience was of independent living. I asked Mohsin Kamal, who was also playing league cricket, to move in; we connected with the local Pakistani community, so that food and company were never a problem. I also became more comfortable with the English I had first learnt at Cathedral School. By far the most memorable parts of my season were visits to the *Tuxedo Princess*, the ship-turned-nightclub on the nearby Tyne, frequented by celebrities like Mick Hucknall and Rick Astley, sportsmen like Daley Thompson and Frank Bruno, and members of Frankie Goes to Hollywood and The Chippendales. I was not in the same category, but nightclub memories from New Zealand came flooding back during evenings on 'The Boat'.

By the time I returned to Lahore, I had turned twenty and grown up a great deal. There was a divide in the Pakistani team at the time between those who spoke mostly English, like Imran, Mudassar, Zaheer and Mohsin Khan, and those who did not, such as Saleem Malik. I now identified with the former group more. It was a little step in confidence, ahead of what loomed as a momentous summer.

Our guests in Pakistan were again the West Indies, this time for three Tests, which would be critical for Imran's prestige. He basically hand-picked the team. They were his guys. For instance, he loved Saleem Yousuf, who became my roommate. Sally was maybe not the best keeper, but he was fearless, would bat anywhere, was always positive and always put the team first. We needed those attitudes to stand strong against Viv Richards's team, which had won seven Tests on the trot.

In Faisalabad, they looked like making it eight: we were reduced to ten men when Walsh broke Saleem's left arm, then were bowled out for 159. On the second afternoon, the visitors were 20 runs ahead on the first innings with six wickets in hand. Just then, however, the ball started reversing sharply, and I took the last five wickets. These included Viv from round the wicket, which I had started trying at Burnopfield, finding it a good way to help me complete my action: he nicked one to Sally trying to run it down to third man. Thrown in as nightwatchman, Sally then batted forty-six overs for his maiden Test 50, although we were still only 135 to the good when I came out to join Imran.

Imran was so intent in that series. No matter what number he was batting, he would pad up when we lost our first wicket and have someone start bouncing a tennis ball at him, which he would smash into a wall. He had made 61 of our first innings runs. Now I caught his confidence, hit a few through the covers early, then grew more and more ambitious. Tauseef Ahmed hung in with me a while, then Saleem came out with his arm in plaster – the roar round Iqbal Stadium when, shaping up left-handed, he managed to block his first ball, gave me chills. He was clearly in great pain; Viv had refused him a runner.

I walked down the wicket to see if he was alright. 'Saleem *bhai*, just get a single!' I said.

'I'm trying,' he responded through gritted teeth.

While we were talking, the keeper Jeff Dujon took the bails off to claim a run-out; the West Indies were disgusted when the umpires said no. For the next forty minutes, we urged each other on. Turning to face the other way, Saleem survived fifteen balls and managed to eke out three singles while we added 32 runs. I slogged Marshall over his head and Gray over mid-wicket for sixes before I was stumped for 66, my first Test half-century, just before tea.

By now the crumbling pitch was tailor-made for Qadir. Baoo was such a curious mix. He could be taciturn, sometimes aloof, maybe a little self-conscious about his relatively humble background. He was a terrible fielder. He could bat but never took it seriously, and was an appalling runner between wickets. But at his best, in favourable conditions, he was irresistible: you could hear the ball spinning as it left his hand; he smothered batsmen with variations and badgered umpires with appeals. Having trapped Haynes himself, Imran threw the ball to Qadir for the sixth over. By stumps the game was basically over: even Viv could make nothing of him as the West Indies collapsed for 53. It was the West Indies's second defeat in thirty-seven Tests. I was surprised to receive the man of the match award. But I did so in English – another little milestone in my career.

Imran was ecstatic – so ecstatic he now took another bold step. Beating the West Indies was not enough. He wanted it achieved in such a way that nobody could doubt its legitimacy. Visiting teams were always blaming defeat in Pakistan on umpiring. Imran's pride would not allow that. To this end, he insisted that, for the final two tests, the BCCP draft umpires from India: VK Ramaswamy and PD Reporter. We did not care. But Imran was determined to set an example. He believed in independent umpires and saw no reason that his own country could not lead the way.

In fact, the West Indies needed no help from anyone. On an uneven pitch at Gaddafi Stadium, in a match without so much as a half-century partnership, they beat us in two and a half days. Marshall was unbelievably good. As he barged in, you could start fixating on the gold jewellery dancing round his neck. He rushed you, confused you, scared you. I remember in the second innings of that match, Imran scolding our opener Rizwan-uz-Zaman for going out to bat without a helmet. When Rizwan returned soon after, having had his middle pole knocked out of the ground, Imran said solemnly: 'You have to respect fast bowlers.' None was worthier of respect than Marshall. You never felt safe around him. He may well be the greatest I saw. Still, we had drawn the series, and, a year on from succeeding Javed, Imran's stature had never been greater.

CHAPTER 3

IMRAN, VIV AND ME

Wasim, he was very, very special ...

Viv Richards

I never saw a cricketer with such talent as Wasim Akram. Everything about him was completely natural. I had had to completely rebuild my action early in my career. He arrived on the scene with an action he hardly had to alter and a passion for the game that never dimmed. What I taught him was the art of taking wickets and the importance of self-discipline – how he had to work if he was to fulfil his enormous potential. In his era, Wasim was as good as anyone in the world.

Imran Khan

It was a period of unrest in South Asia. India and Pakistan were jostling militarily on their border. Both countries nourished nuclear ambitions. General Zia had identified with Imran's team, and pushed a policy called 'Cricket for Peace' to normalise diplomatic relations. As part of it, we were sent to play five Tests in India – as it turned out, the last series of that duration involving our two countries. That gave our captain a kind of quasi-ambassadorial status – in India, he was the personification of Pakistan.

I got a taste of Imran's eminence when we landed in Mumbai in February 1987. Rather than stay at the Taj Land's End, he hung out with the philanthropist and hostess Parmeshwar Godrej, whose husband was one of India's wealthiest consumer goods industrialists. On our first night in India, Imran drove me in his sponsored car to the Godrej's massive pile on Malabar Hill, where a party was held to fete him: all the great and the good of Bollywood, all of whom I recognised from a lifetime of watching Indian movies, all of them clustered round my skipper. Later in the tour, in Jaipur, he filmed a commercial for Cinthol, a 'freshness soap' that Godrej Group created in Imran's honour. It was probably a greater blow for diplomatic relations than Zia turning up to watch the subsequent Test.

For all that Imran looked after me, he never showed

any favouritism. When the team went to Faridabad for a warm-up match against a Board President's XI, he remained with me in Mumbai to undertake a demanding regime of laps, sprints, and bowling and batting sessions. I even felt slightly uneasy about my place at the time. Saleem Jaffar, a tall left-arm bowler a few years older than I was, had recently emerged, taking eighty wickets in a first-class season. When I was chosen ahead of him for the First Test at Chepauk, I felt I had something to prove, and helped Imran add 112 for the eighth wicket, hitting five sixes and six fours in 62. Imran went on to an unbeaten 135, hitting five sixes and fourteen fours, putting on 81 for the last wicket with Tauseef. What a cricketer.

I then bowled fast – probably as fast as I had to that point. You'd hardly have known it, for India piled up 527: Srikkanth hitting 123, Gavaskar 91, Dilip Vengsarkar 96 and Mohinder Amarnath 89. But the pitch was hard and bare, surprisingly bouncy, and I got the ball to reverse. Though I took only the one wicket, the keeper Kiran More, I heard Gavaskar telling my skipper: 'This guy is *quick*.' Mohinder, who Imran told me was the toughest of their players, mentally and physically, certainly proved it, opening his shirt afterwards to show me the bruises I'd inflicted on his chest. I went on to take five for 96 at Kolkata – my fourth Test five-for.

The Tests in Kolkata, Jaipur and Ahmedabad, however, were also high-scoring draws, making eleven consecutive stalemates between the two countries – such was the assumed shame of defeat that nobody was prepared to take any risks. Imran had called for a reinforcement from Lahore recommended by Javed: the 39-year-old left-hander Younis Ahmed, fully seventeen years after his previous Test appearance. Alas, he batted like an old man, making a painstaking 40 as we crawled to four for 134 off eighty-six overs on the first day at Gujarat Stadium, then spending four and a half hours over an undefeated 34 on the last day. Imran kept sending messages to the middle urging him to accelerate; Younis kept ignoring them. 'What sort of cricket was that?' he roared at Younis after a final day in which only 110 runs were scored. Imran was especially irked when Kapil Dev accused us of 'negative cricket', because he knew his rival captain was right.

Another Javed recommendation paid off: the experienced, slow left-armer Iqbal Qasim. Abdul Qadir had struggled since his coup against the West Indies, so we included Qasim for the final Test in Bangalore. We also chose Saleem Jaffar. He did not bowl a ball, and Imran and I only got through eighteen overs between us: the pitch ragged square from the first day, when Maninder Singh took seven for 27 as we made our lowest total against India, 116. India were two for 71 early on the second day before Qasim and Tauseef restricted their lead to 29, and our batters battled into the middle of the third day to set India 221 to win. I yorked Srikkanth and got Mohinder with a leg cutter, before Tauseef bowled Vengsarkar and trapped More to leave India four for 99 at the close.

With the Test, and the nations, so delicately balanced, you might have expected some tension between the teams, both of whom were staying at the Taj. In fact, the atmosphere was festive. Rest day fell during Holi, India's festival of love, which we Pakistanis had only seen in Bollywood movies, but in which we joined with enthusiasm. We threw so much colour at each other that it was still staining the water when I was washing my hair months later. When Maninder and Ejaz helped me tip Ravi from his sun lounge into the pool, the water went first blue then black. Imran locked himself in his room, so Sunny sent a girl up to knock, knowing Imran could not resist opening the door; when he did, we poured in, throwing colour everywhere. Some things I never got to the bottom of. Later in the evening we were lazing by the pool when Javed came running past, followed by Qadir brandishing a knife – a small knife but still a knife. Who knows what that was about? It all came back to me when the quizmaster Gautam Bhimani, son of the great Kishore and then a young commentator, posted a picture recently of the two of us youthfully dye-stained. In this day and age, when politicians have rendered cricket relations between India and Pakistan all but impossible, such fraternity must be hard to believe. But as far as the players were concerned, 'Cricket for Peace' was actually more than an empty slogan.

The next day we squeaked home by 16 runs to win Pakistan's second only series victory in India, Qasim and Tauseef taking nine wickets each. This was despite a five-and-a-half-hour epic by Sunny: his 96 was his final Test innings, ended only by a ball from Qasim that leapt off a length. No batsman I ever saw was so defensively complete as Gavaskar. His technique was precise; his concentration was total. When I got him out for the first time a few days later in a one-day international at Hyderabad, I felt like I had really earned it, and it capped off my tour. We had been made to feel almost as welcome as Imran: Ejaz and I had even done a shoot for an Indian film magazine, striking poses like Anil Kapoor, who after *Mashaal* had become our favourite actor. We received some quite extraordinary gifts. When I was man of the match in a one-day international at Nagpur – I hit poor Chetan Sharma for 25 in an over – I was presented with a huge scale model of the Taj Mahal.

Mind you, the souvenir I cherished from that game was a bail, which the umpire gave me when I broke it bowling Mohammad Azharuddin.

The crowd at Allama Iqbal Airport when we returned was put at 60,000, and three days' celebration followed. We were feted by General Zia, who presented us with gold medals and purses of 40,000 rupees each. Imran did not accompany us to the UAE for the subsequent six-match Sharjah Cup also involving India with England and Australia, but it proved a memorable one for me. Between the West Indies and India series, Pakistan had detoured to Perth for an eight-day limited-overs quadrangular, the Benson & Hedges Challenge, to coincide with yachting's America's Cup in that city: we lost the final, but I bowled swiftly under the lights, and it happened that Lancashire CCC was in the market for an international pace bowler to share the workload with Patrick Patterson. England's physio at the time, Laurie Brown, was a staunch Mancunian who had spent twenty years at Manchester United. It was he who now beckoned me from behind a palm tree at the Sharjah Continental to meet Neil Fairbrother, who was making his debut for England in that tournament.

'Would you be interested in playing for Lancashire?' Neil asked.

I misunderstood him. 'I'd love to play Lancashire League,' I replied. 'Who for?'

'No,' said Neil. 'For the county. We'd like you to join us at Lancashire, to play in the County Championship.'

County cricket then had the aura of the Indian Premier League today. It was the world's only full-time professional circuit, and only the very elite of overseas players played – Imran, at Sussex, and Javed, at Glamorgan, were the only

Pakistanis involved. I could hardly believe I had been asked, and so far ahead of time. Pakistan were shortly to tour England. Neil and Laurie were offering me a contract to start in 1988 and lasting for six years – though I did not know it at the time, it was the longest contract ever offered to an international cricketer. I can still remember the terms. I was to start on £20,000, with Lancashire to pay the tax, and provide airfares, accommodation and a car. The money was irrelevant. I had no need of it; I lived under my father's roof. But to play cricket all the time? Three one-day competitions? The offer was irresistible: having no agent, I simply left negotiations to our team manager, Haseeb Ahsan.

Lancashire could hardly have been more welcoming. The day before the First Test at Old Trafford, they threw me a twenty-first birthday. I had not bowled a ball for them, and they not only wheeled out a huge cake in the Red Rose Suite, but had secretly flown my brothers, sister and parents in for the occasion – Naeem was then studying in London, but the rest had been brought all the way from Pakistan, and put up in the Hotel Britannia. It was incredible to see my mother and father, so long estranged, together, and I warmed immediately to Lancashire chairman Bob Bennett. A kind, soft-spoken man, he had played for Lancashire during the 1960s, and now lived on the Isle of Man. He was a true cricket lover.

Of the Pakistani team, English cricket was not nearly so welcoming. On landing we took six hours to clear customs as sniffer dogs went through our every item of luggage, and we were deposited in a poky dive called Kensington Close Hotel – a huge contrast to the hotels we were used to in the UAE and India. There were ugly skirmishes during the Texaco Trophy match at Edgbaston between Pakistani supporters and English 'supporters' with shaven heads and heavy boots, who were identified as members of the brutish, racist National Front. When Neil Foster nicked a boundary off me to win the game in the last over, there was pandemonium, the umpires being bowled over by the on-rushing mob. It might have unsettled a less united team when, for example, we were booed taking a warm-up lap before a day's play in the Manchester Test.

Our requests regarding umpires were disregarded. Imran, who had been dissatisfied with them five years earlier, requested that David Constant and Ken Palmer be replaced on the panel; the Test and County Cricket Board imperiously refused. Personally, I liked the English umpires, like David Shepherd, Dickie Bird, John Holder and Merv Kitchen. I respected that they were hard to impress with lbw appeals on the front foot. Shep also admitted that because my trailing leg blocked their vision of the front line when I bowled over the wicket, I probably got away with a few no balls over the years. Which was fine with me too!

Under Imran, however, we were a tight unit – he was his usual commanding self. But Javed was also heavily involved – his corner of the room was always the centre of noise, fun, stupid jokes, crazy ideas. I once asked Imran why he preferred sending Javed to field at third man. He smiled: 'Javed will come up with a thousand schemes during a match, and if one of them works I will read about it in a newspaper.' Pakistani cricketers had once been notoriously finicky travellers. I remember an under-23s tour of Sri Lanka from which a player, Hafaz Shahid, had to be sent home because he could not bear the smell of coconut oil. But now Imran's shrewdness was apparent. As a result of my season with Burnopfield, I was used to England. I even liked it. Every second day, Ejaz and I would go to an Angus Steakhouse and order a pepper steak with French fries and creamy cauliflower.

I felt good about my cricket too. I started experimenting with my run-up. At Old Trafford, I explained to Imran that I felt I was wasting my first eight steps. I was just jogging in. Instead I should sprint in from seventeen paces. 'Are you sure it does not affect your pace?' he asked. I said I did not think so, but he insisted on having me pelt in at him in the nets for a couple of overs. At the end of it, he nodded: 'Okay, give the shorter run a go.' That consent was all I needed; maybe I had grown in confidence, to the degree that I no longer needed a long run. I got my fiftieth Test wicket the next day, having David Gower caught by Sally; Imran was shortly to take his 300th. That was at Headingley, in a match I'll never forget.

Rain had washed away the first two matches. At Headingley the sun poked through, and the square and outfield were dry – perfect conditions for reverse swing. Imran was simply incredible. He took three wickets in his first spell; I took two, including England's captain Mike Gatting with a ball that came back very late. In our celebratory huddle, Javed chipped me: 'Why can you not bowl that ball all the time?' Imran interceded in that deep voice of his: 'Javed, you cannot always bowl exactly what you want.' Yet in that game, it seemed like he could. For the third time in the series I also hit Ian Botham on the left boot, which prevented him from bowling in conditions he'd have enjoyed. I remember the look on his face as he went down: 'What the fuck is wrong with you?' it seemed to say. Nothing was wrong. He was the opposition's most dangerous player. As such he was my number one target.

I contributed 66 to an unassailable lead of 217, including two sixes off Phil Edmonds into the old dressing room, and sixes off Neil Foster and Graham Dilley as well. We then burst through England a second time, so that I was left to bowl to Dilley as last man. 'Bowl him outswingers,' Imran suggested. I did. He missed every ball. Next over Imran bowled Dilley with something full and straight to finish with match figures of ten for 77. Though we were outplayed at Birmingham, Imran and I kept England from obtaining a fourth-innings target of 124 in eighteen overs, ensuring us at least a share of the series. The captain glowed at putting the disappointments of 1982, when Pakistan had lost to England 1–2, behind him.

• • •

Two days before the Oval Test, I started to feel unwell. I ignored the pain in my belly near the top of my groin until the second day, when it turned out I needed my appendix taken out – a painful operation after which I could hardly breathe for three days and not travel for a month. By the time I got back to Pakistan, preparations were well underway for the first World Cup on the Subcontinent, hosted jointly by Pakistan, India and Sri Lanka. Needless to say, the first two of those meeting in the final was the organiser's dream. Sponsors had invested accordingly. In those days, with only one television station in Pakistan, PTV, a commercial was a massive deal. I received 200,000 rupees to advertise an energy glucose drink called Rafan. Imran, of course, outdid me, doing a fashion shoot for *Vogue*, and also turning up one day in a red Ferrari after having been made a brand ambassador for Pepsi.

Through the group stages, it looked like we were cruising. We beat Sri Lanka convincingly in Hyderabad and Faisalabad, England assuredly in Rawalpindi and Karachi. Against the West Indies in Lahore, we were bailed out by a fearless half-century from Sally, who was dropped from three consecutive balls. Great as they were, we felt we had a slight edge over Viv's team at this point, although our eventual win was a gift from Courtney Walsh. We needed 14 to win from the last over with our last pair, Qadir and Jaffar, at the wicket, and finally two from the last ball. As he ran in, Walsh refrained from running Jaffar out at the bowler's end, when he would have been well entitled to. Qadir promptly hit the winning runs. That was typical of Courtney, a thorough gentleman, although Viv lay on his back on the pitch with tears in his eyes afterwards. Our celebrations raged all night.

There was a feeling of destiny about what we were doing. Imran, Javed and I were guests at a soiree hosted by Yousuf Salahuddin, grandson of the poet Allama Iqbal and son of a senior justice of the Supreme Court, in the vast courtyard of his 400-year-old haveli behind the fort in the centre of Lahore. Imran had the team he wanted. If you were playing, you always felt he rated you, and he had favourites: he thought, for instance, that Mansoor Akhtar was the country's most talented batsman, and was determined to persevere with him come what may. But after we lost our return match against the West Indies in Karachi, we grew strangely diffident ahead of our semi-final against Australia. There was no team dinner the night before. 'Go to your room,' Imran said simply. 'Don't meet anyone. Get to sleep.' I could not sleep. Having successfully held expectations at bay for a month, I tossed and turned all night. I had chipped a bone in my foot and so was uncomfortable as well as anxious.

Australia played well, but we let them. Mudassar withdrew on the morning of the match, which cost us his 'golden arm'; instead we decided to rely for our spare overs on Saleem Malik, who bowled what we called 'mixed pakoras', and as an opener on Mansoor, who was in no form at all. In the nineteenth over, a ball from Qadir glanced off Dean Jones's pad and hit Sally flush in the face. Javed did a good job in his stead, but was clearly exhausted by the effort: he was subdued in our reply, taking 104 balls for 70.

What people remember most clearly is Imran's miscounting the overs and leaving the last to Jaffar, whose first five had gone for 39. Steve Waugh took him for 18, then dismissed Saleem with his first ball. Mansoor sent Ramiz back and ran him out, then was bowled by Craig McDermott, who also bowled me after I'd slogged two sixes. When Imran was caught at the wicket off one of Allan Border's little tweakers, he stood motionless for a moment, like a martyred saint. We slid to defeat by 18 runs with an over to spare.

Imran staggered us afterwards by announcing his retirement, which felt like a blow of national proportions. As our bus returned to the Lahore Hilton that night, you saw people slumped in disappointment, shaking their heads, bereft. The general mood lifted a little the following day when England beat India in the other semi-final. But I sank into something akin to a depression. Without Imran, it wasn't just that I didn't want to play or practise – I did not want to go out of doors. He was the source of all my confidence as a man as well as a player. I broke down with a groin strain during the second match of the one-day series against England, and I was mostly a dispirited onlooker during the unruly Tests that followed, marred by chequered umpiring and poor behaviour.

Imran was eventually roused by a challenge. He brooded a while. He received petitions, including from General Zia himself. Having hosted the West Indies in a drawn series, he could see the sense in a sequel. Javed, again, had to give the captaincy up, but he too was stimulated by the prospect of a Caribbean tour. To prepare for combating the West Indian fast bowlers, our greatest batter went into the nets at Gaddafi Stadium and placed a marble slab on the pitch, off which he had a ball bounced at short range from differing angles. He got his hook into order. He got used to fending off the chin, off the collarbone. That was what facing their pace was like – survival of the fittest.

My groin was still troubling me, while Imran had lost some conditioning during his break. We were heavily beaten in the one-day international series, including at Port of Spain in Trinidad and Tobago, where Imran's eight overs were looted for 76. We were jogging round Queen's Park the next day when Imran noticed that the bowling analyses were still on the scoreboard. 'Sisterfuckers!' he seethed. He looked round the group and chose its most junior member, seamer Zakir Khan, to get the scores taken down. Nobody dared laugh. The silence was total. I can still hear the scrape of Zakir's spikes on the steps, then the manual lowering of each of the numbers until the captain was satisfied.

Suddenly, however, the tide turned. Against all expectations, we won the Test at Bourda in Georgetown, Guyana. Stuck on 99 for thirty-eight minutes, Javed made a brave century. Despite an infection in his foot, Imran took eleven for 121. The West Indies, unusually ragged, were furious. When we went in to knock off our 30-run victory target, Patrick Patterson bowled as swiftly as I ever saw him, and at our county I often saw him. Ramiz attempted a pull shot that went for six off his top edge, over the wicketkeeper's head. On the hosts, though, we soon inflicted a first home defeat in a decade.

My first tour to the region was eye-opening. Parts of the West Indies were incomparably beautiful; so were certain West Indians. In Guyana, a young woman flew Imran, Ejaz and myself on a private plane over the forest. Imran then vanished with her, while Ejaz and I amused ourselves swimming and boating in a river. But I did not warm to the Caribbean. The crowds were very hostile, the conditions poor. Lunch at the ground was not only mediocre, you could not access it without a ticket; when I misplaced my ticket a couple of times, I went hungry. The pitches were nothing special either. In the Trinidad Test I bowled left-arm spin, and was annoyed when Sally missed a stumping because Viv then crunched me for consecutive boundaries. After Sally appealed for an lbw, Viv shaped up as if to fight him. Between times he was magnificent. I finally trapped him lbw for 123 with the second new ball.

I enjoyed my rivalry with Viv. He had the broadest shoulders, the biggest swagger. Nobody occupied the crease like him. Nobody chewed gum like him – it was like he was chomping down on you. Still, maybe he was just a little past his peak, and that cap was an invitation to bounce him. In the Third Test at Bridgetown, Barbados, I had him caught at fine leg by Mudassar in the first innings, then threw myself into bowling the penultimate over of the fourth day in West Indies's second innings, knocking his cap off and following through with a 'Fuck off' for good measure.

Suddenly Viv seemed to swell in size. 'Don't swear at me, man,' he rumbled. 'Or I'll kill you.'

I did not know Viv well at this stage, but I knew him well enough to understand that he was not a man to say anything lightly. 'What do I do with Viv?' I asked Imran at mid-off anxiously as I walked back. 'He said he's going to kill me.'

'Don't worry,' said Imran. 'I am with you. Give him another.'

So I did, and a few more for good measure, amid lots of mutual snarling, before stumps were drawn. I was sitting in the dressing room afterwards, halfway through getting changed, when the attendant rushed up to me. 'Someone wants to see you outside,' he said gravely.

Literally with one shoe on and the other off, I asked naively: 'Who?'

'You'd better come,' the attendant said.

The great man's bare torso was glistening with sweat; he held a bat on his shoulder, wore a snarl on his face. Not waiting for him to open his mouth, I ducked back into the dressing room to where Imran was sitting. 'It's Viv,' I said anxiously. 'He was serious. He wants to kill me.'

A smile crossed my captain's face. 'It's your fight,' he said. 'You sort it out.'

There was no avoiding it. I returned to Viv with a grovelling apology on my lips. 'I'm sorry, Viv,' I stammered. 'It will never happen again.'

'Make sure it doesn't,' he said intently. 'This is your last warning.'

I wasn't so intimidated that I didn't enjoy it when I bowled him the next morning, and we looked certain winners when the West Indies were eight for 207 chasing 266, but then Dujon survived an lbw shout against Qadir to compile a series-levelling partnership with Winston Benjamin. We were then absolutely baffled when police turned up in our dressing room to question Qadir, who after his appeal was rejected had thrown a punch at a heckling spectator. Though he had not actually connected, our team manager Intikhab Alam had to find money to get the charges withdrawn.

It was a suitable note on which to finish a series I'll never forget for the brutality, and the brilliance, of the cricket: the speed of the rising Curtly Ambrose; the tenacity of the old stager Javed in his back-to-back hundreds; being at the non-striker's end when Sally hooked two sixes then had his nose broken by Marshall. The home and away tests that Pakistan and the West Indies played in the 1980s were as close as anything came to a world Test championship – the West Indies, remember, were on their way to blackwashing England in their home summer. I was on the same trajectory. On 4 May 1988, I landed at Heathrow from Barbados for my long-awaited rendezvous with Lancashire.

CHAPTER 4

WASIM FOR ENGLAND

Wasim was, by any estimation, a great cricketer. He was the most brilliant, inventive left-arm fast bowler the game has known: quick with the new ball, and a prodigious swinger of the old ball, both ways. He was highly competitive to play against, and in combination with Waqar Younis offered one of the most potent new-ball threats the game has known. He was a hugely popular teammate at Lancashire, where he played for a decade in the late 1980s and 1990s. He threw himself into life in the north of England and retains a house there still, a measure of his affection for the county. Some of the happiest times of my career were alongside Wasim playing for Lancashire.

Mike Atherton

Waiting at arrivals was the county coach Alan Ormrod, an opening batsman who had retired three years earlier after playing 500 first-class matches. Bob Bennett had sent him to meet me, and I warmed to him immediately on our drive to the Nottingham Forte Posthouse. I was to be introduced to my teammates in a place where, I was to discover, a lot of a county team's time was spent – in the bar.

In the bar? I thought. What kind of team gets ready in the bar?

I soon found out. There they all were, players with whom I would spend so many of the succeeding years. There was Neil Fairbrother, who had recruited me; there was captain David Hughes, swing bowler Paul Allott and keeper Warren Hegg; there were the wily pros Jack Simmons and Mike Watkinson; there were our gutsy openers Graeme Fowler and Gehan Mendis. Each had ordered their favourite tipple. I, to their amusement, asked for a glass of milk. I tried to commit their nicknames to memory: Harvey (Fairbrother), Yozzer (Hughes), Walt (Allott), Chooky (Hegg), Simmo (Simmons), Winker (Watkinson), Foxy (Fowler), Dix (Mendis) et al.

Next day, I started going quietly about my work at Trent Bridge, and to my teammates' bemusement got the Dukes ball reversing. What was I doing? Could they do it too?

I started explaining. The important thing was that the square had to be dry, so that the ball made as little contact with dampness as possible; if the ball got even slightly wet, whether from grass or palms or pants, it would do nothing. But bouncing a throw in so that the rough side hit an abrasive square accelerated the process; if by accident you hit the shiny side, you had to try to smooth it as much as possible.

They were no less bemused, if less inclined to imitation, when I introduced my Imran-inspired training regime. They noted that I would always take the oldest balls out of the training bag: the older the better when you were experimenting with reverse swing. They noted that when it rained, I either headed out to run laps or in to bowl in the indoor nets, usually to Gehan, a fine player.

'You're crazy!' they'd joke. 'You've got six months. Just relax.'

I couldn't do it. 'I can't relax,' I would say. 'I'm not built that way.'

They did find one rather cunning way to slow me down, at least temporarily, keeping completely straight faces when I complained about the heaviness of my cricket coffin. After a few weeks I found that a prankster had secreted several bricks in it. Mind you, everyone's favourite prank was persuading me that on being introduced to a woman it was polite to ask: 'So, do you like shagging?'

I had a good season. I started taking my batting more seriously after I made my maiden first-class century: 116 not out against Somerset, in my first outing at Old Trafford. I almost made another at Southport against Surrey. On 98 I absolutely nailed one to deep mid-wicket where David Ward was grazing, having not heard his captain call him in off the boundary. My consolation was a hat-trick in the same game. I bowled a lot: 2450 balls in all, for fifty-one wickets. The only downside was that I aggravated my chronic groin problems, had to miss some games, and would eventually be ruled out of the Tests we hosted against Australia later in the year.

Most fascinating was the cultural contrast of first-class systems. Players in domestic cricket in Pakistan don't really form strong bonds; English county cricket was a genuine community. In Pakistan, I was accustomed to wandering round in whatever I wanted to wear; at Lancashire, the expectation was a navy blue jacket and red rose tie every day. The staff were part of everything. The room attendant, Ron Spriggs, had my tea, toast and clean laundry waiting for me every morning. The groundsman, Peter Marron, would let guys loose with their golf clubs on the outfield when we won. You were expected to put in your time at the bar every evening with teammates and opponents. One of the twelfth man's jobs was to have the first round ready when everyone arrived, from Walt's pint of Stella to Harvey's bottle of Bud; there, every night, would be my pint of milk until, after a few months, I buckled, and started having the occasion tipple just to be social. Daily life depended heavily on running gags. The boys never let me forget the occasion of the awarding of my county cap by Lancashire divinity Cyril Washbrook. 'Ladies and gentlemen,' he told the audience, 'please welcome Wasli Akrow.'

The travel was ceaseless. Everyone had a car; nobody was a poorer driver than I was. It took me years to come to terms with the idea of road rules, which in Pakistan simply didn't exist. Everyone drove with one eye on a map; nobody got lost more than me. I once became so disoriented on the

M60 that I abandoned my old-model Volvo and simply called a cab to get me the rest of the way. There was, nonetheless, always a solid core of members who would follow us to offer support during four-day matches, and reliable contingents at our limited-overs fixtures. There was a tradition of overseas players, like Farokh Engineer and Clive Lloyd, becoming honorary Lancastrians. When I played Sunday League matches, which I loved because the restricted run was exactly the length of my shortened approach, fans chanted 'Wasim for England'.

Could I be 'for England', as it were? There were hurdles to surmount. For a while I was self-conscious about the communal showers and baths. I also found I couldn't eat the lunches of soup, cold meat and salad at the ground. One day I started tucking into the pasta when a teammate told me it contained bacon – I hastily spat it out. Mind you, my faith also came in handy at times. My first roommate was Peter Martin, a great guy and a terrific seam bowler, but a terrible snorer. I felt self-conscious about complaining until I came up with a graceful solution, explaining that I was worried I might disturb Peter by getting up at nights to pray. I was quickly granted a single room. Eventually I even got a nickname – 'King', which I both appreciated and was slightly embarrassed by.

I was determined to go beyond my experience at Burnopfield and become part of my teammates' social circle, so when a Pakistani friend began bringing delicacies to the dressing room I would share them. I accepted invitations to their homes. 'Would you like a cooper?' said Harvey's mother by way of introduction. Cooper? Ah ha, cuppa! Yes, I would love a cuppa tea. Golf? Never played it Harvey, but sure. A left-hander is a left-hander. I started buying clothes, new shoes, trying to look a little smarter, trying to sound a little more polished. I had made a good friend in Chishty's son Ahsan, a year younger than me but Birmingham-educated and English-speaking. He often joined me on the road. One day when driving between games, I asked him: 'Will you help me improve my English?' He said: 'Sure, providing you help me learn Punjabi.' So we did. He also cajoled me into getting a decent haircut – it was goodbye to my old mullet, never to be seen again.

Finally, after traipsing from one temporary dwelling to another, from the Trafford Hotel to a pub on Dunham Road, I decided to buy some property. Sufi Sadiq was a local accountant and a friend of Imran's who did my taxes free of charge. 'Why don't you buy a house?' he asked one day.

'But I don't have a penny,' I protested.

Patiently, Sufi explained mortgages to me, how I could borrow against my £4000 a month, guaranteed for six seasons. From an elderly couple in St Margaret's Close, Altrincham, near the Fairbrothers, I acquired a four-bedroom townhouse. I bought some very ugly furniture, including black couches which clashed violently with the pink, flowery carpet. A girlfriend painted a mural on a wall. The house has changed a lot since, but I still own it, and I'm still proud of it – my boys grew up there, and I feel very much at home.

At first, I was a little worried about looking after myself. The nearest McDonald's, whose Filet-O-Fish was my staple diet, was a little far away. Then the county secretary, a lovely woman named Rose, fixed me up with crockery, cutlery, pots and pans, and my father sent over a family friend, Qasim, to be my domestic helper. He had a variety of duties, including coming with me when I wanted to bowl extra overs in the nets and retrieving balls for me. Qasim was a poor cook but an old charmer, and eventually married an English woman in the same street.

Of course, in those early days, I did suffer for my naivety. One afternoon I was wandering through the pet section of a big retail warehouse when I came across a cage of marmosets – fluffy New World monkeys from South America. They looked cute, seemed playful. I thought some animal company might be nice, so I told the shop assistant I liked them. 'Have four,' he said. There were two problems. Firstly, they stank. Secondly, they could not be left at home, relying as they did on a constant supply of crickets. My constant supply of cricket had to take precedence. In fact, that constancy was taking its toll. Injury caused the longest gap in my Test career – eighteen months – and in the interim I had to be nursed in one-day cricket. I had a heart problem too.

With Imran one night, I went to a party at Abdul Rahman Bukhatir's house in Karachi. Among the guests were next-door neighbours the Mufti family, including 21-year-old Huma, daughter of a Pakistani father, a successful chartered accountant who ran a Nissan franchise, and his Croatian wife. I was immediately smitten, captivated by both her beauty and her intelligence. In fact, after a brief flirtation, she went to study European history, English literature and psychology at London's University College, while I peeled off to play a Benson & Hedges World Series Cup in Australia and an Asia Cup in Bangladesh. Our lives were headed in different directions, she explained to me matter-of-factly. I was devastated – I mourned for months.

Soon after I arrived for my second season at Old Trafford in April 1989, a message was passed on to me by the switchboard: a girl had left her number, with the advice

Huma: so beautiful, so smart.

KAMAL SHARMA

that if I was in London she would be happy to have dinner. I drove to London the next day – it helped, given my poor sense of direction, that her father had bought her a little apartment near Lord's, in Oslo Court off St John's Wood Road near Regent's Park. I was so determined to spend every waking moment with Huma that after each day's play of Lancashire's first county match at Edgbaston, I drove from Birmingham to London, then drove back the next morning at 5 am.

Huma was *the* girl. She was so confident, so mature; she read and listened widely; she knew I was a cricketer but it did not faze her. Imran, whose life was so full of beautiful women, had always counselled against early marriage. 'Don't get married until you are at least twenty-eight, Waz,' he had told me. 'It is too distracting.' I confess I was thoroughly distracted that summer, but my cricket was a good advertisement for the endorphins released by love: my sixty-two first-class wickets cost less than 18 as we finished fourth in the championship, and I took a record twenty-seven wickets at 14 as we won the Sunday League.

When we returned to Pakistan later in the year, I stayed in a friend's flat in Karachi in order to be near Huma, to meet her friends, to watch the educated elite at close quarters. My mother knew merely that we were good friends, although she must have had suspicions. Till this point in my life, Imran had been my only partnership. Now I had a second, and was about to form a third.

• • •

The next decade in Pakistan would be defined by rivalry. General Zia had been killed in August 1988 in a mysterious plane crash near Bahawalpur, heralding the restoration of democracy – or, at least, the Pakistani version of it. Benazir Bhutto's revived PPP and Nawaz Sharif's Islamic Democratic Alliance alternated in power. There also emerged, out of student politics, the Mohajir Qaumi Movement, strong in Sindh, and with fluctuating allegiances. Always, of course, there was the rivalry with India, played out bloodily in disputes over Kashmir which culminated in the Kargil War in 1999. Finally, there was cricket.

At the top of the 1988–89 season in Pakistan, I played the domestic limited-overs competition, the Wills Cup, for Pakistan International Airlines. I also watched some of it on television, including a game between United Bank and Habib Bank in Gujranwala where a very good domestic player, Agha Zahid, was completely beaten for pace hooking a bouncer, the edge flying down to third man. That same young quick, Waqar Younis, was bowling a couple of weeks later when I turned on the television at Imran's house in Zaman Park, and United Bank were playing Delhi in the Super Wills Final at Gaddafi Stadium. 'Watch him, skipper,'

I told Imran. 'He's quick.' Imran was so intrigued that after I left he went to the ground, intercepted Waqar as he came off, and invited him to a training camp for the national squad a few days hence.

At that stage, I think I was as fast as anyone around. During the World Series Cup at Bellerive, Hobart in December 1988, I bowled a spell that stands out in my memory, when everything clicked, and the ball flew. Viv Richards was batting without a helmet, as always. I came round the wicket and angled one in at his left shoulder. I knew it would be called a no ball – bouncers were in those days – but I wanted to make an impact. I did. Viv went back as if to hook, then realised it was too quick even for him – he later said it was the quickest ball he ever received. You'd never have known it. Viv made even his evasive action look elegant. He squared his shoulders and chomped his gum. Since then he's confessed that he still has 'nightmares about it every now and again'. From a man who could be a nightmare to bowl to, I cherish that compliment.

I also knew pace when I saw it, and Waqar had it. He was seventeen years old, broad-shouldered, strong-legged. He ran 30 metres to bowl, and his stock ball was full and fast, even if at that stage he was overfond of the bouncer. He was quiet too – as quiet as I'd been five years earlier. He hailed from Burewala, a small cotton-growing town on the Punjab's Sutlej River, and was self-conscious about having only four fingers on one hand – jumping from a bridge to swim in a canal when younger, he'd gotten the finger caught in a crack. Anyway, I was already proud of him. He was my guy. I'd spotted him. When we went to Sharjah for the Champions Trophy in October 1989, I wanted him to play. For Waqar it was actually a homecoming. He had grown up in the UAE, studied at Sharjah College. But the heat and his desperation to impress in that debut match got the better of him; he cramped up after four very swift overs, and the West Indies were five for 209 chasing 251.

I remember that game for Imran's uncanny intuition. From round the wicket, I knocked over the leg stumps of Jeff Dujon and Malcolm Marshall with consecutive balls that swung back late, then asked Imran how to approach the hat-trick ball, to be faced by Curtly Ambrose. 'He will expect the inswinger,' said Imran. 'Bowl him an outswinger.' It pitched middle and hit off, just as prophesied – only the fourth hat-trick in ODI cricket. In the penultimate over I bowled Courtney Walsh to win the game by 11 runs. Next day against India, having taken three for 30, I was sent in at the fall of the first wicket against India, hit my second ball from my old friend Ravi for six, then three more. My 37 off twenty-three balls set up a comfortable victory.

As we went on, however, Waqar became the talk. He was frighteningly fast, and had arrived just as the edge was coming off Imran's pace, and others like Zakir, Aaqib Javed and Ata-ur-Rehman were emerging to challenge for a place. With Saleem making a hundred, we smashed India in the final. There was also a young leg-spinner, Mushtaq Ahmed, who loomed as a successor to Abdul Qadir, with the same bouncy approach, the same finger-licking habit, the same beseeching appeal.

These were timely emergences. It was a period which required a constant infusion of new blood, when tours and tournaments were scheduled hard up against one another, and official travel days were almost unknown. Let me give you a sense of it. The night of that Champions Trophy final, we flew 3000 kilometres from Dubai, arrived in

Bhubaneswar near midnight, then boarded a bus at 5.30 am for a two-hour journey to Barabati Stadium, Cuttack, where we were to commence the Nehru Cup. This was a pretty big deal, the next best thing to a World Cup – only New Zealand among the Test nations was not involved. But we were shattered. Worse, no sooner had we wearily lost our opening game to England than we were on our way to the airport for an overnight flight to Mumbai to play Australia the following day.

Amazingly, we found something, beat the World Cup holders, and again headed straight to the airport, finding ourselves on a plane to Amritsar with the West Indies, who had beaten India the same day. Everyone was tired. Everyone was testy. As we rose to our feet on landing, I saw Ambrose hurl Qadir back into his seat and start throwing punches. Apparently Abdul had been tossing screwed-up bits of paper at the back of Ambrose's conspicuous head during the flight. Viv had to separate them; Imran stood to one side in tears of laughter. To add to the stress, the Punjab had recently been the scene of sectarian violence, so we had to be helicoptered to an army camp and afforded an armed escort to the ground.

We were all a bit of a mess by this stage, lost the match in Jalandhar, just edged Sri Lanka in Lucknow, then went straight to the airport and arrived at the Taj Bengal in Kolkata near midnight ready for a 7.45 am bus to Eden Gardens. In this, our last qualifying match, we needed to beat the hosts. Our eyes were out on stalks. We could barely put one foot in front of the other. But the big crowd and the do-or-die occasion lifted us. India were none for 120 chasing 280 when I ran out Kris Srikkanth, and their last eight wickets fell for 47 to gain us the last semi-final spot.

Waqar then bowled furiously against England in Nagpur, and we had effectively crashed India's party. We returned to Kolkata to meet the West Indies in the final of a tournament being held to mark the centenary of India's first prime minister.

In his last ODI in India, Imran was just superb. In front of 70,000 spectators, he dismissed Viv, Dujon and Gus Logie, and piloted us to the brink of a win with 55 not out, so that we needed four off three balls when I joined him. 'Waz,' he said sternly, 'take a single and leave it to me. Don't hit across the line. We have only Qadir, Aaqib and Mushie left.' I tried to do the right thing, honestly. I pulled back to dab on the off side, but Viv followed me, put one in my arc, and I really had no choice but to swipe him for six over mid-wicket. Imran stared daggers at me all the way off. I tried to look nonchalant – after all, what could I do? The captain's humour was restored by the US$40,000 winners' cheque – a king's ransom in those days – and the individual awards for match and series.

Looking back, I think that this Nehru Cup, now long forgotten, was one of our most remarkable and auspicious achievements as a team. In nineteen days, we had won nine out of eleven one-day internationals in seven different cities separated by 50,000 kilometres. Two and a half years later, many of the same players were involved in lifting a World Cup; it wasn't a coincidence.

· · ·

The guard was changing in India too, reflected in the party they brought to Pakistan soon after. At National Stadium in Karachi, we got our first glimpse of Sachin Tendulkar, who was purportedly sixteen but looked about twelve. Waqar, who was also making his Test debut, the day before his eighteenth birthday, roused himself to a fearsome spell that day. He beat the bat repeatedly. He hit Tendulkar on the helmet. Imran put me in at second slip, where I dropped a chance that absolutely flew. Some Indian players at the time were nervous around pace. I dismissed Srikkanth seven times in eight innings in that series, and on the eighth occasion caught him at fine leg off Imran. But Tendulkar looked increasingly comfortable. When Imran sent India in on a green top at Faisalabad, the prodigy made the most composed half-century you can imagine. On another sporting pitch at Sialkot, Waqar hit Tendulkar in the face, drawing blood; after taking painkillers overnight, Tendulkar came back and made a composed 57. In a match at Peshawar in the one-day series, he took 28 off the penultimate over from Qadir, leaving me to defend 14 in the last. Fortunately I closed the innings out.

The weakness in our cricket at the time was fielding. We had no culture of slip catching. The cordon was chosen according to seniority. That's how I ended up being tried there, although I was never comfortable. Traditionally it had not mattered much. Our leading pace bowlers, Imran included, had depended on bringing the ball into the bat; now that Waqar and I were swinging it both ways, it became more of a factor. Our fielders in this series against India dropped two dozen catches in four Tests; it became a surprise if anything stuck, and four times the visitors escaped with draws after conceding first-innings deficits. For our next opponents, Australia, we would need to be many times better. I would need to be too.

CHAPTER 5

AN ALL-ROUNDER AT LAST

I hold Wasim Akram in the highest regard. So much so that if there is reincarnation, I would want to come back as him! Not only a great bloke, but probably the greatest left-arm quick the cricket world has seen.

Allan Border

I had high hopes for three forthcoming Tests down under, for which I was visiting Australia a fourth time. The ball was coming out well, and my batting seemed at last to be catching up with my bowling. The division of labour in Pakistan had traditionally been absolute: if you bowled, you did not bat. The result was very fit bowlers but also very long tails. Imran was the great exception. County cricket had changed my attitude. Everyone at Lancashire was expected to be able to hold a bat, especially an overseas pro. There were so many games that you could bat multiple times in a week, and experiment with your approach – and while you can slog your way to 30, you can't slog your way to 100.

I'd also benefited from the freedom that county cricket offered my bowling. I tutored myself in pace variations after watching the West Indian Franklyn Stephenson, who must be the best cricketer to never play a Test match. He was a phenomenal player for Nottinghamshire: superb in the field, a powerful hitter, and a pace bowler whose slower delivery nobody could pick. He had these huge hands in which he'd hide the ball, and he would release it out the back with top spin so it dipped – sometimes he would bowl guys as they ducked under the ball. When I asked him how he did it, he told me. The only trouble was that his accent was so thick I could not understand him. Too embarrassed to ask again, I decided to have a go in the nets following what I thought he had said, inevitably bowling a fair few full tosses and hitting a few guys. 'Fuck off Waz!' they'd grumble. Gradually, though, it became a crucial part of my armoury in the Sunday League, alongside the cutter I already bowled.

There was a fantastic variety of techniques in county cricket. The first time I saw Peter Willey from Northants, he stood chest-on to me as I stood at the end of my run, toes pointing down the pitch – I could not believe it was his stance. I hated bowling to Kim Barnett from Derbyshire. He moved round the crease constantly so you never saw his stumps, and he was a beautiful striker of the ball too. So many players, so many challenges. You had to experiment. Having come round the wicket to right-handers for years, for instance, I also decided in England to try it against left-handers. 'Why can't I bowl round the wicket to a left-hander?' I asked Imran. 'The ball will go away with the angle, but if I can get it to straighten even slightly, there's a chance of a lbw or bowled.' I was thinking ahead to those moments I might need a variation on a pitch offering no assistance – like, it turned out, the one I encountered on the first day of play in Melbourne on 12 January 1990.

That morning, I remember, the Kookaburra did nothing – on a slow pitch, it went gun-barrel straight. Australia were none for 90 when, suddenly, I started reversing it from round the wicket. Geoff Marsh nicked an outswinger, David Boon padded up to an inswinger, and to the left-handed Border I stayed at the same angle and *just* beat the outside edge. 'He's not going to get any closer to a hat-trick than that,' said Richie Benaud, commentating – he wasn't wrong. I did eventually get my man, driving at an away swinger, then picked up Peter Sleep, Merv Hughes and Terry Alderman to obtain my best Test figures, six for 62, despite four catches going down.

When I came in to bat on the second afternoon, unfortunately, we were six for 65. Unlike us, the Australians had caught everything on offer. We'd perhaps never had a better chance to put Australia under pressure at home, but our batters had bottled it. The guy who battled hardest was Tauseef, who hung around for more than two hours at number nine. When we came in at teatime, Imran said loudly in the dressing room: 'Why can't you guys bat like Tauseef? He plays straight or he lets it go. Simple.' Two balls into the final session, Carl Rackemann hit Tauseef in the midriff; worse, he was wearing a Pakistani box and it disintegrated.

'Tauseef *bhai*, are you all right?' I asked. I swear his eyes were watering.

GETTY/BOB THOMAS

Main stage: during my eleven for 160 against Australia at the MCG in January 1990.

'This is Imran's fault,' he said breathlessly. 'Why did he have to praise me? Look what's happened.'

In the second innings I picked up Dean Jones lbw, Steve Waugh caught trying to leave, and Ian Healy mis-hooking. Yorking Sleep and bouncing out Merv left me with eleven for 160 from 71.4 overs. But even with a seven-and-a-half-hour century from my roommate Ejaz Ahmed, we could do no better than narrow our margin of defeat to 92 runs. Nor did we make the most of winning the toss at Adelaide Oval, and this time when I came in the score was six for 187. With little to come, I played my shots for sixty-eight balls, making 52 of our last 70 runs.

Australia had taken the lead by the end of the second day, and I was limping from the pain in my groin. Still we fought. I picked up five for 100, including both David Boon and Steve Waugh padding up as the ball tailed back late, although Aamer Malik dropped Dean Jones at 19 going on 116. What was I saying about catching?

The match was in the balance when I joined Imran early on the fourth day – we had just wiped off our deficit, the pitch had settled right down, and my captain at the other end always made me play sensibly. When I was 12, I punched one back to Greg Campbell, who just got an outstretched finger on it – it was the only semblance of a chance I offered. Otherwise, I planted my front foot and drove – through point, through cover, straight, once so hard that my captain could not get out of the way and wore it on the shoulder. As always, he was my conscience, with a caution every over. 'Pick your shots,' he said. 'Play straight. Don't slog.' When the off-spinner Peter Taylor bowled, I was dying to hit him against the spin, but Imran simply would not let me. I blocked. I picked up singles.

Finally I cleared my front leg and sent the ball over wide mid-on – a big hit on the Oval's long, straight boundaries. Imran nodded: 'Good shot. But be careful. There's a hundred for you here.' It was the first time I'd thought of it, and Imran would set the example. On a misfield at mid-off, I charged through to get my captain his 100th run; not long after, I pulled Merv for four to bring up my century. I did not know quite how to celebrate. I stuck both arms awkwardly in the air but quickly pulled them down, feeling self-conscious. Imran shook my hand briskly, although I could see he was proud. When Campbell bowled me off my pads, I'd made 123 out of our four-hour, 191-run partnership. Imran, aged thirty-seven, batted eight hours for his 136, on top of having bowled twenty-seven overs. Who could not be inspired playing with such a man? Had Mushtaq Ahmed accepted a return chance from Dean Jones on the last day, we might even have squared the series. As it was, Dean completed a brace of centuries, and this Test and the next were drawn.

Somewhat to my surprise, I was named man of the series, and Australia was the kind of place where you got recognised. I tried not to mind it, although the trappings and circles of fame didn't come naturally to me. I remember as our bus pulled into the MCG car park one day, we saw a red Ferrari we came to know was Dean Jones's – a brash car for a brash player. Subconsciously I compared it to my Suzuki at home. I still felt awkward, unworldly. One day in Sydney, Imran took me to the famous fish restaurant Doyle's. Oysters? Calamari? I could make nothing of them. I stuck to bread and butter. Nor could I make much of the guest I was sitting next to: balding, bespectacled, unassuming. 'He's Elton John,' Imran confided. I was none the wiser.

In the middle, I was completely at ease. For the first time in my life I felt more than a tailender who could hit. I was confident of my defence. On that bedrock I could build. In the first final of the World Series Cup, I came in at five for 50 and made my maiden one-day half-century. I scored 86 of 109 runs added while I was at the crease, including five fours and three sixes, in seventy-six balls. Batting at number three in the second final, I made 36 off thirty. By tour's end, in fact, I was more comfortable batting than bowling because my groin was really troubling me, and only painkilling injections were keeping me going.

Intikhab Alam went in search of a surgeon and located a sports physician involved with the Sydney Roosters and Newcastle Knights, Neil Halpin. Halpin agreed to operate providing I joined him on the west coast of Tasmania, where he was doing six months' charity work. So I flew to Hobart, where Halpin collected me for the four-hour drive to Queenstown. There he relieved the strain on the left side of my groin by cutting one of the adductor muscles away from the pelvis. I was a long way from home but well looked after: Halpin was a great guy, and a local Indian family fed me. I made a quick recovery, even though in hindsight I probably rushed back: I reappeared in the Austral-Asia Cup six weeks after the operation, when I was still experiencing postoperative pain. I was limping in the final when I slogged an unbeaten 49 off thirty-five balls, then yorked Merv Hughes, Rackemann and Alderman from round the wicket in a hat-trick – my second in just over six months.

In my absence, Waqar had really hit his straps. He had taken fifteen wickets for 94 in three Tests, and been recruited by Surrey. Bowling his bouncer more sparingly and developing a fiendish reverse swinging yorker, he took

240 first-class wickets at 17 in the next eighteen months. It was good to see another Pakistani on the county circuit, particularly one I had helped identify and foster. We would drop into our own language when we saw each other, chat about this and that. He got me out in our Benson & Hedges Cup quarter-final at Old Trafford, but we ended up winning thanks to a brilliant innings from my Altrincham neighbour Harvey, who was then even better in the semi. Because Waqar and I were rivals too, we followed each other's performances, used them as a spur, set ourselves to win big games, grab big wickets.

The Benson & Hedges Cup became Lancashire's target that season. We had a terrific one-day team, not only internationals like Harvey, Daffy DeFreitas and the young Mike Atherton, but also our keeper Warren Hegg, this super-proud Lancastrian, and Ian Austin, a short, stout but improbably agile cricketer with a lot of one-day smarts and a wonderful throwing arm. We were ably led by David Hughes, who knew just what to do and when, and used me as a first-change bowler to maximise my opportunities for reverse swing.

I'd not realised what a big deal one-day finals were. We were all outfitted for new suits. There was a send-off for the team at Old Trafford. Members followed us on coaches to St John's Wood to raise a great chant of 'Lanky-Lanky-Lanky-Lancashire' throughout the day. Having my breakfast on the Saturday morning in the Danubius Hotel across the road from Lord's, I spread the newspapers out and read about the big contest of the final: me versus Worcestershire's Graeme Hick. I'd played against him, of course, and we shared a bat-maker in Duncan Fearnley. Born in Zimbabwe, he was still a year off qualifying for England, but was comfortably the championship's tallest scorer. He'd scored 1000 runs in May; he'd made 405 not out in a single innings against Somerset. The only thing was that counties could then only play one international at a time; if you saw them off, there was not much else to stop a batter seriously intent on run-making. I sensed Hick was vulnerable to the yorker – a tall man, he stood with his bat off the ground. I sensed I could unsettle him with a bouncer – a stiff mover, he found it hard to evade. Even on the slow county pitches, a bouncer was a good option because the uneven bounce made it unpredictable. I'd actually seldom felt so confident of a one-on-one contest. I went into the game convinced Hick was mine.

In fact, Worcestershire sent us in, and we had a battle early on against their seamers: Botham, plus Phil Newport and Neal Radford, both of whom played for England. Winker Watkinson held us together through the middle, then the sun came out and we got away in the last ten overs, thanks to Chooky and Daffy; I managed 28 off twenty-one balls, including a six off Radford into the top tier of the Members. Worcestershire were none for 27 chasing our 241 when David Hughes brought me on at the Nursery End. In my first over I got some extra bounce, and Chooky caught Tim Curtis.

As Hick took guard, I was almost pawing at the ground. I sprinted in so hard that I overstepped, but the bouncer was just about perfect. Hick swayed back, and I could see in his attitude he understood the stakes of the contest too. He stooped a little. He looked away. With the next ball I nearly yorked him, and he scuttled off strike with a leg bye. The third ball I bowled him jagged away sharply: he had to play, could only nick, and I was running so fast I reached the slips fielders before he had passed them on the way to the pavilion. Only Botham delayed us long after that and, later in the afternoon, David Hughes held the cup aloft. Such was the congestion of the English cricket schedule back then, we hosted Worcestershire in the Sunday League the next day. This time I bowled Hick off an inside edge, and we won again with ten overs to spare. Later in the summer we added the NatWest Trophy to the cabinet at Old Trafford.

There were some grim days and bleak places in county cricket: the two showers at Derby; the distant car park at Leicester; the long, long drives. When I wanted to see Huma in London during games, I used to enlist my friend Ahsan, a sensible guy and a non-drinker, who would borrow his mother's car and ferry me from wherever I was to St John's Wood and back. There were days I would return to Altrincham at 5 am, then head for Old Trafford having had only a couple of hours' sleep. On one occasion I needed to return to Manchester from Derby in a hurry, and asked Ahsan to collect me – the drive was not so far but would take too long on the team bus. As he picked me up, the rain started falling, but we chatted happily for an hour, then two hours, then three. Finally I said: 'Hey, I'm hungry. Can we pull in at a roadhouse?' While I was doing so, Ahsan asked a staff member: 'So how far are we from Manchester?' The staff member said: 'Manchester? You're nearly in Scotland!' We'd been driving three hours in the wrong direction. What should have taken an hour took six.

The Lancashire guys were right. I gradually fell in with a culture that looked forward to rain, with Ian Austin as our chief meteorologist. 'Coming from that direction, twenty minutes,' he would say, and never be wrong. But those finals we played are among the best memories of cricket I have.

• • •

Now that Waqar and I were on the county circuit, there was more talk among professionals about reverse swing. There was actually nothing so mysterious about it. 1990 was a dry summer in England. The outfields were parched, the ball scuffed readily; my fielders, by now, knew what to do. We'd even cured our off-spinner Gary Yates of licking his fingers between deliveries.

With this came muffled muttering about how we were achieving swing with old balls – when an opponent achieved reverse swing, especially a Pakistani one, it was convenient to blame 'ball tampering'. New Zealand took that course when we hosted them in October 1990 after Waqar and I took fifteen wickets between us in Karachi, and Waqar took seven for 86 in the second innings in Lahore. In Faisalabad, the New Zealand medium-pacer Chris Pringle took a customised bottle top to the ball at drinks and, when the umpires did not inspect it, kept on scratching until he had taken seven for 52 on debut. Waqar retaliated with a matchwinning twelve for 130. We did nothing out of the ordinary in that series. Probably the key to Waqar's success was that we were using Pakistani balls, Grays, which were rock-hard: unusually for Pakistan, all the edges carried; still more unusually for Pakistan, they were caught.

I did not, in fact, bowl particularly well. I was coming to realise that I'd rushed my comeback. What I'd not realised was that the adductor surgery had left me with a left leg only half as strong as my right. I had always bowled to get fit, not vice versa. I needed to find a way to compensate, so I visited London for remedial work, and was instructed in scientific weight training. I came back, gingerly, alongside Imran in three home Tests against the West Indies.

I remember that summer in Pakistan for the batting of three men often left out of calculations when you're talking about the very elite. I never saw a batsman play reverse swing better than Martin Crowe. 'How do you do it?' I asked him eventually. 'Somehow we can't stop you.'

His answer illustrated what a great player he was: 'I've got a simple technique for you guys. I get on the front foot and play for the inswinger. That's the danger ball in Pakistan because nothing is going over the top of the stumps. If you beat me on the outside six balls out of six, I don't care. Because if I guard my stumps for three or four overs, you and Waqar lose patience and bounce me, which is what I want you to do.'

That was Martin: he was so confident he could tell you what he was doing and still challenge you to beat him. Had he come from a country other than New Zealand, he would now be an all-time great, up there with Viv, Tendulkar and Brian Lara.

In Karachi, Saleem Malik made as good a century against the West Indies as you'd see, as we raced to a win. He could make batting look so easy: light on his feet, opening up the off side with his wrists. His cricket brain was super-sharp, and he had wonderful tactical instincts. As I've said, his weakness was personality. Had he been a simple, straightforward guy, he'd also be regarded as one of the best of all time, such was his talent. But he was sneaky, untrustworthy, was often unpleasant to deal with, would talk behind your back. Imran nicknamed him 'Rat' for the facial resemblance, but it fitted in other respects too.

The other centurion in that game, Desmond Haynes, who was leading the West Indies in the absence of an injured Viv, was an interesting contrast. He wasn't an elegant player. He was a battler, brave and gutsy, a rock with a great front-foot technique. He also happened to be a terrific human being. Again, personality matters. The West Indies missed a trick in not making him a long-term captain rather than Richie Richardson. He led them to a terrific win in Faisalabad, where Ambrose, Walsh, Marshall and Ian Bishop were frightening – Javed, who was starting to struggle, asked Imran to demote him in the second innings, then did not play the next Test.

Frankly, the visitors should have won. We almost had to follow on in Lahore, and the only way I could keep the West Indies from romping away was by taking their last four second-innings wickets in five balls. Ironically, it was my captain who cost me the hat-trick. I had Dujon caught behind off a cutter, and stayed round the wicket to trap Ambrose lbw with an inswinger – Curtly, as always, was furious to be given out, and stalked off as though cheated of a century. To Bishop I bowled an outswinger on which he turned the bat too early, but Imran for some reason was slow to sight the leading edge and went for it unsuccessfully with one hand. 'Bad luck skipper,' I said loyally. But with some luck I might have improved on four wickets in five balls, which I achieved in my next over by yorking Marshall and Walsh.

The West Indies had ignored Imran's campaign for third-country umpires, so the series had two locals, which may have eased our task a little. Still, Imran and I were thrown together on the last day when Pakistan were six for 187 chasing 345 on a pitch with widening cracks. Having grafted 38 in two and a half hours in the first innings, I made 21 not out in an hour as Imran made 58 not out in nearly five hours. It felt like we batted for days. But as never before, I felt capable of that.

● ● ●

By now I was grooved into cricket twelve months of the year; sometimes it felt like thirteen. My next stop was Perth, where Lancashire were starting their pre-season with some matches against Western Australia. The super quick WACA was hardly the ideal preparation for soft English pitches in April, but everyone bought into the idea of a sunny holiday. I roomed at the Perth Sheraton with Hegg's deputy John Stanworth, who cockily told me that his nickname was 'John Shagworth', then proceeded to enjoy no action whatsoever.

Maybe I'd picked up some swagger too. I was a world-class player; I probably thought I should develop the manner to go with it. I also took the whispering about reverse swing personally. Had Australia or England prospered from a new skill, the cricket world would have stood and applauded. We were seen as sneaky, tricky, deceptive. Sometimes I rose to the bait. One of the most irritating characters around in those days was Dermot Reeve, who led Warwickshire and who strutted around like he'd invented captaincy. He was always looking for ways to ruffle and distract you. I was fielding at fine leg when we were playing at Edgbaston one day, and he walked around in front of the pavilion until he was in earshot and started waving a bottle opener, calling out: 'Did you need this? Hey Waz, do you need this?' I wanted to punch him. David Lloyd, who'd succeeded Alan Ormrod as our coach, wanted to as well.

Stresses came with being a high-profile overseas player. I zoomed to fifty first-class wickets that summer. I also made

122 off 165 balls against Hampshire at Basingstoke. Then, in the first round of the summer's NatWest Trophy, against Dorset at Dean Park, I was hit by a gentle full toss. It broke a bone in my foot – something I usually inflicted on others. It slowed me down at a crucial moment, on the eve of another Benson & Hedges Cup final against Worcestershire. There was enormous excitement at the prospect of another trophy, among our members and also among Pakistani fans, always so warm, patriotic and demanding. I had so many entreaties from my countrymen, and was so anxious not to let anyone down, that I spent £500 of my own money buying tickets. The match was an anticlimax. The day was overcast and the pitch moist – conditions better suited to their attack's conventional swing than my reverse swing – and I was held back to bowl second change, by which time Hick had played himself in.

Frustration welled up ten days later when we had our return match against Warwickshire at Old Trafford, and I ran foul of both umpires: Ken Palmer's brother Roy, and Nigel Plews. Needless to say, the sight of Reeve raised my hackles, and I started bouncing him, only for Palmer to tell me to 'spread them out', then give me an official warning when I didn't. Sensing my annoyance, Neil Fairbrother swapped me to the other end, only for Plews to warn me a second time. The pitch was slow, the ball was soft, and the bouncers posed no threat to anyone. I'd also seen players chew umpires out – these were the days before the ICC code of conduct, and there was a fair bit of latitude – and I snapped back. When Plews later admonished me for bowling a bouncer at tailender Tim Munton, I irritatedly bowled another, and he issued me a third warning, which entailed my removal from the attack. Within his earshot, I mumbled: 'Shit umpiring.'

Plews was an ex-policeman who umpired like one. Nothing happened straight away, but then the story appeared in the newspapers, and even on *News at Ten*. Lancashire suddenly felt as though they had to penalise me and, rather than impose a suspension, and thereby also handicap themselves, they fined me £1000. I paid, grumblingly. I also annoyed some members by withdrawing from the Sunday League final because my foot injury had not healed. It introduced a note of disharmony to what had previously been a very happy relationship. I brooded a little. Cricket could be a stern teacher.

CHAPTER 6

1992 AND ALL THAT

'Who's the best bowler you ever faced?' Unsurprisingly, that is the most frequently asked question that comes my way. Without blinking, the answer is simple. 'Wasim Akram.'

Left arm. Fast. Very fast. Swung the ball both ways. Brutal bouncer. Competitive animal, like all the best of them. When he wasn't bowling a lightning fast yorker or bouncer, his line and length was immaculate. Facing Wasim was like batting in a fishing net. You couldn't go anywhere. You couldn't score. Basically, it was a nightmare.

Adding to your woes, was the understanding that, behind the killer eyes and cobra-striking wrist, was one of the good guys. A gentleman who off the field was always smiling and offering a kind word of encouragement or a humble answer to his greatness. This made it harder to get into the fight. The smiling, gentleman assassin was in a class of his own.

Justin Langer

Our route to the 1992 World Cup was, frankly, bizarre. Immediately beforehand we hosted Sri Lanka in three Tests on terribly slow pitches – nothing like what we were preparing for, and more use to our visitors than us. Then we gathered for a five-day training camp in Lahore, which was almost as punishing. Finally, we travelled to Australia well ahead of our first game, basing ourselves at the Boulevard Hotel in King's Cross, and training more or less every day for three weeks at North Sydney Oval.

There were the usual undercurrents about the choice of the initial group. We left behind two very good players in Saeed Anwar and Shoaib Mohammed; nor, at first, did we bring Javed, for reasons that weren't altogether clear. It looked like an experimental squad, with lots of options and no obvious XI, and the first selection decision turned out to be involuntary. Waqar, who had arrived on the tour with a sore back aggravated by the training camp, proved to have stress fractures in his lower vertebrae and had to be sent home. He was followed by Saleem Jaffar, Shahid Saeed and Akram Raza, who were judged surplus to requirements. We played some lacklustre warm-up matches, winning one in six, and passing 200 just once. I was struggling badly with the white ball, there being one in use at each end in this tournament to counteract complaints about its deterioration. It was hard to get any better because the Board of Control for Cricket in Pakistan had us training almost exclusively with old balls. New balls were deemed 'too expensive'.

To outward appearances, then, Pakistan were making up the numbers. Co-hosts Australia and New Zealand had organised everything to suit themselves; other teams were compelled to rove like Bedouins. Still, there was a strange buoyancy about our team. We were young, unfancied, uninhibited, with talent that would underpin our next generation: Aamir Sohail; Inzamam-ul-Haq; Moin Khan; Aaqib Javed; Mushtaq Ahmed; and Iqbal Sikander, a Pakistan International Airlines teammate whom I had recommended as a back-up spinner. Australia was a fun place to tour because we could go anywhere, eat anything, do anything, even if we didn't often take advantage of that – with my roommate Ejaz Ahmed, I watched *Backdraft* and *Naked Gun 2 1/2* on video so often we could almost recite the dialogue. Ejaz also had a boom box he brought to training, so that we practised to the mighty qawwalis of Nusrat Fateh Ali Khan.

Above all there was the other Khan, Imran, who was totally in charge, completely confident, even a little forbidding. It's hard to explain to the current generation how powerful Pakistan's captain was in those days. Intikhab Alam was nominally 'manager' but did little more than hit a few high catches and distribute the 'dailies' – the per-diems that players, even Javed, greedily hoarded. Imran was Pakistan cricket front and back – our captain, our coach, our chief selector, and our conscience too. He had become obsessed with building a cancer hospital in Lahore named for his mother, Shaukat Khanum, whom he had lost to the disease in 1985. The government had offered land, but erection of the building and employment of personnel would have to come from private philanthropy. He enlisted us in the idea – not so strange given that one of the Five Pillars of Islam, *zakat*, is annual charitable donation. For a youthful group it was an inspiring vision, and reinforced a sense I think Imran wanted to instil: that we were on a mission, that it involved more than cricket, that God Almighty would help us. Favourite Australia losing their opening match in New Zealand seemed like another omen.

Of course, we were going to have to help ourselves first, and we didn't. Imran himself was struggling with a damaged shoulder which required daily injections. Then Javed arrived unexpectedly and not only replaced official vice-captain Saleem Malik but stood in for the injured Imran in the first game. We were a mess. On a dead MCG pitch against the West Indies, we limped to two for 220. Ramiz Raja went from 23 to 47 in singles, and dawdled 157 balls over a hundred. The white ball swung like crazy for ten overs – I gave away seven wides – then, after the lacquer was knocked off, it became impossible to polish. We dropped Desmond Haynes from consecutive balls and were unable to take a wicket, although I broke Brian Lara's foot with a yorker.

Imran came back for our next match, against Zimbabwe, but was wary of overexerting himself, so neither bowled nor batted. Javed and Aamir Sohail did the job, adding 145 for the third wicket. I disposed of their two best players, Andy Flower and Andy Pycroft, in my fifth over. But when we went to Adelaide Oval to play England, Imran rested himself again, and we fell apart. The pitch had sweated under the covers during the previous day's rain, and the sheen of green sent a tremor through our batters when we lost the toss. We should have scraped 150 together at least; we could not make half that. Our 74 was the lowest by a Test nation in the World Cup. I had Graham Gooch caught at the wicket, but at lunch England needed 58 to win with nine wickets in hand.

The timing of this World Cup, however, was unusual. It was late in the Australian summer, after their Test series and their World Series Cup, spilling into a phase of more uncertain weather. Perhaps because there had only ever been one washout in three previous cups, the organisers had not allowed for reserve days, or arrived at a fair system for revising rain-affected targets – ridiculously, you had to chase what your opponent made in their most productive overs. Adelaide Oval ground staff did not even bother covering the bowlers' run-ups, further delaying a restart and making time a factor: both teams needed to bat a minimum of fifteen overs, which had to be completed by 5.45 pm, for the game to have a result. So it was that fate – Imran's idea that God would look after us – gave us another chance.

When the match resumed at 4.45 pm, England needed 50 from thirteen overs. Rain returned almost instantly. We emerged again at 5.12 pm. The rain resumed after two overs. Time ticked away, finally expired, and we shared the points of a game we were bound to lose. We slipped away with a mixture of shame and relief. Rain falling elsewhere that day did us a further good turn. India were disadvantaged by a downpour at the Gabba against Australia – chasing 237, they lost three overs to rain but had only three runs shaved off their target, and ended up going down by a run.

India got their own back in Sydney a few days later when we mismanaged a chase against them. From two for 105 in pursuit of seven for 216, we contrived to lose by 43 runs. I went wicketless; Imran was run out for zero. Outwardly, he betrayed nothing. The field, he insisted, was still open: the West Indies were faltering; South Africa had lost to Sri Lanka; Australia were about to lose to England. He gathered us in a circle at the end of our SCG game and insisted, in that deep voice and with that commanding presence, that we remained in line for the semi-finals. 'We need to win two of our next three games,' he argued. 'And when we play New Zealand in New Zealand, we know we can beat them.'

At that point New Zealand were unbeaten, so that was a confident call. Again we wanted to believe him. Ramadan began the next day. We knew that meant that Pakistanis at home would be awake all night and sleeping a lot of the day, so watching us all the more closely: the country would be behind us, depending on us, needing us. The Qur'an cut us some slack: because we were training, we were allowed to eat; but we fasted on non-playing days and prayed together, so as to deserve any good fortune that came our way.

The way we were playing, we hardly did. We sent South Africa in at the Gabba, and donated the game to them. Still struggling with the white ball, I conceded seven wides and two no balls; when rain made it slippery, we gave up at least 30 runs in the field. This time it was we who suffered by the run rate adjustment system. An hour's break when we were two for 74 in twenty-two overs chasing 212 cost us fourteen overs, but resulted in our target shrinking by only 18 runs. God was testing us. We at least got a glimpse in that match of the powers of Inzamam-ul-Haq, who had just turned twenty-two, and in those days was a disarmingly slim and limber figure. He took 48 off forty-five balls, then tried for a single into the covers and was famously run out by a diving Jonty Rhodes. When Imran was caught behind in the same over, it triggered a match-losing collapse.

'Did you not see it was Jonty?' Imran chided Inzy when they were watching later.

'Imran *bhai*,' Inzy replied solemnly, 'how was I to know he was going to throw himself at the stumps from ten metres away?' I was with Inzy. It was just extraordinary.

By now, our faith in Imran was being tested. Even if we won all our remaining games, we were depending on other results to go our way. Bookmakers ranked us 40–1 to make the last four. We had to drag ourselves across the continent and three time zones to get to Perth to play the home team. Our batsmen were out of form; our fielding was lamentable; I had struggled all the way through the tournament with my direction. But over breakfast with Ejaz and Mushtaq at the Parmelia Hilton, I opened the paper and a headline caught my eye: 'Imran: I Want Wasim to Bowl Fast'. He had told the press that I was too concerned about wides and no balls; my job was to bowl quick and intimidate. It was a public mandate. He had told the world, not just me. I checked anyway. 'Yes, that's what I want from you,' he said. 'I don't want line and length. That is for me and Aaqib. You are fast. So bowl fast.' Imran had clearly given thought to how best to motivate each of us, because it was at the toss that he appeared in a T-shirt across which a tiger was emblazoned.

We lost our way a little with the bat after a good start: we should have made more than nine for 220 off fifty overs, having been three for 157 off thirty-seven. But I did as I was asked. I bowled as fast as I could without worrying about the extras, and even with five wides and four no balls took two for 28. Attack was now our watchword. Mushtaq bowled his variations boldly, and got the crucial wicket when Dean Jones tried to hit him over the top. The 48-run victory kept us in touch, and England beating South Africa the next day meant that two semi-final places remained open. We were wasteful when we then played Sri Lanka at the WACA, but did enough to win in the last over with me and Ejaz at the wicket.

So off we went, this time across four time zones, to Christchurch, but in surprisingly good shape. We would still need providence, in the form of Australia beating the West Indies, in order to go deeper in the cup. If the home team beat the West Indies by more than 33 runs and we lost, in fact, Australia still had a glimmer of a semi-final berth. But, as Imran had insisted all along, we had New Zealand's measure. Their pitches suited us; their post-Hadlee attack was not quick; Martin Crowe was their key wicket. And for us the task was clear. We *had* to win; by losing, perversely, they could obtain a home semi-final. We were a cornered tiger against a cagey kiwi. I wonder if this took the edge off their performance ever so slightly. It certainly added some edge to ours. The day before the match we trained to the strains of Nusrat Fateh Ali Khan, then went go-karting. They were unbeaten; we felt strangely unbeatable. 'Leave it to God,' Imran told us, 'and we will be all right.'

New Zealand's winning formula had been based on chases led by Mark Greatbatch, a powerful left-handed hitter, taking on the pace bowlers. So when Imran won the toss, he sent the home side in, with a plan to use Mushtaq early. Aaqib went for 16 in the first over, thanks to Greatbatch, but he quickly nicked off the other opener Rod Latham. I removed first Andrew Jones and then Martin Crowe to leave them three for 39. Now Mushtaq did the trick. He puzzled Greatbatch and becalmed Ken Rutherford, who in his desperation to get off strike pushed it wide of me at mid-on. I swooped and ran him out.

From eight for 106, the New Zealanders clawed their way back into the match thanks to their ninth-wicket pair, Gavin Larsen and Danny Morrison, but I came back to finish the innings for 166. We had been typically profligate, conceding 42 extras, but uncharacteristically dashing in the field. Still, nobody was more uncharacteristically dashing than Ramiz Raja, who was unrecognisable from the stodgy figure of our opening match in making 119 not out with sixteen fours. I hardly saw him bat better. We overtook the New Zealanders with thirty-two deliveries to spare, then retired to our hotel to discover our fate.

This may have been the hardest part of that World Cup – not the playing but the watching. We needed Australia to win big at the MCG, but not too big. David Boon made a fine century and they swelled towards a strong total. Then the West Indies fought back, replying fluently – so fluently that Ejaz, Mushtaq and I could watch no more and went out to dinner. From two for 59, however, the West Indies started to falter against Mike Whitney – a bustling, combative left-armer with whom we'd tangled in Perth, where he'd been fined for sledging. Now we were cheering him on. He yanked out Richardson, Carl Hooper, Keith Arthurton and Gus Logie, and when Lara was run out in a mix-up, we knew we would be flying to Auckland for a semi-final rematch against New Zealand. As a joke, we sent Whitney a telegram offering to pay his fine. We were in such high humour that on our way out to a nightclub we introduced ourselves to the cab driver and I wrote a note for him: 'Pakistan will win the World Cup. Signed Wasim Akram.'

By now we were feeling the long-term attrition of the tournament. Imran and Javed were inspiring to watch as they prepared, brainstorming their options, polishing their skills, and suffering injection after injection to alleviate their various aches and pains. They were dragging us with them. On the morning of the semi-final, an hour before the toss, a wan Inzy presented to the captain. 'Skipper I'm not well,' he said. 'I have a fever. I've been up all night puking, wasn't able to sleep. I can't play.'

Inzy had not had a great World Cup, but we had stuck with him at first drop because his talent was obvious. You saw him in the nets and he had so much time, so much power. Anyway, Imran fixed him with his gaze. 'Listen,' he said, 'I don't care if your head's fallen off. You're playing today. Have a couple of tablets. We need you for this game.' Then he announced to the dressing room: 'I am batting three today.' I'm not sure he'd had it in mind to that point, but his selflessness was inspiring. He was the cornered tiger springing; all we had to do was follow. I beat Greatbatch three times in my first over. We were sharp and keen, relishing the game's high stakes.

We ended up chasing a few more than we should have. Eden Park, a box-shaped Rugby stadium, is fearfully difficult to defend. Crowe and Rutherford combined for a controlled century stand. Then Crowe pulled a hamstring and I had Rutherford caught behind, but we allowed New Zealand to double their score in the last fifteen overs, and lost Sohail early in our reply. Imran joined Ramiz in a steady partnership but we kept taking our foot off the accelerator, so that when we reached four for 140 at the end of the thirty-fifth over we basically needed to do as our hosts had. One thing in our favour was that Crowe, a wonderfully subtle captain, was off the field nursing his leg. In his absence, the bowling changes were reluctant and the fielding a little lethargic. We were there because they'd let us; they were there because we had already beaten them once.

Our match winner was Inzy, who hit a 37-ball 60. He flailed Danny Morrison, their quickest bowler; he mauled Dipak Patel, who had been almost unhittable for the tournament; he cover-drove Chris Harris for six. Though Inzy fell responding to an overoptimistic call from Javed, Moin looted an unbeaten eleven-ball 20 to get us home with an over to spare. Ejaz pulled out our boom box in the dressing room and we celebrated our final berth to the tune of Nusrat's 'Allah Hoo'. I gathered a swag of coins in order to ring my parents in Pakistan and Huma in England from a payphone – it was cheaper than ringing from the hotel. On the spur of the moment, she decided to fly to Melbourne and book a room in the Hilton where the team was staying.

By the time we got there, we knew we would be playing England, who'd beaten South Africa in another rain-affected match – an interruption in play infamously changed South Africa's equation from 22 in thirteen deliveries to 22 off one. We were not displeased. While Gooch's team had morally beaten us in Adelaide, their attack was far less potent than South Africa's, and their batting had collapsed against Zimbabwe. I was more pleased still when Huma arrived, although we were almost comically anxious about Pakistani groupies. At one stage Huma, Ejaz and I were coming down in the lift when friends of Huma's parents stepped in. I very nearly panicked. Much as they were a feature of Imran's life, girlfriends are not part of Pakistani culture.

It was great to have Huma in Melbourne. Over the past few years, she'd been practising on me some of the relaxation techniques she had learnt in psychology. She would say that natural talent would take me only so far, that mental conditioning was every bit as important, if not more. In a soft voice, she'd encourage me to think of a time or a place where I'd been happy or successful. I wasn't to think about the opposition or the scenario. The objective was a feeling of achievement and wellbeing that I could take onto the field; I should be able to visualise what I wanted to do, then do it. She got me to think about my breathing. She got me to think about my body language, and the opposition's. I'm not sure I would have accepted direction from a professional, but from Huma it came naturally. She knew me so well: what worked, what didn't. The day before the final we went shopping and I invested in a Nike tracksuit. You could never get a tracksuit from the Board of Control; we still tended to train in whites. But I thought I looked pretty good, and the 'Just Do It' sticker summed up how I was feeling.

From Imran we had firm direction. 'Go to bed by midnight,' he told us on the eve of the match. 'Have breakfast by ten. Be ready to go.' Ejaz had been told he was playing ahead of Iqbal Sikander, so we both went to bed with dreams of a World Cup. I don't know about him but I slept well. Sometimes in my career I awoke with a knotted stomach and a lump in my throat. Not this time. I felt fresh. I felt relaxed. I felt like I could fly.

• • •

The Melbourne Cricket Ground is unique in its history. It hosted the inaugural Test match, the very first one-day international. Attendance at the Boxing Day Test is an annual rite for Australians, the high point of every summer. But the MCG had never hosted such a game as this World Cup final.

MARK RAY

Easy does it: I've never felt so calm and confident before a big match as I did before the 1992 World Cup final.

For England vs Pakistan, it was effectively a neutral venue. Who to cheer? How to feel at the end? The atmosphere, in fact, was surprisingly welcoming. A lot of Australians who had bought tickets in the reasonable expectation that they would be watching their team, now seemed to have offered us their temporary allegiance. Ejaz and I got lots of encouragement on our short walk down the hill from the Hilton. Imran walked in wearing his cornered tiger T-shirt again, and gave us his stump speech: 'What does a tiger do when it's cornered? It attacks. We can't be on the back foot today. Be aggressive today in everything you do.'

After a few words from Javed, we walked out for the warm-ups. In those days, everyone did their own thing before a match. You wandered round, had a look at the pitch, maybe took a few high catches, did some stretches and run-throughs. On this occasion I saw my Lancashire teammate

Neil Fairbrother with his bat and gloves. 'Hey Harvey!' I called to him. 'I'll throw you some!' I could see his eyes widen. 'What?' he said. I picked up some balls, gave him fifteen or so throwdowns, wished him luck and went on my way. I wasn't playing a mind game or trying to put pressure on him. I was simply in such a mellow frame of mind that I could not see a reason not to be friendly.

No team batting second had won a cup final, so Imran was pleased to win the toss and bat, also with an eye on the weather and our lack of experience batting under lights. He believed in runs on the board; he foresaw me, Inzy and Moin coming in for the last ten overs to take advantage of a base built by the top order. Still, we made heavy weather of the occasion, slipping to two for 24 after nine overs, and it might have been worse had Steve Bucknor granted either of two lbw appeals against Javed by Derek Pringle.

Then, just after the mid-point of our innings, a fateful moment. Imran, despite what he'd told us about tigers in corners, had eked out nine in sixteen overs when he top-edged to backward square leg – by that point, he and Javed had been limping along at less than three an over. Gooch ran back under the swirling ball but could not hold the catch as it descended over his shoulder. We were shouting, screaming even. It seemed that the Almighty really was on our side.

From that moment, the acceleration began. We were two for 77 in the twenty-eighth over when Imran hit their left-arm spinner Richard Illingworth into the Members. It was like a bugle sounding a charge. By the time Javed got out reverse-sweeping in the fortieth over, we were going at better than four an over; we went at eight an over in the last ten, just as we had planned – Inzy making 42 off thirty-five, and me slogging 33 off nineteen. I charged Botham and hit him through the covers, then hit a full toss over mid-wicket for four. With an over to go I got down on one knee and carved Chris Lewis over cow corner, then pounded the next ball back past him. Pringle bowled an excellent last over in which he yorked Inzy, then Saleem had me run out. But we had set England the task of scoring at five an over – something beyond our wildest fantasies ninety minutes earlier. The dressing room at the break was noisy, almost euphoric.

As Imran threw me the ball, I was excited – too excited. As I started over the wicket, I began feeling cramps in my hamstring, struggled with my follow-through, and dragged the ball down. I bowled two wides. Gooch cut my third ball for three. As I walked back, I called to Imran that I thought I should swap to round the wicket, because it would help me complete my action. He nodded, and it did feel better. Although the first ball of my second over was a wide and the third a no ball, it was coming out fast and swerving late. I hit Botham on the pads, hurried his defence, then got one to zoom past his outside edge, accompanied by a loud noise. Even as Botham gestured that the ball had touched his sleeve, umpire Brian Aldridge did not hesitate to raise his finger. We had our breakthrough.

Alec Stewart cut a wider one to the boundary, but in the next fifteen deliveries we kept England to a single run. From the other end, Aaqib was also swinging the ball. Our fielding was unrecognisable from the unit that had been so bad against South Africa. Our captain was completely in charge. Stewart nicked me noisily to Moin, but Aldridge frustrated us by keeping his finger down. Imran held up his hand. We settled obediently. Aaqib nicked Stewart off in the next over.

Moin was unable to accept a thick nick from Gooch, so a second wicket eluded me in that first spell of 5–0–21–1 – figures swollen by five wides and three no balls. I did not care. I had made a statement about how we would tackle our task – defending by attacking. Mushie now came on to bowl the spell of his life, defeating Hick with a googly and Gooch with a leg break. Aaqib's catch of the latter felt like God was watching over us. He was a slow mover, a lousy catcher. Yet he ran 20 metres, grabbed Gooch's top-edged sweep with a single outstretched hand, then challenged us to catch him as he celebrated. At the end of the twenty-first over, England were four for 69, needing 181 from 174 balls.

Still, we knew how dangerous Harvey and Allan Lamb were as a pair. They would take the game deep. The outfield was quick, and we had shown how you could accelerate. They took toll of Imran, and picked off second-stringers Sohail and Ejaz, putting on 72 in fourteen overs to keep England's hopes alive. We grew a little frustrated. When we took a drinks break at the end of the thirty-fourth over, I said to Imran: 'I think I should come back, maybe just for a couple … Which end is it reversing from?' He gave me the ball to come on at the Pavilion End, to Harvey, just near where I had been giving him throwdowns in the afternoon. I started over the wicket, and at once the ball began swinging sharply. Harvey, jabbing down late, worked the fourth ball to fine leg for a single. As he walked down the pitch to talk to Lamb, he would have heard me tell the umpire I was coming round the wicket. As I walked back to my mark, the big screen showed the attendance: 87,132, a cup final record. All of them were paying attention. I welcomed that feeling.

Funnily enough, over the years I had never bowled terribly much to Lamb. Harvey later told me what he'd told his partner: 'Just cover your stumps and see him out. He will bowl outswing to you from wide of the crease.' I can imagine Lamb being sceptical a bowler could do that. I stormed in. Lamb came half-forward and played down the line. The ball went away late, clipping the outside of off. Nobody could quite believe it, not even me. We stood as a group, transfixed by the replay on the big screen, until Moin slapped my hands with his gloves. How about that? Javed said that only Bradman could have played it. As the next batsman – Chris Lewis – came out, we were smiling, laughing, on top again.

'I think I should bowl the yorker,' I said to Imran as I walked back.

'No,' my captain replied. 'He'll be expecting the yorker. Bowl length to him, inswing.'

So I thought of that ball. At the top of my mark, I visualised it just as Huma had told me. Imran was right: Lewis was expecting something full, and his front foot moved late, leaving a gap for the ball to breach on the way to the stumps. Huma was right too: as it shattered the stumps, it was as though I had already seen the delivery. There was no hat-trick for me that day – the first ball of my next over hit Harvey on the pad but was missing leg. Harvey later said that he picked my inswinger from the cock of my wrist – he knew my variations from years of fielding at slip for Lancashire – but it still beat him for pace. My follow-through carried me all the way down the pitch so that when he looked up I was just a few yards away – I gave him a smile. By the time I finished my two overs, the World Cup was as good as ours. When Aaqib got Harvey a few overs later, the asking rate was 10; when I came back to bowl the forty-fifth over, conceding four singles, it was 12.4. When

Imran took the last wicket in the final over to consummate our 22-run win, we sank to our knees, in relief and thanks, before our God. It was the eighteenth day of Ramadan, and late afternoon in Pakistan. People were about to break their fasts, as we had broken ours in the World Cup.

Funny, but I also thought about that Christchurch cab driver. 'Remember me, buddy,' I'd said to him. I wonder if he did.

• • •

The victory speech Imran gave that night has achieved a strange notoriety, in that rather than extol his players, he concentrated on what success meant for his personal goal of completing his cancer hospital. I can honestly say that the speech meant nothing to any of us, even to me as man of the match. We were not listening, so busy were we celebrating. There were no replays to watch; there was nothing to read on social media; there was nothing even to do, once we had finished playing 'Allah Hoo' on Ejaz's beat box. Melbourne in those days was dead after midnight. There was nowhere to go once we had been turned out of our dressing room and walked up the hill to the Hilton. I ended up calling the physiotherapist to get a sleeping pill so I could get some rest.

Imran's remarks only began to become an issue as we wended our way home via Singapore, where the Pakistani ambassador hosted a dinner that, it soon emerged, was to raise funds for Shaukat Khanum. We were in the bus on the way to Changi Airport afterwards when Javed and Ramiz called me over. They were seething. If there was money to be raised off the back of cricket success, it should be theirs. It was true that they had had outstanding tournaments: Javed had made 437 runs at 62, Ramiz 349 at 58. But I was upset. 'Ramiz *bhai*, Javed *bhai*,' I said, 'I am not talking about this.' I went and sat on my own at the front of the bus. I guess I had shown where my loyalties lay.

When we landed at Karachi, we were advised that we were just stopping over. There would be a three-hour wait before we boarded a private flight to Saudi Arabia, where we were to meet the prime minister: Nawaz Sharif headed the conservative Islamic Democratic Alliance, the PPP's rivals, and was intent on accompanying us for umrah. We hardly had a say in it. Still, for two days it was not such an imposition, and we did feel that the victory was owed to a higher power.

When we arrived back in Lahore, the tarmac at Allama Iqbal Airport was thronged with thousands of well-wishers, not to mention a host of officials, and the bus journey to the Pearl Intercontinental, which usually takes twenty minutes, took seven hours. Seven hours! You could not see the trees, let alone the road, for people. For company, at least, we had Waqar, who had greeted us at the airport, tearful at having not been part of the campaign, but excited to be reunited with us. The whole of the city, it seemed, was out – the whole of the country, in fact, as we toured other cities, other provinces, being plied with cash, medals, jewels, other gifts. The official prize money for the World Cup then was miserable: each squad member received about US$1800. It was our countrymen who were most generous. Each of us received a plot of land in Islamabad.

In the end, then, Imran's fundraising hardly mattered. There was plenty to go round. But it had opened a rift between him and his senior players which never closed – and he knew it. When he invited the team to the tree-planting ceremony at Shaukat Khanum, there was a sense of things not being said. When he hosted a party in honour of the victorious team in London, he pointedly did not invite Javed, Ramiz and Saleem. Frankly, you could tell that Imran was finished with cricket. He had bigger plans, greater ambitions. We in the team would be charting our future path alone.

CHAPTER 7

A RELUCTANT CAPTAIN

I'm often asked, 'What is your all-time greatest team?' I start with Akram and go from there.

David Lloyd

Imran and Javed, comrades and rivals, had had an uneasy
relationship: supreme on the field, testy off it, and in a sense
always uneven. Imran's teams always had Javed; Javed's
teams, after a while, never had Imran. Still, now Javed had
undiluted control, which he had always coveted.

It was one of Javed's characteristics that he knew
everything about everything, whether it was batting or
bowling, player management or sports medicine. I'd had a
taste of this when we'd arrived in England for the World Cup.
My right leg was sore. I took painkillers but could obtain
no relief. After the first one-day international, I told Javed
I did not think I could play the second. He was furious. He
claimed that I was feigning injury in order to undermine
him, perhaps out of loyalty to Imran. I was lucky – the tour
manager, Khalid Mahmood, was a senior civil servant,
a Harvard graduate and an instinctive problem-solver.
'I'm confident that if Wasim says he is injured, then he is
injured,' Mahmood told Javed and team manager Intikhab.
'But let us make sure.' When X-rays at Cromwell Hospital
revealed a hairline fracture entailing two weeks with my leg
in plaster, Mahmood not only advised Javed to bring me
some flowers but rang Huma to keep me company – it was
one of the reasons I thought him the best administrator I
encountered.

Javed need not have worried. He had inherited a terrific team, fast coming into its own: first-rate batting from Ramiz, Saleem, Inzy, Sohail, Ejaz and Asif Mujtaba; a world-class leg spinner in Mushtaq Ahmed; a tenacious keeper-batter in Moin Khan; and myself, Waqar and Aaqib Javed, who had just played a season with Hampshire, thoroughly experienced in English conditions. We had also developed, for Pakistan, a degree of consistency, and a determination to win everything. That summer in England, the brewer Tetley sponsored the tour matches: we had been offered a £100,000 bonus for winning ten of our thirteen matches, which we easily secured.

Reverse swing remained a huge advantage for us. Five years on from 1987, England had still not caught up. They still prepared pitches on these big dry squares; they still gave us the option of Readers balls, which we took every time we could. Conventional away swing was a skill I'd not mastered. When I came back against Notts after recovering from my stress fractures, I remember bowling off three steps, just retrieving my rhythm. I took four for zero in nine overs floating up these outswingers, with a little push away, which I alternated with quicker inducers. I was skipper that day so could do as I pleased, but trying the same for the Lord's Test displeased my new captain. 'What the heck are you doing?' Javed shouted, running from slip.

'I'm trying to get it to go away,' I explained.

'Forget about that,' he fumed. 'I want you to sprint in. If you're just jogging in, the batsmen can set up. They can prop on the front foot and leave. It's your quick arm action that unsettles batsmen. You're a fast bowler. I want you to bowl quick.'

'Okay, Javed *bhai*,' I said.

Perhaps he was still annoyed about the flowers. I got Graham Gooch straight away, but I struggled until late in the Test when I yorked Jack Russell, had Phil DeFreitas caught at slip and bowled Devon Malcolm in four balls.

We dominated that Lord's Test, then almost lost on the fourth afternoon. I came in when Inzy ran himself out to leave us five for 62 chasing 138, and lost Sohail as a partner straight away. The England players were aggressive, boisterous. You could see that they felt they were going to burgle a win. Ian Salisbury got Moin, Malcolm got Mushtaq, and Waqar took guard, thronged with fielders, with us needing 43. 'You just block,' I told Waqar. 'There is no hurry. There's a whole other day to go.'

England had a useful attack: Lewis and DeFreitas were skilful bowlers, Malcolm was very swift, and Salisbury was a better leg spinner than he was given credit for, although I could spot his googly and flipper. I swept him, and hit Lewis straight for boundaries. Looking round the field, I glimpsed the body language of the English players change. They were no longer so sure of themselves. Waqar then drove Malcolm superbly on the up, and the field started falling back, offering more gaps.

I had bad days and good days at Lord's but always loved playing there. Huma was watching this Test. I could see where she was sitting, with her friends in the Compton–Edrich Stands. I could see her smile; I could see her cheer. It was like she was alongside me – I was drawing on the self-confidence she had helped build. Towards the end, Gooch brought Salisbury back. When he looped one into the rough, I smashed it through the covers for the winning runs, and from Ejaz's beat box poured the strains of 'Allah Hoo' again. My main embarrassment was, as a Muslim, being handed a huge magnum of champagne as man of the match. One of Huma's friends, Asin Gigdi, eventually smuggled it back to her flat in St John's Wood.

There is nothing quite like beating England at Lord's, although playing them at Old Trafford, my home ground, which we did next, came close. I took five wickets on a very flat pitch and got a great reception, even when I dismissed my county teammate Mike Atherton. Poor Mike. I used to bounce the hell out of him. It was nothing personal; in fact it was the opposite. He was such a good man I felt obliged to really crank it up against him just to prove that I gave my fellow Lancastrians no quarter. Still, it was turning into a testy series. Our fans were conspicuous again – we used to joke that we enjoyed more ardent support in England than at home. Our success affirmed them amid the everyday racism of their lives. And umpiring, as always when England and Pakistan were involved, became an issue.

I'm bound to say that umpiring in those days was very difficult. The umpire did everything. They supervised the front line; they adjudged run-outs, stumpings, lbws, caught-behinds, low catches. There was no Decision Review System; the third umpire was auxiliary, not active. It was why independent umpires were a cause we believed in. England had some outstanding officials, probably the best in the world, but insisted on a rotation policy that kept putting less experienced and sometimes more prickly umpires in charge. The Manchester Test was Ken Palmer's debut, and his first decision, against Ramiz, was a shocker – so bad we did not even know what it was for. Was it lbw? Turned out to be caught behind. It was neither. Worse, Palmer was officious, humourless, rude. In the second innings, he warned Aaqib for bowling bouncers at Devon – not in a

calm, sober manner, but by barking at him: 'Hey! Come on!'
Aaqib began to remonstrate: no batsman himself, he had
copped his share of bouncers from Malcolm. Javed pitched
in, as he did with any conflict on the field – like I said, he
knew everything about everything. It grew very heated.
At the end of the over, Palmer seemed to throw Aaqib his
jumper – in fact, he had got it caught in his belt in the act
of trying to hand it back, but it became the cue for more
shouting and finger pointing.

The media response was immediate and partisan, as
it had been in 1987, as it always was where Pakistan was
concerned. Javed had overreacted, although as players we
rather approved of our captain, our elder, taking it on
himself, showing that he cared. But the general context was
ongoing English paranoia about reverse swing. They showed
no curiosity about the skill involved. They didn't observe,
for instance, how we only ever had one man polish the ball,
how we took care to hold the ball in our fingers but never in
our palm. They did not grasp how quickly the side of a ball
could deteriorate if you neglected it, bowled the odd cross-
seam ball, bounce-returned it to the keeper. They simply
derided us as 'cheating Pakis'. The sole exception was Geoff
Boycott, who stuck steadfastly by his view that Waqar and I
could 'bowl England out with an orange'.

Had England given it a moment's thought, they'd
have realised how easy we were to counteract. In fact,
they proceeded to win the Headingley Test because they
provided, on the one occasion that summer, conditions that
did not suit us: a lush square that favoured conventional
sideways movement. I picked up only one wicket – Athers,
luckless as ever, who I got with one of the best balls I ever
bowled – but otherwise simply could not control the swing.

There was then a horrendous umpiring decision during England's short fourth-innings chase, when Goochy was caught 2 metres short of his ground but given not out by Ken Palmer's older brother Roy. Two further reprieves of David Gower so enraged Moin and Rashid Latif that they were penalised by the ICC referee.

The best English players played us well because they stuck to simple methods. Gooch was always outstanding. He kept his back-lift short, defended his stumps, backed his patience against yours, and sold his wicket dearly. You had to be out, out, out, out, then maybe in, but you'd get bored, bowl in too often, and he'd pick you off. His opening partner, Alec Stewart, was fit, strong and brave, had quick hands, loved to pull and drive. Later he told me he felt he had to: 'I always attacked you guys at the start because I knew we needed runs before it started reversing.' He wasn't wrong, because in game after game we blew their tail away by bowling fast and full. On another dry, quick wicket at the Oval in the Fifth Test, we took the last six of the first innings for 25, and the last five of the second innings for 21. I took nine for 103. The hostile press coverage was a huge motivation. Call me a cheat? I'll bowl faster and more fiercely than ever.

The paranoia reached its climax in the fourth one-day international at Lord's, a peculiar game spread by rain over two days. We eked out five for 204 between showers on the first day. The outfield was so damp when we bowled the next day that the ball did nothing. We tried to get it swinging conventionally but without success; it certainly would not reverse, and we were annoyed when the ball was gashed when hit to the boundary by Botham.

Allan Lamb had been dropped from England's Test side after Lord's and developed a bit of an obsession with ball tampering. Years earlier at Northants, he had had as a teammate Sarfraz Nawaz, who had apparently boasted of his prowess at doctoring the ball. We noticed that Lamb seemed to watch us very closely as we tried to pick mud out of the seam, then cast meaningful glances at umpires Ken Palmer and John Hampshire. That the ball was doing nothing at all he seemed not to notice. It's now a matter of history that, at lunch, Palmer and Hampshire agreed with third umpire Don Oslear that the ball should be replaced under Law 42.5: 'No-one shall rub the ball on the ground, or use any artificial substance, or take any other action to alter the condition of the ball.'

It should have been a standard ball change, but after the summer's innuendo, the officials seemed to panic. They reported the damage to the ball to Deryck Murray, the match referee, who was exceedingly risk-averse. They consulted TCCB chief executive Alan Smith, whose secretive, bureaucratic manner was summed up by him once telling a journalist: 'No comment, but don't quote me on that.' Khalid Mahmood, who had been at the official lunch with Denis Compton and Ted Dexter, then got wind of the situation and asked Smith if he could talk to the umpires. Mahmood had studied law at Harvard and had an encyclopaedic knowledge of cricket's statutes. He asked the officials if they had seen any bowler or fielder handling the ball suspiciously. When they confirmed they had not, he argued that it would be inappropriate to invoke Law 42.5, with its hint of criminality. They should instead apply Law 4.5, which allows for the ball to be replaced if 'the umpires agree that it has become unfit for play through normal use'. The TCCB hurried off to consult its own lawyers. The result was that nobody said anything.

As is often the case, the cover-up caused more trouble than the conspiracy, which wasn't a conspiracy at all. Far from having our nefarious plans foiled by the replacement ball, it worked in our favour. After lunch, Waqar and I split four for 10 to win the match by three runs. That did not stop Botham, who rang the press box to tip them off about the lunchtime confab, and Lamb, who turned the tale into lucrative tabloid tittle-tattle in *The Daily Mirror* by claiming that we had 'repeatedly tampered with the ball to produce the murderous late swing that won them the Test series'. It was the English cricket establishment at its sneaky, self-protecting worst, aggravated by a match referee who left us neither convicted nor cleared. Imran was so outraged by our treatment, he prophesied that Pakistan would never tour England again. A statement was prepared for Waqar and myself to sign, and I quote it because I still stand by it:

> We have played in this country for both Lancashire and Surrey County cricket clubs and have bowled hundreds of overs for both counties. We have played in numerous county and Test games on a variety of grounds throughout the world; we have taken hundreds of wickets on all different types of surfaces. At no time has any umpire, official or administrator had cause to allege we have done anything illegal … It is significant that these allegations are only now being made after we have beaten England in a Test series. When we have been on the losing side in county or Test cricket nothing has been said.
>
> It is very convenient to blame the failure of the English players' batting techniques on us. The simple truth is that we have bowled extremely professionally throughout the last series against England. We are amazed that a fellow

professional has stooped so low as to make such unfounded comments in the papers. We can only guess at Allan Lamb's motives for his articles in *The Daily Mirror*, but we hope they are nothing so base as money or even worse our nationality.

There was nothing suspicious about us winning. We were simply the better team. Aamir Sohail's double-century at Old Trafford confirmed the promise he had shown during the World Cup. He had an ideal technique, tight and compact, with all the shots. His problem was that, as would grow clear, he was what Australians would call 'a weird cat' – selfish, ambitious, never happy, always complaining about something. It's a shame. At his best, he was scintillating. He should really have been a superstar.

Inzy established himself too. I remember coming out to bat with him at Old Trafford when Devon Malcolm was bowling. Devon was as fast as anyone at the time. He bowled a West Indian length and probably didn't attack the stumps enough, but he had a big heart and a steepling bounce. Anyway, as I'm standing at the non-striker's end, he bowls a ball that absolutely takes off, and Alec Stewart takes it above head height. I thought, in that way you do: Might be a good idea to watch this rather than face it. 'Inzy *bhai*,' I said at the end of the over. 'I've got a plan. You face Devon. I'll see off the other guy.' Who happened to be Graham Gooch, bowling his little mediums. I can imagine the response from some players, but Inzy just said: 'Done deal.' And he played Devon superbly, with all the time in the world, while Jack Russell stumped me off Goochy – serves me right maybe. But that was Inzy. Even at that stage, he was completely composed, elegant, never hurried. That could show between the wickets, of course, and Inzy grew a bit sensitive about his reputation for run-outs. In fact, I always thought his running was fine; it was his calling that was a bit erratic. But in all other respects he was the natural successor to Javed as our number one batsman.

The team was also really contented. Perhaps the dissolution of the Imran–Javed axis had something to do with it. There were, for the moment, no agendas, no rivalries. We had fun together. We had silly nicknames for each other: Inzy was 'Moose', because his first response to any question was an all-purpose moose-like grunt. We played silly pranks. One day, Waqar and I collected all the little bottles of hotel perfume and aftershave we could find and emptied them into the beds in the room that Mushie and Aaqib were sharing. The odour was so overwhelming that they had to ask for a new room. It was all good, light-hearted, youthful fun. The tour ended in a remarkably mellow fashion in the Netherlands, where we went for a few games and a lot of relaxation. I remember very little about the trip because, to be quite honest, you could order marijuana in Amsterdam as easily as coffee in Melbourne – it was on the cafe menus. 'Do whatever you want,' said Javed. I do recall that it was cold, but after a while we didn't feel it.

• • •

Pakistani cricket is associated with the capacity to strike back from nowhere. It also has an amazing knack for self-harm from positions of apparent stability. The team that in 1992 won the World Cup under Imran and routed England under Javed was about to pull itself apart, preluding some of the darkest days in our cricket history. For thirteen years, Imran and Javed had alternated the captaincy with only a brief interruption by Zaheer Abbas; over the next eight years, the captaincy would change hands fourteen times among seven individuals.

There was some ill-feeling at the end of the 1992 tour of England, when we distributed our £100,000 Tetley Challenge bonus. Javed, always very money-minded, devised a system whereby most of the pool was scooped up by the senior players. Moin, Waqar, Aaqib and Mushie complained. Javed, as he could be, was dismissive. It was a sour note on which to finish the trip, and on which to begin our next – returning to Australia, the scene of our triumph eight months earlier, to make a threesome with Australia and West Indies for the World Series Cup.

The visit started satisfactorily. We beat the West Indies in the first game comfortably, with me taking four for 46, and tied a memorable game against Australia, Asif Mujtaba hitting the last ball of the match for six. Then we played a hideous match against the West Indies, losing by four runs after throwing away seven wickets in thirty-five balls, including four run-outs. From then on, we could not win a thing. We saw banners at the SCG: 'Javed! Think about Imran'; 'Give the World Cup to the Windies'. Between times we squeezed in a one-day series in New Zealand, where I took a matchwinning five for 19 in the first match, but we collapsed hopelessly in the next two. Waqar and I won an ill-tempered Test at Hamilton with five wickets each, as New Zealand, minus an injured Martin Crowe, folded for 93 chasing 127. But it was a poor tour for a team that should have been auditioning to succeed the West Indies, by now without Richards, Marshall and Gordon Greenidge, as the world's best. Everyone was poor. We were on a roll again – this time downhill.

On the flight home, Javed took me aside. Was I interested in becoming his vice-captain, with an eye to my succeeding him? I had stood in for him a couple of times; he was clearly nearer the end than the beginning. I liked the idea of learning from him. I did not know the Board of Control's leaders – chairman Wasim Hasan Shah, a retired chief justice; and secretary Shahid Rafi, a senior bureaucrat – but thought I could work on gradually gaining their confidence. Little did I know, I already had it. No sooner had we returned than I was summoned to Shah's office at Gaddafi Stadium and offered the captaincy of my country. Apparently the players were disillusioned with Javed. He was too tough, too abrasive, too stingy. It was Shah's decision. He had bypassed chairman of selectors Majid Khan, who promptly resigned, then later agreed to continue under sufferance – a sufferance I felt.

I was dumbfounded. I had barely accustomed myself to the idea of being deputy. There I was on the cover of *Pakistan Cricketer*: 'Wasim Akram Takes Over as Pakistan's New Captain: When the Axe Falls the Scapegoats Lose Their Heads'. Yet I had no particular knack for managing people; I had no experience dealing with the media. I did not feel like I could say no, but I did not say yes with any confidence. Javed was, publicly, furious. He blamed Imran. He accused Shah and Rafi of 'destroying Pakistan cricket'. He loudly countenanced retiring. In the event, he did not, coming with us on a brief tour to Sharjah, where we won the Wills Sharjah Trophy against Sri Lanka and Zimbabwe, and a longer trip to South Africa, where we were part of the triangular Total International Series, which went from good to bad to worse.

I had always looked forward to touring South Africa. The names of the venues – Wanderers, Newlands, Kingsmead –

had such a marvellous ring. We also had the measure of the home team, which lacked international experience. In Durban, Waqar roared through their lower order, taking five for 25; in East London, I shut them out with five for 16. On the West Indies, however, we could make no impression, and lost four consecutive matches. The surface in Durban was poor, but not poor enough to justify us being bowled out for 43 in nineteen overs. The game was over before noon. I was furious, and handled it badly. I refused to attend the presentation ceremony. I demanded a three-hour practice session afterwards. I was trying to be a disciplinarian, without really knowing how. I was trying, really, to be Imran, without anything like Imran's aura and background. The aggravating factor was that I felt no support from any of the senior players. Javed was still bitter; Ramiz Raja and Saleem Malik, who at first had been excluded from the party then mysteriously reinstated, had their own designs on the captaincy. And Waqar ...

Waqar and I had always been good teammates without being especially close. We loved bowling together. We admired one another's skills. But he was more than five years my junior, closer in age and disposition to Aaqib, Mushie and Sohail. His naming as vice-captain now created a second centre of power in the team, and in some ways a stronger one, as I was isolated, reluctant and struggling. Vice-captains are a perennial bane of Pakistani cricket. They are seldom supportive, often ambitious, and sometimes mischievous. In all my terms of captaincy, virtually every deputy I had concealed a dagger.

In hindsight, I was trying to look the part. When we chose our team for the West Indies tour in April 1993, I even exercised the Pakistani captain's prerogative of picking somebody from nowhere – I had spotted Aamer Nazir bowling at a pre-tour camp, and liked his turn of speed. But from the minute we arrived, Waqar and Javed made clear their lack of respect for me. They were disruptive in meetings; they were late to board the bus. Waqar thought it was cool; Javed just didn't care. It made enforcing discipline impossible. At length, I rang Imran in London: 'What should I do, skipper?' His advice, as ever, was that the cornered tiger attacks: 'Don't worry. Fine them.' So I had Khalid Mahmood fine each of them US$500 for persistent unpunctuality. It was terribly difficult for me. Javed had helped discover me; I had helped discover Waqar; and I was, of course, not Imran.

We had some success. For the first time in the Caribbean, we squared an ODI series, coming back from 0–2 down, and should have won it at Bourda. I bowled a yorker to Carl Hooper that he squeezed out but, as spectators came from nowhere after fording the fence, I fumbled a return from substitute fielder Zahid Fazal, leaving the scores level. The scenes afterwards were of total chaos, carried on in deliberations about the result. Strictly speaking, the West Indies should have won, having lost fewer wickets, but ICC referee Raman Subba Row declared a tie in view of the crowd's interference.

Still feeling a little rattled, we caught a small plane from Georgetown to Barbados, then another to Grenada, the most southerly of the Windward Islands, where we expected to play a three-day game against the West Indies under-23s. We arrived about 4 pm on 8 April, were greeted by the local association president, Walter St John, and then whisked to the Coyaba Beach Resort in the capital St George. Nearby Grand Anse Beach looked a pleasant refuge, and I headed for the water with Waqar, Mushy, Moin and Aaqib. We took a personal stereo. We ordered some chicken wings from the hotel restaurant. We were offered a bottle of rum. The night was passing pleasantly when we were joined by a couple of English women, Susan Ross and Joan Coughlin. They were office secretaries on a package tour and in their early forties, although to our naive gaze they looked far younger. As the clock struck ten and Moin returned to the hotel to fetch more CDs, one of the ladies said: 'Would you like a joint?' At first we said that we didn't usually smoke. Then we thought: Oh well, surely there's no harm in a puff ...

Before we knew it, we were surrounded by plain-clothes policemen shouting orders and brandishing guns. Waqar and Aaqib looked shocked. Mushie started crying. I stood up quickly, in such a hurry that I tripped over, gashed my forehead on the metal edge of a sunbed, and started to bleed copiously. The police had us turn our pockets out on the spot. Nothing incriminating emerged, but next to one of the women's bags were a few butts, which the police collected in an ice bucket as evidence. They dragged us to the nearby Umbrella Cafe where a senior officer began barking at us: 'You're the Pakistan cricket team aren't you? You're not smiling now!'

We were frogmarched twenty minutes along a dirt track beside the beach to the station. On the way, the police arrested a known dealer, a man called Irwin Wilson, whom they perhaps suspected was the original supplier of the joints – they beat him savagely in front of us. When we arrived at the station, we were split up for questioning, which was belligerent and intimidating. For my bleeding forehead I was not offered so much as a tissue.

What had happened? It seemed pretty simple. Most hotels in the Caribbean have a private beach on which you grow accustomed to doing as you please; although we were unaware of it, Grand Anse was a public beach. Still, why had the police been loitering there? This was a region where people smoked weed at home, in the street, even at the cricket ground. You could not help feeling suspicious. Had someone at the hotel seen us, smelled the dope and called the cops? Had it been a teammate? Had it been a tabloid newspaper? Nothing would have surprised me. Certainly the police were revelling in the attention.

About 11 pm, Moin woke Khalid Mahmood, who hurried to the station with Javed and Mudassar. They were informed that we were to be charged with 'constructive possession of a controlled drug' – that is, although we had no drugs on us, drugs had been found nearby. Mahmood rang St John, who hastily procured a lawyer, Derek Knight QC, and posted our £2400 bail. At about 2.30 am, I was escorted to a hospital to receive four stitches in my forehead, after which I followed everyone else back to the Coyaba.

About half an hour later, the phone rang in Mahmood's room. It was a reporter from a Caribbean television network seeking a comment. Our manager, slightly irked, told him to wait until the morning. After another fifteen minutes, St John rang: the network was reporting this as a 'no comment', which made us look evasive. Mahmood changed tack and got on the front foot. He challenged the charge, doing this everywhere for the next twenty-four hours, making sure it was understood that we had not 'possessed' anything at all.

The story mushroomed. The BCCP sent a lawyer, Ashram Karim. Pakistan's embassy in Washington sent a police representative, Khawar Zaman. A host of English tabloids sent journalists – they already thought we were 'cheating Pakis', and they had no difficulty believing we were drug abusers too. Huma's father rang from Japan. 'I don't want to worry you,' he said levelly, 'but you're on CNN.' The secretary of the ICC, Col. John Stephenson, gave a spluttering interview demanding that 'Pakistan take firm action against the players involved'. Said Stephenson: 'If the players are guilty, I would hope that Pakistan authorities will set an example. The Pakistan management must suspend them and send them home. If they don't take appropriate action, we will stamp our feet like mad and lay it on the line to them.' He said he would insist that Lancashire suspend me and that Surrey suspend Waqar.

We had a team meeting. Feet were stamped here too. Javed and Ramiz wanted us to go home in protest at our treatment. They had some support. Afterwards, I rang Imran.

'I know what's happened,' he said when I began to explain.

'Javed and Ramiz want us to abandon the tour, skipper,' I complained. 'What should I do?'

'No, you are in the Caribbean to play cricket,' said Imran. 'Whatever happened, happened. But the long-term consequences of your leaving would be too severe.'

So I stuck to my guns. It would have suited others had I led the team home and become associated with a shameful withdrawal. A local East Indian businessman, Amral Khan, retained a prominent human rights lawyer from Trinidad, Ramesh Maharaj, to advise Mahmood. Maharaj urged us to fight the charges. We had neither bought nor sold nor trafficked. We had only been close by some evidence that on its own meant nothing. Mahmood went to see the prime minister of Grenada, Nicholas Brathwaite, and his attorney-general, Francis Alexis. Through the window of the prime-ministerial residence, he saw an expanse of nicely manicured grass. 'Did you know, prime minister, who would be responsible if an illegal substance was found on your lawn?' he said. 'You would.'

'Is that so?' Brathwaite asked Alexis, who confirmed it was.

'But the point is that my players were not in their house,' Mahmood continued. 'They were not even in their hotel. They were on a beach, open to everyone, used by thousands of people. So the charge is ridiculous. They could have been charged with using drugs, in which case I would have sought a drug test. But no test was taken and it is now too late.'

After a further meeting between Maharaj and the acting director of public prosecution, the charges were dropped, on 12 April, even as we defeated the under-23s. I told you Mahmood was a good administrator.

We were not sorry to say goodbye to Grenada when we set off for Trinidad. Some players were still disgruntled by the whole affair. Mahmood requested of the West Indies Cricket Board of Control executive secretary Steve Comancho that the First Test in Port of Spain be delayed a day so that we could pick ourselves up. Meanwhile, *The Sun* came to the Hilton to interview Waqar and myself. Ironically this caused us further problems at home, because I referred to having taken a drink. 'I do have an occasional beer,' I said. 'But on this tour has been the first time in my life I've drunk rum. It is the famous drink of the Caribbean, so we thought we would give it a try. We normally drink milk in the dressing room after a day's play.' I'd thought I was being honest. Wrong move. Some in Pakistan were more severe about drink than dope. The bad publicity only abated when we started the series well, knocking the West Indies over for 127 on the first day, taking all ten wickets for 63.

Unfortunately, our batters immediately ceded that advantage back, and we lost the First and Second Tests by big margins. Our best performers were Inzy, who made his first century, and Basit Ali, who averaged 50 in his first series. But on this tour you saw the worst of Pakistan – no-one smiling, everyone muttering, lots of emotional blackmail, a lack of maturity even in success. Basit, for instance, was a good player, out of Karachi, an apprentice Javed. He was also a smart-arse – one series and he thought he was invincible and could take anyone on, including his captain.

•   •   •

Pat Cummins's appointment as Australian skipper in late 2021 once again raised the issue of the taboo on bowler captains. I'm bound to say that, yes, I found it hard, at least in my first term. I was only twenty-six, with little experience and little support. My bowling suffered because I had so much on my mind – fielding placements, bowling changes, the state of the match, of the team, of the ball, of the media. I was walking back to my mark thinking about everything *except* what I was about to bowl, and after a day in the field I was exhausted. Later I'll talk about the advantages I believe a bowler captain enjoys, but that time around I remember it was a relief to get to Lancashire where the decisions were Harvey's to take. I took fifty-nine county championship wickets at less than 20 out of sheer relief.

I was now enjoying the authority that came with being a senior player and a young veteran of the circuit. One Sunday we were badly beaten at the Oval: I took four for 32, but Surrey walloped us by 165 runs. Next day, a bit quiet, we set off on our coach bound for Leicester. As we approached Marble Arch I suddenly had an idea. 'Stop the bus!' I shouted. 'Stop the bus!' The driver duly pulled over. With all eyes on me I announced: 'Best kebabs in London!' I led the boys to Ranoush on Edgware Road – a favourite of Pakistani teams past and present – where we fortified ourselves for the rest of the journey. The following day we played our Benson & Hedges Cup semi-final at Grace Road. Harvey made 64 not out and I took five for 10 off seven overs. Harvey and Bumble (David Lloyd) have since become regular Ranoush customers.

At the end of the season I returned to Pakistan to, at last, marry Huma – a celebration that took three weeks, with receptions in Karachi and Lahore. But it was depressing afterwards to return to the atmosphere of dressing room selfishness. I held on to the leadership for the Pepsi Champions Trophy in Sharjah, where I was bowler of the tournament despite getting my hand broken by a full toss, and the home series against Zimbabwe in December 1993, which we won well. Still, I remember how, during the training camp before the Tests, I happened to walk into the dressing room to overhear Inzy, Basit and Saeed Anwar planning. There would be flat, dry pitches, they were saying, which would guarantee them nice fat hundreds – that way lay healthy, respectable averages and consistent selection. I confounded them. To the groundsman I expressed a preference for pitches with grass and pace. When my wishes prevailed, that further antagonised my players.

I missed the First Test of the series, nursing my hand. Waqar captained in my stead, and took thirteen for 135 on the pitch I'd commissioned, going on to take twenty-seven wickets over the three Tests. Mushie and Aaqib pointedly continued calling him 'skipper' when I came back. I later learnt from Ejaz that there had been a cabal, where Mushie, Aaqib, Ramiz, Waqar, Saleem, Inzy, Basit, Saeed and Rashid Latif had sworn on the Qur'an that they would never play under my captaincy again; Mujtaba apparently sat in the meeting without saying anything. The newspapers reflected the various agendas at work: players had begun cultivating journalists (and vice versa), promoting themselves, undermining others. The selectors choosing the team for the forthcoming tour to New Zealand then dumped Javed as a player. In fact, despite florid press conferences, public protests and private audiences with prime minister Benazir Bhutto and newly appointed president Farooq Khan Leghari, he had played his last Test.

The outcome was a very Pakistani one. Leghari dissolved the BCCP and appointed an ad-hoc committee of Javed Burki, Arif Ali Abbasi and Zafar Altaf, three former grandees, who were empowered to start again as the Pakistan Cricket Board. Burki eventually became chairman and Abbasi the CEO. I was blindsided by this, and by the captaincy getting caught up in the general push for change. I was so oblivious, in fact, that Huma and I hosted a party for the squad bound for New Zealand, where everyone ate, drank, danced and sang into the early hours of the morning. When I arrived the following morning at the training camp at Gaddafi Stadium, there were the mutinous nine, sheepish and self-conscious in their blazers and ties, having just conveyed to the PCB their decision that they would never play under my 'domineering' captaincy again. The board would not back me; I essentially had to resign. Saleem, a compromise candidate, was appointed captain, with the studiously neutral Mujtaba as his deputy.

Imran was furious on my behalf. 'Don't make the tour,' he told me. 'They can't force you to go.' For the first time in my career, I ignored his advice. I was resolved to play, determined to show that my detractors had not gotten to me. It is not always a good trait, but I have my mother's stubbornness: push me one way and I will lean the other. I decided I would take Huma to New Zealand. She was all I needed. I took twenty-five wickets in three Tests at 17, including my best Test figures – seven for 119 off thirty-seven overs at Wellington. I did not celebrate any of them; I avoided high-fives; I would not talk to Saleem except to get the ball off him and to set my field; with the rest of the team I barely shared a word. It worked. Saleem, Inzy, Basit and Saeed made centuries as we won 2–1. But it was a strange, chilly tour. Imran's cousin Majid Khan came along as tour manager, but he communicated little more than I did. The cousins had a decade-long feud dating back to Imran leaving Majid out of a Test team in England. Majid remained an aloof figure, nose always in a book, who made sudden, unilateral decisions, and was firmly convinced that money sullied everything. When we were offered a bottled water sponsorship by Pepsi, for example, he turned it down on the grounds there was nothing wrong with tap water.

My sole concession to the collective was, at Imran's request, taking an interest in the teenage pace bowler Ata-ur-Rehman. 'He's young and comes from a poor background,' Imran told me. 'Make sure you look after him.' We had some things in common. He was from Lahore. He had played for PACO Shaheen. We probably could have used him in the last Test, at Christchurch, where Waqar and I, weary from bowling 270 overs in eighteen days, let New Zealand chase 324 for the loss of five wickets. It turned out that I would regret ever knowing him.

CHAPTER 8

DIRTY MONEY

Only an elite few bowlers forced you into the mindset of surviving rather than dominating. Wasim Akram used stealth, skill, strength and stamina to never allow you as a batsman to settle and feel relaxed at the crease. It felt like he bowled from 20 yards, not 22, by using his broad shoulders, fast-twitch muscle fibres and flexible wrists to produce outrageous movement through the air both ways, searing yorkers and targeted bouncers. To make matters more complicated, he could switch from over to around the wicket randomly and regularly to disorient you, to get you second-guessing what was about to happen. He had an unrivalled repertoire of subtlety, to go with imposing body language and a willingness to critique and comment on a batsman when needed. He demanded respect, and history will judge him as one of the finest fast bowlers the game has produced.

Steve Waugh

The first hint I had of corrupt undercurrents in cricket in Pakistan was before the final of the Austral-Asia Cup in April 1990. For a few days beforehand, there were rumours in Sharjah that we would lose to Australia, and they eventually reached the ears of Javed, who told Imran. Imran gathered us in the dressing room and stated flatly that, to ensure we all played our best, he would be betting the £14,000 prize money we had accumulated so far in the cup on ourselves to win. We duly won, and collected – a good day's work, or so it seemed to me.

What I hadn't realised, and most outsiders still don't, was how susceptible our system was to malpractice – because, frankly, Pakistani society was. When you became a member of Pakistan's cricket team, you joined a very tiny elite of the population, around which whirled a swirl of satellites. You had money. You had glamour. You had access. These were all things outsiders craved, so you were of intense interest to well-wishers and ill-wishers alike. When you were introduced to someone, how did you tell the difference? When you were offered nice things, how did you know what you could safely accept? You often defaulted to trusting those you'd known longest – family and long-term friends. But they could be just as dangerous. They could get under your guard because of your sense of obligation to them. More Pakistani cricket careers have suffered for a want of advice than a want of talent.

I had benefited from what in hindsight was a period of relative continuity in Pakistani cricket. For all their differences, Imran and Javed were uncompromising leaders who set high standards, which I felt honoured living up to. By the time rumours of malfeasance began recirculating, the power dynamic in the team was very different. Imran had retired, Javed had been sidelined, I had been forced to resign, and Saleem had the captaincy but without great respect. It was a team in which nobody was in charge, but a number of people thought they should be, and they were surrounded by hangers-on and yes-men.

It was also a team, I confess, in which I had little interest. Although I had never coveted the captaincy, and had then made a poor fist of the job, I was bitter about the circumstances of my demotion. Teammates with whom I had played for many years, whom I'd regarded as friends, whom I'd welcomed into my home, had in the very next breath refused to play under my captaincy – and the PCB had allowed it to happen. How was I now to play alongside them? The only way, Huma counselled me, was to regard them not as friends, still less as allies, but simply as 'colleagues'. And so, for the years 1994 to 1996, I was in the Pakistani team but not of it. I bowled. I batted. I contributed my skills. I gave as little as possible of myself. I went to team meetings and barely spoke; off the field I avoided my teammates as much as I could. Least of all would I bow down before whomever was in charge, who was constantly changing anyway.

While I was keeping my distance, other agendas advanced. As always happens when Pakistan loses a Test, rumours swirled around our failure to bowl New

Zealand out on the last day at Christchurch in February 1994. The simple fact is that Waqar and I were tired, we fielded poorly, and the hosts batted well. Saleem Malik had also picked his friend Akram Raza, an off-spinner, who struggled in the conditions. But still the rumours came. A couple of days before the last ODI of the BNZ Series, Ata-ur-Rehman came to see me. 'The next match is fixed,' he said. 'Everyone in the team is talking about it.' I did not know how seriously to take him. Ata was a nice enough guy but, as Australians say, not the brightest crayon in the box. I probably dismissed him a little lightly. Today I see the sense in one of my mother's sayings: 'Better to have a clever enemy than a stupid friend.'

Rashid Latif would later claim that the night before that last ODI, he answered a summons to Saleem's room where inducements were dangled before Waqar, Inzy, Basit and Akram Raza. Who knows whether this was true? Rashid Latif was a strange character – very good at keeping wicket, very good at manipulating journalists with tidbits of 'inside information'. His sister was heavily involved in the Mohajir Qaumi Movement. He had a similarly overdeveloped instinct for politicking. One thing I can say categorically isn't true is Ata's claim, not to be aired for four years, that I offered him 3–4 lakh rupees to bowl badly. The reason we *did* lose the game was not because anyone bowled badly; it was because we were bundled out for 145.

Disengaged as I was, I did begin hearing disturbing rumours. On 14 April 1994, the day before an Austral-Asia Cup match against India, I was at Sharjah's Holiday Inn. Some of the gloss of the early days of cricket in the Persian Gulf had worn off. We were in three-star rather than five-star hotels now. There was no security, no privacy – the foyers were always crowded with people; you never knew who might ring your room. I answered a call, and a disembodied voice said: 'You're going to lose tomorrow.' When I asked who it was, the voice said: 'You know.' I honestly had no idea. I told whomever it was to go away, that if he did not I would call the police, and I did not take the call seriously. But when Intikhab said that he had received a similar call, he ordered a team meeting. You could tell that Intikhab was alarmed: this was as firm as he ever got. 'We're going to beat India tomorrow,' he said. 'And if anyone knows anything about these calls they should say now.' Although nobody came forward, he doubled down by staking the US$10,000 losers' cheque on the outcome of the final a week later. Here, again, we defeated England.

When I returned to Pakistan from England for a training camp in July, I talked to Imran about all this. What if it was true, that people were selling games? I knew it was possible. Some of my teammates were terribly naive and unsophisticated – as, indeed, I had been. Mushie, for example, was from a family of ten children. When first he joined the national squad, he had never used a lift. The first time I saw him he was standing self-consciously in a hotel foyer with his room key, not knowing where to go or what to do; I helped him find his way. So what should I do now? 'Keep out of it and look after your own performance,' Imran advised. 'Make sure that nobody can say you're not trying.' When we went to Sri Lanka for a Test series, I did my damnedest. I took five for 43 on a terribly slow pitch in Colombo, where the home team picked just one medium-pacer, who did not take a wicket. Waqar and I shared twenty-seven wickets in the two Tests, bowling unchanged through the first innings in Kandy.

After we'd disposed of the hosts in the Tests and ODIs, most of us loitered for two weeks at the Taj awaiting the Singer Trophy. It was another strange interlude – people everywhere, all seemingly with reasons to be there, not all of these clear. Huma and I even went to Malé in the Maldives for four days. Later there were allegations of deals done with players by a former first-class cricketer, Saleem Pervez, and a bookmaker, Aftab Butt. I knew the former by sight and briefly met him once; I was unaware of the latter. But the Singer Trophy would later be infamous for its infiltration by betting interests, with a nearby casino a favoured haunt: it was there that MK Gupta, aka John the Bookie, introduced himself to the Australians Mark Waugh and Shane Warne. I know that some of their Aussie countrymen were sceptical of the offer they spoke of receiving – of thousands of dollars simply for the pleasure they had given, then later for a little bit of seemingly insignificant information. But believe me, it was standard. A player from South Asia was in more or less constant receipt of gifts and favours. Only later might they find some strings were attached.

The atmosphere had an effect on how we saw things too. When Pakistan played Australia, it was a decidedly odd match. We were two for 80 chasing their seven for 179 when Saeed Anwar retired with cramps that appeared to infect everyone. Although the pitch wore badly, it seemed baffling that batsmen as fluent as Saleem (22 off fifty-one balls) and Basit (zero off thirteen balls) should so lose their way. Waqar had earlier taken none for 43 off eight overs. Intikhab called the three of them together after the game, having received another alarming call from a gambler claiming to have lost money on the match, and tackled them about their performances. Intikhab would later claim that Basit admitted taking a bribe (which Basit denied).

At the time, all I felt was a sense of unease and mutual suspicion. It is a weird, unearthly feeling to take the field with team members you're wary of. You watch everything they do. You study their reactions. When they make a mistake, you wonder. When they say something, you reflect. Part of you is curious. Part of you doesn't want to know. Cricket is unpredictable. Your question then becomes: how unpredictable is it, really? In that game against Australia, I took three for 24 off my full complement and made 16 off thirty-three, getting bowled trying to slog Glenn McGrath after we got bogged down against Shane Warne and Steve Waugh. I knew I was trying. I knew others were too. But was everyone?

What *was* dismaying was that we could be so good. Saeed Anwar had emerged as a dashing opening partner for Aamir Sohail; Inzy was in fine form; and my old friend Ejaz was back. On returning to Pakistan, we faced the Australians. They were a rising team – within a year they would do what we had never quite succeeded in doing: beating the West Indies in the Caribbean. Just before the close of day three in the First Test at National Stadium, they were 252 ahead with eight second-innings wickets in hand. Then Waqar and I got the ball reversing. He yorked Mark Waugh, and I picked up Michael Bevan and Steve Waugh in the next over on the way to five for 53.

This should, by rights, be regarded as one of the greatest Tests of all time – its associations, sadly, are unsavoury. We were left to chase 314 on a turning wicket, and needed 159 from our last seven wickets going into the last day with Shane Warne and Tim May in harness and our best batter in

Saleem just out. That evening, Warne and May would later report, Saleem offered them money to bowl badly. So far as I'm aware, nobody else knew; I certainly didn't. I accepted it at face value when Inzy put on 57 for the last wicket with Mushie to win us the game, and celebrated heartily. I did the same after our later win in the ODI at Rawalpindi before which, it was later claimed, Saleem had offered Mark Waugh money for his wicket. In fact, I never saw Saleem bat better than in that series. He made 237 in Rawalpindi and 143 in Lahore to secure us against Test defeats and preserve our lead. It's quite possible that our then captain was the outstanding batter in the world in 1994; nobody was more composed against Warne, who had just emerged as the world's best spinner and perhaps the world's best bowler. It makes what came later so confounding and so tragic.

I bowled fast in those Tests on very flat wickets. I bowled a spell to Steve Waugh in Rawalpindi that I rate among my best. I had been off the field getting treatment and had to wait for a chance to bowl, so by the time I did I was in the mood to absolutely bomb him. In his autobiography, Steve says: 'Wasim either didn't like me, or I was in the wrong place at the wrong time.' A bit of both, Steve. I did used to hate him – not personally, of course, but professionally. He was so damn gutsy. He didn't look great but he was always there, behind the line, blocking your path. He could look uncomfortable against the bouncer and would wear it on the body. But gradually I realised he wasn't actually vulnerable – he had simply cut the hook out as too risky. He knew he was a key wicket; he sold it dearly. Still, we had been able to work around him. The win felt like one of our best achievements. I went to London for a sinus operation afterwards feeling reasonably confident of our prospects on a tour of South Africa and Zimbabwe. At least, I thought, the trip could not be as bad as the last time. I was wrong – it was worse.

• • •

I arrived in Johannesburg just in time for a best-of-three final series in the Mandela Trophy. After surgery I was hardly match-fit, but what was more worrying was that we had reverted. I felt, again, like a complete outsider. There was none of the banter and laughter you associate with a contented cricket team. People were looking over their shoulders; people would stop talking when you entered the room. I took on the silent code. Huma was not there, so I had no confidant at all. Fine, I thought, I'll keep to myself, go out alone, do my best to enjoy my spare time – South Africa was a party country in those days with a vibrant nightlife. But there were events I could not overlook.

We knew from the previous summer that runs on the board counted in ODIs in South Africa. Hansie Cronje's guys liked first innings. They were an excellent defensive team, tight with the ball and athletic in the field; they lacked the batting quality to chase well. The ball, what's more, really hooped under their mediocre floodlights. Yet when we won the toss at Wanderers, we elected to chase, and did so disastrously: Ejaz and Basit holed out in the deep; Saleem, Rashid Latif and Aamir Sohail were run out; we lost six for 22.

Recriminations were in the air when we convened ahead of the second final in Newlands, Cape Town. Intikhab suggested that everyone swear their honesty on a holy amulet. But Saleem somehow failed to present for this ceremony until after he had won the toss. This time the case for batting was even stronger: there was a chance of rain, and the rain adjustment formula South Africa had adopted, post the World Cup, was overwhelmingly favourable to the team batting first. Cronje tossed the coin and saw Saleem win again, and put his hand to his head, then did a double take when Saleem said: 'We will field first.' People in the dressing room shook their heads in disbelief. Saleem had also included his friend Akram Raza ahead of Kabir Khan – an off-spinner ahead of a left-arm pace bowler on a pitch with bounce and carry. Chasing 266, we slumped to six for 42 in bowling conditions we would have flourished in, and suffered a 157-run defeat.

Saleem was inscrutable. You'd ask him what was going on and he would just shrug it off. Everything was fine. Nothing was amiss. His deputy Latif, in contrast, was in a state of permanent umbrage, which was almost worse. On 14 January 1995, a report appeared in *Frontier News* by Usman Shirazi, a Karachi journalist with whom Rashid was so close that they were sharing a room: 'Vice-captain Planning to Return in Disgust'. It advertised that Rashid intended quitting the tour out of disenchantment with rifts in the team – rifts he was at least partly responsible for, and had certainly done nothing to repair. 'What's all this about the toss and bets?' someone blurted at the next team meeting. I tried to talk over the raised voices. 'Guys, what's going on?' I said. 'Can't we just enjoy playing our cricket and be nice to each other?' As the accusations and counter-accusations roiled, I got up and walked out. I was disgusted, bored, sick of it. What had I done to deserve these teammates? Having undermined me, they were now bent on undermining each other.

A few days ahead of our Test at Wanderers, Waqar and Rashid both declared themselves unfit, the former going home with spinal stress fractures, the latter complaining of a sore back. Moin came in but not Kabir nor Ata, the back-up pace bowlers: instead the selectors summoned Aamer Nazir, who flew fourteen hours from Pakistan via London, landed on the morning of the match, and did not arrive at the ground until thirty-five minutes after the start. Poor Aamer – he had potential. But he suffered cramps after seven overs, reducing us to a three-man attack. When our batters capitulated twice, we were beaten by 324 runs. A Pakistani captain can afford few such defeats. It was a huge blow to Saleem. It was correspondingly to the advantage of Rashid Latif, who had pre-emptively distanced himself, and also Aamir Sohail, his eyes always on a chance of advancement.

By the time we got to Harare for the first of three Tests against Zimbabwe, we could hardly look at each other. Although they had not previously won a Test, Zimbabwe was then a pretty reasonable team, with the Flowers, the Strangs, David Houghton and Heath Streak. I remember bowling seven consecutive maidens to Andy and Grant Flower, who left me on length until I was worn out, on their way to a matchwinning partnership of 269. Apparently bookmakers in Bombay voided all bets on the Test, so convinced were they of malpractice: actually, I've little reason to think that our defeat was due to anything other than our general demoralisation and lack of application with the bat, plus some amazing catching by our opponents. I was cranky in Bulawayo, took eight for 83, broke Houghton's thumb, was reprimanded for snatching my cap from the umpire. But all hell broke loose on the first day of the Third Test, on 15 February, when a story burst from Australia that Warne and Tim May had accused Saleem of offering them money to underperform during their previous year's tour of Pakistan. Mark Waugh's allegation about the ODI in Rawalpindi was then also made public.

Frankly I had no idea who to believe. Much as I admired his batting, I had never had much time for Saleem as a person. And why would the Australians have made up the allegations? There's no doubt Saleem was jolted. He denied everything. 'I never socialise with anyone,' he said. 'I am a quiet person.' But there was now no avoiding the issue. It was all very well to be pointing at each other, but now others were doing the pointing – it really was every man for himself. One morning we gathered in our hotel foyer for a pleasure trip to Victoria Falls. Rashid was not there, nor was Basit Ali. It turned out that Rashid had announced his 'retirement' because he was 'not enjoying international cricket any more', and he'd taken Basit back to Pakistan with him. Sohail was quoted as saying he 'could name so many players in the present national team who have been bribed to lose matches'.

The PCB attempted a quick fix. Saleem Altaf, a board representative, arrived from Lahore and told everyone to say nothing, presumably in order that he could report that there was no substance to the fixing allegations. Saleem and Intikhab were sacked, although not for corruption per se – rather they were being held responsible for on-field results. Out went Saleem's friend Akram Raza and his brother-in-law Ejaz too. For the Pepsi Asia Cup, with Rashid and Basit momentarily 'retired', our new leadership ticket was Moin Khan and Saeed Anwar, with the veteran Khalid Ibadulla as our team manager.

Me, I was fed up. I had arranged for Huma to join me from Manchester. She was actually in the air when I learnt

that the PCB had decreed wives would not be permitted
to join us in Sharjah. I went to the new chairman, Zulfiqar
Bukhari, and said I had put up with enough – if the decision
was not changed, I would simply not play. Zulfiqar was a
decent man, an Aitchison-educated diplomat appointed
by president Leghari: not about to add needlessly to his
board's troubles, he diplomatically consented to Huma's
presence. But after we bossed India and Bangladesh, we
lost Moin to chickenpox and were outplayed by Sri Lanka,
failing to make a final in the Gulf for the first time in six
years. India, to our further chagrin, took the cup. I took
some tough tours in my career, but I never left one with a
sense of such relief.

• • •

Moving on to Lancashire was like going on holidays. It
turned out to be my best season for them – simply, I think,
because of the joy of finding myself among cricketers I
liked and trusted, and loyal fans who supported us come
what may. You'd see them one day at Old Trafford, then
the next day at Hove, then the next week at Edgbaston –
always cheerful, never impatient. I bowled 4309 deliveries
in the summer of 1995, took eighty-one first-class wickets
at 19.7, and forty-three one-day wickets at 18.4. Led by a
fine all-rounder in Winker Watkinson, we were fourth in
the championship and the Sunday League, quarter-finalists
in the NatWest, winners of the Benson & Hedges. We had
a top-class top order, including Harvey, Athers and John
Crawley; shrewd short-form players, including Ian Austin
and Gary Yates; and Chooky Hegg still keeping wickets to
the highest standard. The last three helped me get us over

the line in a Benson & Hedges quarter-final against our old rivals at Worcestershire, when we needed 93 off the last eleven overs at Worcester – an almost unthinkable equation in those days. I made 64 off forty-seven balls, putting on 34 with Ian and 69 with Chooky. Then Winker would not let any of us in the dressing room leave our seats as Chooky and Gary took 26 off the last twenty balls to win. We had a massive night's celebration, which ended with the cathedral lights blazing, and the need to find rooms at a local hostelry because driving was out of the question.

We also had a terrific coach, David Lloyd. As well as being very funny, Bumble was wonderfully astute: we evolved the tactic of Winker bowling his new off-breaks into the rough left by my follow-through. He had a great eye for talent. In a game at Portsmouth, we blooded a new all-rounder whom Bumble strongly recommended. 'This lad's got hands like bookets,' he insisted, so we posted him at slip where he promptly put down his first two chances. 'Fuck off out of there, Freddie,' I said finally – for it was, of course, seventeen-year-old Andrew Flintoff. I took seven for 52 so my annoyance didn't last long, and I could soon see what Bumble saw. Freddie had a sound enough batting technique to open for us in the Sunday League, and the height and strength to be genuinely quick. He was reluctant to bowl at the time, but I talked him into it: 'Fuck, man, you've got real pace. Have a go.' He was playing for England within three years.

Huma and I were very comfortable in Altrincham. St Margaret's Close was a charming L-shaped cluster of nine houses. We formed a strong bond with our next-door neighbours Ivor and Pam Davis, and their young daughters Caz and Kate. Huma made friends easily: she had tremendous grace and warmth. The smells from her kitchen and the sounds of her favourite music would waft through the Davis family's windows – they could tell she was in a good mood if she played Supertramp's *Breakfast in America*. We were ten minutes from the airport, fifteen minutes from central Manchester, twenty minutes from Old Trafford. We would spend time at Dunham Massey, this beautiful National Trust manor house where deer grazed on the grounds. It was almost possible to forget about Pakistani cricket – it seemed like everyone was waiting for the ICC to do something, but they were typically ineffectual, and Saleem was now threatening legal action if his suspension was not rescinded.

I arrived in Peshawar the day before the First Test against Sri Lanka to find that we had a new captain, Ramiz Raja, and a new team manager, Mushtaq Mohammad, although the same old pettifogging attitudes. Unlike at Lancashire, where for years I'd always had my own hotel room, here I was expected to share: sixty Tests and nearly 200 ODIs and I had the same entitlements as a guy making his debut. It was typical of Majid Khan's penny-pinching ways and I told him so, to the point that I got what I wanted. I honoured my side of the bargain by taking the man of the match award with seven for 79, and making 36 in a handy partnership with Moin. But I broke down in Faisalabad with a shoulder injury, Waqar was still struggling with his back, and we sustained our first home series defeat in fifteen years despite a brave century from Moin in Sialkot. In my absence we also lost our home one-day series against Sri Lanka, then failed to make the final of the Pepsi Champions Trophy in Sharjah. Aamir Sohail refused to play the last two games, claiming an injury, but apparently out of disenchantment with Ramiz's captaincy. Finally, under pressure because of accusations against Saleem, Arif Ali Abbasi announced a commission of inquiry chaired by Fakhruddin Ebrahim, a former Supreme Court judge, law minister and governor of Sindh. It did not get us far. Saleem simply denied everything. The Australian Cricket Board refused to send Warne, Mark Waugh and May to Pakistan to testify – though we were not to know this, part of the ACB's reluctance was due to Warne and Waugh being compromised by their relations, for which they had been secretly fined, with John the Bookie. 'The mountain doesn't come to Moses,' said Abbasi. From that point on, the outcome was inevitable.

On 21 October 1995, Ebrahim presented a nine-page report: because of the non-cooperation of the Australians, the judge said he had no choice but to conclude that the allegations against Saleem Malik were 'not worthy of any credence and must be rejected as unfounded', having been 'concocted for reasons best known to the "accusers"'. The PCB added to the chaos by sacking not just Ramiz and Mushtaq but also Majid as tour manager while the players were at a training camp on the eve of a planned six-week tour of Australia. Saeed Anwar had come down with typhoid. Waqar was still suffering the after-effects of his back injury. Who would take on the job of leading this rabble?

I would.

CHAPTER 9

TAKING ON THE WORLD

Wasim and Lancashire is a long love affair.
Teammates loved him. Supporters loved him.
He loved them back. Our games were never
over until Wasim had bowled his last ball.

Neil Fairbrother

Of course I would. I had failed as captain the first time round. I had let the position get to me. I had tried, really, to be someone I wasn't, overcompensating for my insecurities by posing as a disciplinarian, a strong man. With a bit of maturity, and a lot of advice from Huma, I had learnt from that. Now I wanted to be like Imran, but in my own way: to skipper successfully as myself. Besides – and I don't mind admitting it – I enjoyed the irony of captaining a team many of whose members had sworn on the Qur'an two years earlier that they would never play under my leadership again, and on behalf of a board that had failed then to back me. The Qur'an itself teaches that 'whoever pardons and makes reconciliation – his reward is [due] from Allah'.

Still, I had my price. I advised Bukhari and Abbasi that I would accept the job only on the condition that I held it for at least a year, encompassing the World Cup as well as tours of Australia, New Zealand and England. We had turned over six captains in two years. The obsession with short-term fixes had to stop if we were ever to break out of our malaise. I accepted Aamir Sohail as vice-captain with misgivings, but was glad to have the placid Intikhab back as team manager. That would leave most of the coaching and selection to me. It was agreed that Saleem would now join us after the tour's first week, accompanied by the young pace bowler Mohammad Akram, so as to minimise distraction.

Like so many previous Pakistani teams, we struggled in the Australian conditions, almost losing our two warm-up games, and being overwhelmed at the Gabba in the First Test, where the bounce Shane Warne obtained made him almost unplayable. We dropped eight catches, including Michael Slater three times in the first hour. Saleem inevitably became an object of contention. He felt the hostility. He split the webbing of his left hand in the field, did not bat in the first innings, and made a duck in the second to the hosts' visible and audible satisfaction. When the teams went out to shake hands at the end of the match, he did not join them.

'I feel sorry for Wasim Akram,' wrote Imran in the *Daily Telegraph*, 'because our game will be in ruins if we are thrashed by Australia ... The talent has been squandered and there has been this constant squabbling over the captaincy and other issues.' He was right about the squabbling, but I continued believing the talent was there, and was determined to put the best face on things. I was frank with the media, which I found fair and reasonable. I liked my counterpart Mark Taylor, a good man and an underrated batter. I enjoyed Australia. I particularly like Hobart, where we played the Second Test in December 1995 – it's so peaceful and picturesque.

In all the debate about whether fast bowlers can make good captains, critics ignore a key reality – the opportunity we have to lead by example. Batters have it, of course, but it only takes one ball to stop them. The fast-bowling captain can captain from the front, and, if they are good enough with the ball, control phases of the game by their efforts.

I remember opening the bowling at Hobart's Bellerive Oval in that Second Test, setting myself the task of coming into the breeze, and running in hard – it was something I'd learnt from Malcolm Marshall, who sprinted in from first ball to last, never bowling a loosener, always compelling the batter to play. The first ball hooped back a long way and trapped Slater plumb in front, but Darrell Hair said not out – umpires in those days, a contrast to now, were boringly difficult to satisfy. I pushed one across Slater; the rest forced defensive strokes, with the last an inswinging yorker that hit him on the back foot. In a video on YouTube, you can see how excited I am to get him lbw. There couldn't be clearer leadership by example.

Waqar later broke Warne's toe with a yorker to reduce Australia to ten fit men, and Mushie took nine for 198, but fielding again cost us, and the hosts won with a day to spare. We had work to do but were catching up. Sydney was then a duel between Mushie, with nine for 186, and Warne, eight for 121, with us prevailing by 74 runs. Ejaz, whom we'd brought as injury cover for Saleem, batted more than seven hours for 137; I got off the mark with four fours in an over from Craig McDermott, then went out and yorked Slater in the first over again. Australia needed 126 on the last day; we needed seven wickets, and knocked them over for 51 before lunch. It was a hugely satisfying win when so many factors had been against us, and there was a surprising spirit of good fellowship between the teams afterwards, tinged with our relief, as we mingled to shake hands in the outfield. Sri Lanka's subsequent fortunes in Australia, with Hair no-balling Muttiah Muralitharan at the MCG on Boxing Day, showed how badly it could all have gone.

I then took five for 53 at Lancaster Park in Christchurch as we rolled over New Zealand in a one-off Test, with Mushie this time taking ten for 171, and Ejaz making another fine century, putting on 140 with Inzy. It was the kind of performance for which Pakistan, for good and bad, has a reputation: we had gone from a shocking rabble to one of the favourites for the World Cup, which we were not only defending but co-hosting with India and Sri Lanka. It's possible, in fact, that the miracle of 1992 had conditioned Pakistani fans to expect a repeat. There seemed omens everywhere: Imran hosted his friend the Princess of Wales at a lavish charity dinner in Lahore, raising money for Shaukat Khanum; Pasban-e-Pakistan, an Islamic political movement, sacrificed a camel to improve our prospects. On paper, we were actually a stronger side than four years earlier: Waqar was available, and the core of our team was considerably more experienced. Certainly the World Cup did not seem to place huge initial demands on us. The addition of three associate members had resulted in the splitting of the competition into groups of six, of which four went through to the knockout stage. We were in Group B with a strong South Africa, a useful New Zealand, and a weak England, Netherlands and UAE, so we were virtually bound to proceed to a quarter-final.

Unfortunately, we put obstacles in our own path. I had a top five that picked itself in Sohail, Saeed, Ejaz, Inzy and Saleem. As we were likelier to be short of wickets than runs, I wanted to play five bowlers, and imagined pairing Mushie's leg spin with the off-spin of my PIA teammate Saqlain Mushtaq. Though Saqlain was only nineteen, it was clear he was a precocious talent: aggressive, confident, skilful. At PIA I had seen him bowl a ball that seemed to turn *away* from the bat. Then I saw another, and another. I asked him what it was. 'It is the one I bowl with my third finger,' he said. I was fascinated. That *doosra* – Punjabi for 'the other one' – was a potential match-winner. However, we then heard that the selectors were under pressure from the chief minister of Sindh, Syed Abdullah Ali Shah, to recall Javed, so he could become the only player to have played all six cups.

With all due respect to Javed *bhai*, he was done. He was thirty-eight, twice Saqlain's age. He had not played an international match for two years and had barely recovered from a knee reconstruction. There was no batter he could play ahead of, so we had to gamble on a combination of the part-time variations of Sohail, Ejaz and Saleem as our fifth bowler. Saqlain only played against South Africa when Javed was absent with a sore back, getting two for 38 off ten overs (Jacques Kallis and Gary Kirsten), only to be promptly left out again.

Losing that game after winning the rest left us second in Group B, on course to play India, third-placed in Group B on the run rate, in Bangalore. But in our final group match, a dead rubber against New Zealand at Gaddafi Stadium, I went down to lap-sweep Dion Nash and rose with a strained side. Any fast bowler who has suffered an intercostal injury will know how incapacitating it is. The standard recovery time even now is six weeks. England's Craig White had just strained his side and been sent straight home. I helped Saleem loot 83 from our last ten overs, enough to establish a winning total, but once I'd warmed down I could not take to the field.

You want to believe in miracles at a time like that. After all, Allah had sided with us four years earlier. Now, however,

Where it all began: Back to Mozang in 2014, where I fell in love with cricket, and was talent-spotted in the street.

About a boy: Too young to shave, but fast enough to trouble batters, this is sixteen-year-old me at Gaddafi Stadium, where I'd eventually play nine Tests and eighteen one-day internationals (inset).

The best of frenemies:
Dean Jones was among my victims when I took 5-21 in my first appearance at the Melbourne Cricket Ground on 24 February 1985 (left) and later one of my closest cricket friends (below left). But tussles were never as intense as when Pakistan played India in Sharjah (below right).

NEWSIX/RAY TITUS

GETTY/POPPERFOTO/DAVID MUNDEI

GETTY/POPPERFOTO/PATRICK EAGAR

The spirit of 1987: On my first tour of England, my captain Imran Khan was on a mission and the team right behind him. We celebrated Imran's dismissing Tim Robinson (above, left to right, Shoaib Mohammad, Mudassar Nazar, Saleem Yousuf, Imran, Mansoor Akhtar, Javed Miandad and me) and my upending Ian Botham (below) on the way to victory by an innings and 18 runs.

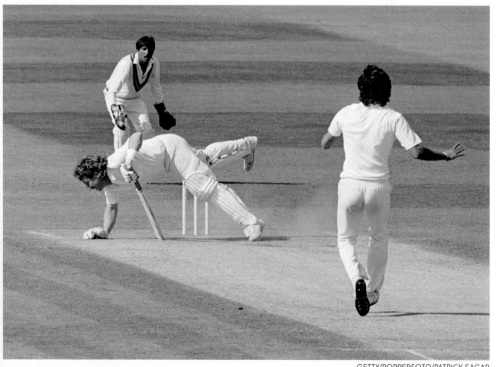

GETTY/POPPERFOTO/PATRICK EAGAR

GETTY/POPPERFOTO/DAVID MUNDEN

The two of us: In the late 1980s, I formed two great partnerships, on the field with Waqar Younis (above) and off the field with Huma Mufti (below). Both taught me a lot.

Cup holders: Back at the MCG on 25 March 1992, I felt like I could fly as we overwhelmed England in the final of the World Cup. Having bowled Chris Lewis (above) to quell our opponents' resistance, I celebrated winning the man of the match award with the mighty Javed (below).

That winning feeling: Embraced by teammates after leading a fightback to win the 1992 Lord's Test. I was, again, man of the match.

Who can you trust?: In New Zealand in 1994 after losing the Pakistan captaincy, I tried to do the right thing by looking after young pace bowler Ata-ur-Rehman (above) – to my cost. The only place I could relax with Huma in these troubled years was with teammates at Lancashire, including my great friend Neil Fairbrother (below).

GETTY/ADRIAN MURRELL

Leading from the front: Back as captain in England in 1996, I led us to a convincing victory, despite resistance from the brave Alec Stewart (above), and culminating in my 300th Test wicket, the rather less distinguished Alan Mullally (below).

GETTY/POPPERFOTO/PATRICK EAGAR

THE AGE/RAY KENNEDY

Trophy hunting: Leading Pakistan to victory in the 1996–97 Tri-Nations Series in Australia included successfully defending 149 at Bellerive Oval (above, I catch Ian Healy off Saqlain Mushtaq). Leading Lancashire to the 1998 Natwest Trophy (below, on the balcony at Lord's) was satisfying too.

GETTY/POPPERFOTO/PATRICK EAGAR

Whitewash: Beating West Indies at home in 1997–98 was a cherished accomplishment. I celebrated the end of Tests in Peshawar (left) and Karachi (above).

So many questions: Australia's 1998 tour of Pakistan became almost a backdrop to dramas about match-fixing. I answered questions from visiting journalists at the High Court in Karachi (above) as well as from inquiry chairman Justice Mohammad Qayyum (below), not helped by the intrigues of my captain Aamir Sohail (facing page, below).

Cricket for peace: It wasn't just a slogan when I led Pakistan to India in January 1999, with former foreign secretary Shaharyar Khan as my manager (above).

New kid on the block: Shoaib Akhtar was our break-out star of the 1999 World Cup, where we failed at the final hurdle (below).

Hopes abandoned: Arriving in Australia for the 1999–2000 tour (above), I felt we had a great chance, but we were thwarted in Hobart by one of the worst umpiring decisions I ever saw (below). Given not out when clearly caught behind, Justin Langer fashioned a match-winning partnership with Adam Gilchrist.

Safe keeping: About some teammates, I was never quite sure; about Moin Khan, my final successor as Test captain (with me, above), I never had any doubts. He was brave, selfless, loyal, and hugely underestimated.

Last hurrahs: My last year of international cricket, as a white ball specialist, had its moments, notably against Australia, including Ricky Ponting caught and bowled first ball under the roof at Docklands (left) and Matthew Hayden bowled in the World Cup (right).

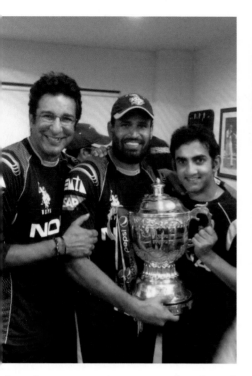

Over but not out: I was part of cricket's future during six years at Kolkata Knight Riders where we won two Indian Premier Leagues (left) while still relishing my friendships of the past with the likes of Brian Lara (right, at the Bushfire Appeal game at Melbourne's Junction Oval, February 2020).

Brush with danger: Life in Pakistan is never dull and can be scary, as when a road rage incident escalated to gunfire when I was en route to National Stadium in August 2015 (giving an interview to police, below).

Family ties: With my beautiful wife Shaniera, dressing up (left) and dressing down (right); with the whole clan, me, Akbar, Tahmoor and Shaniera, holding Aiyla (below).

I was depending on our physiotherapist, Dan Kiesel. Dan, a German Jew, was hardly your standard PCB appointment, but he had come to us from Sri Lanka with a recommendation from Dennis Lillee, and he worked tremendously hard. The quarter-final was only three days away, but Intikhab and I decided to say nothing about the likelihood of my playing, for fear of buoying India and dismaying our own players. In hindsight this was a mistake, and the knowledge that Dan was pumping me painfully full of cortisone probably raised false hopes. I tried to bowl in the nets at Chinnaswamy Stadium on the morning of the match and it was like my ribs were on fire – even coughing and sneezing were excruciating. We discussed a heavy dose of painkillers, but none would last the duration of the match; there was also the risk of further aggravating the injury, with the semi-final and final still to play. An hour before the start, I reluctantly handed the leadership to Sohail, which immediately created an issue because Javed thought he should be captain, and I yielded my place to Ata-ur-Rehman, which in hindsight was tragicomic.

It was not just our first fixture in India since the Nehru Cup final but Bangalore's first floodlit international, and the crowd was deafening. India batted on a very flat wicket that at first they did not take best advantage of, in a cup that was becoming defined by big scores and bold beginnings. In the last three overs, however, our effort fell apart. We gave away 51 runs, Waqar 40 of those. Sohail, having airily banished Javed to third man, lost control in the field. India ended up with eight for 287.

We started as though this was a trifle. Sohail and Saeed Anwar played shots everywhere. We lost Saeed, but with three deliveries of the first fifteen overs remaining we were one for 109. The asking rate was five an over. Javagal Srinath and Anil Kumble, India's two best bowlers, had bowled ten overs already; like us, their captain Mohammad Azharuddin had ten overs to find from part-timers. Our set-up was close to ideal.

To this day, you can see what eventuated on YouTube. First Sohail played and missed with a wild slash at Venkatesh Prasad. Then he pulled back, smashed Prasad through the off side, swaggered down the pitch and gave the bowler a mouthful of cocksure abuse. You can hear Imran on the commentary urging caution – that Sohail must calm down, that Pakistan must not lose a wicket at this point, that it will be harder for a batter just coming in. So what does Sohail do to the last ball of the over? He tries to repeat the previous stroke and has his off-stump knocked out of the ground. 'A very unintelligent piece of cricket from Aamir Sohail,' Imran says sadly.

From there, as I looked on from the dressing room, we started decelerating. Javed and Saleem took fifteen overs to add 52. Sachin Tendulkar and Ajay Jadeja crept quietly through their ten spare-parts overs for 44. Rashid Latif hit a couple of sixes but got stumped – the first of four wickets for eight in fifteen balls. After we'd lost by 39 runs, Javed was the first to point the finger and blamed Sohail, calling him 'an amateur' and 'simply out of his depth'. But there was an easier target. There was me.

An hour or two after the game, Ejaz knocked on my door at the Taj West End and said, 'You need to come with me.' I didn't want to. I didn't want to go anywhere. I was reeling. Ejaz insisted, and I followed him down the corridor to Sohail's room. We stood there outside the door. There was a loud conversation going on inside among members of the team. I recognised the voices of Sohail and Rashid; there were probably four or five others. I was the subject: they were agreeing that they would blame me for the defeat, saying that my withdrawal had been done in collusion with match-fixers.

Who knows what their purpose was? Perhaps Sohail wanted to deflect attention from his own poor captaincy and abject shot. Perhaps Rashid wanted notoriety for being a 'whistleblower'. It's one of the Pakistan cricket team's abiding characteristics. They like to win as much as anyone. But they also know that failure is never altogether bad news – it can always help someone. In this case it was undermining the captain under whom they were playing only reluctantly, having earlier sworn they never would again. This will seem amazing to outsiders, but because there is always a constituency in Pakistan for conspiracy theories, such schemes have a way of bearing fruit. Had I been more conniving, I might have started a rumour that Sohail had sold his wicket. How else to explain such a stupid shot? But frankly I had other things to worry about.

As soon as the match was lost, Pakistan TV began playing mournful sitar tunes – the way that one might on the death of a great leader. Fans were reported to have died of heart attacks. A college student emptied a Kalashnikov into his television set. There was particular unrest in Lahore, which had been eagerly expecting to host us in the final. I was being execrated by politicians. I was being burned in effigy. Posters of me were being defaced. My mother received threatening telephone calls. My home in Model Town was pelted with stones, and I was sued by a neighbour for 'criminal negligence'. Pamphlets were published alleging that I had been paid millions not to play, that I had been dancing in Bangalore's Oasis nightclub the night before the game, even that Huma had masterminded it all. Rumours circulated that we had lost out of fear of retaliation from the Hindu nationalist party, Shiv Sena; that we had been doped with drugged snacks, that we had been infiltrated by spies.

It was a crazy time. Benazir Bhutto tried to soothe injured feelings. 'A game is a game and we should accept the results with grace,' she said. A right-wing mullah, Maulana Naqshbandi, counterclaimed that the nation was being punished for electing a female ruler, an 'obscene' imitation of Indian vulgarity. Sniffing the breeze, Benazir's husband Asif Ali Zardari proceeded to resign from the World Cup organising committee and joined calls for an inquiry into the result. Fake news is not an invention of the digital age – Pakistan was an analogue pioneer.

• • •

Four days after our defeat, while we were still stewing in Bangalore, India lost their semi-final when it was awarded to Sri Lanka because of crowd unrest at Eden Gardens. If that afforded a little solace, we had next to watch our prime minister present the cup to Arjuna Ranatunga, Sri Lanka having convincingly beaten Australia in the final at Gaddafi Stadium. A week later my teammates and I crept into Karachi, with police protection. I hid out with Huma's family. Her father Humayaun Mufti had founded a big medical products company, Venture Pharmaceuticals; he was enormously kind to and protective of me. The PCB, a little unusually, was also supportive. Maybe they needed me. Pakistan had left England four years earlier on sour terms; a return would require delicate handling.

In the intervening period, 'ball tampering' had hardly faded as an issue. Waqar and I were always under the microscope. Lancashire played a peculiar game in June 1993 at Derby where the hosts were two for 243 chasing 379 when I got the ball reversing and took six wickets for 11. The last man, Ole Mortensen, was so agitated that when I bowled him he ran after the ball so he could give it to the umpires, George Sharp and Vanburn Holder, although they could find nothing wrong with it. Derbyshire were still seething two weeks later when they met us in a Benson & Hedges Cup final. Because the ball wasn't reversing, I tried a slower yorker that turned into a full toss, hitting their number four Chris Adams on the shoulder. Umpire Barrie Meyer gave me a warning, I waved my hand to Adams by way of apology, their physiotherapist came out, and the game carried on.

Adams was a good player, but I'd got him padding up at Derby, and he had a temper. Apparently at lunchtime, the BBC was on in the Derbyshire dressing room and the commentators were replaying the incident over and over again, which further steamed him up. I happened to be laughing with a teammate at the lunch table as Adams squeezed past me, and he exploded. 'Do that again and I will knock your fucking head off!' he roared. I stood up and threatened to throw him out the window. Cooler heads prevailed, and after the game ended we shook hands. Having beaten us, the Derbyshire players were in an accommodating mood by then.

Not everything could be settled quite as easily. Having made lurid allegations about us in the *Daily Mirror*, Allan Lamb was sued in the High Court by Sarfraz Nawaz in November 1993, although Sarfraz then withdrew the action in response to umpire Don Oslear testifying that

GETTY/POPPERFOTO/PATRICK EAGAR

Taking It On: pulling a short ball from Chris Lewis in our nine-wicket win in the 1996 Oval Test.

he did consider Law 42.5 to have been broken at Lord's the previous year. This emboldened Lamb to plan a full-scale autobiography, whose contents he promoted as so inflammatory that he would be retiring to prevent the book being censored by the TCCB. Oslear was also publishing his reminiscences, provocatively entitled *Tampering with Cricket.*

Nor could Imran stay out of the news. In Pakistan, he had finally launched Movement for Justice – his long-awaited political drive. But in an interview with Shekhar Gupta in *India Today,* my old skipper was quoted saying that English complaints about ball tampering were underlain by racism, and that protests from Botham, Lamb and Fred Trueman specifically were a result of a 'difference in class and upbringing'. Botham and Lamb sued Imran for libel. Mind you, this probably unsettled England more than it did us. Mike Atherton and David Lloyd, now England's captain and coach respectively, were called to testify in the defamation action the day before the Lord's Test. We carried on regardless.

I was thirty now, almost an elder statesman. I had a genial tour manager, Yawar Saeed, who had been in charge on my first tour. I had an unobtrusive team manager, Nasim ul-Ghani, who had made a Test century as a nightwatchman. Both had played in England: the former for Northants, the latter for Staffordshire. I enjoyed excellent relations with my Lancashire colleagues Athers and Bumble. Athers and I had a running joke when we'd get together to toss for the choice of balls, as we had in 1992, with us preferring the Readers, which scuffed up better, to the Dukes, which were harder. Athers would roll his eyes: 'What other country in the world would do this?' I beat him every time. Even *Wisden* thought this custom absurd, insisting in their tour review that England must 'stop handing away the advantage of the match ball'. Although the Readers were prone to losing shape, we were not complaining – that meant a regular supply of balls to try.

The dry and abrasive square at Lord's and then at the Oval also suited not only our reverse swing but the leg breaks of Mushie, who took seventeen wickets at 26. Soon we were in their heads. They set up for us to bowl full; we started bowling more bouncers. Their non-striking batters evolved signals to their partners, adjusting in which hand they held their bats based on the way the rough side was facing as we ran up; we started hiding the ball as we approached. It was very cat and mouse – although we were always the cat. Only at Leeds, where we drew on a lush square, were England anything like a match for us. Alec Stewart again played finely, although he was lumbered with the gloves again as their selectors had their customary panic. Athers and I got each other out, me playing no shot to one of his ropey leg breaks – good for a bit of mutual leg-pulling.

For once, our playing XI was stable: Sohail was subdued by a finger injury and Rashid was displaced by Moin, who was one of five century scorers, along with Ejaz, Inzy, Saeed and Saleem. All of them averaged over 60. When I took my 299th and 300th wickets – Robert Croft and Alan Mullally – with consecutive deliveries at the Oval, I allowed myself a big celebration. Only Courtney Walsh at the time had as many, and he had not had to survive anything like the feuding and backstabbing I'd experienced. We even prevailed in court: *Botham & Lamb v Imran* rumbled on for fourteen days, enlivened by appearances from not just David Gower, Robin Smith and Derek Pringle, but the Yorkshire antagonists Geoff Boycott and Brian Close, who mainly referred to each other. The jury acquitted Imran of the charge of libel, leaving Botham and Lamb with heavy legal bills. As often happened in those days, we slacked off a little in the one-day internationals, losing the first two and only narrowly winning the third. Uniquely, adjudicator Tom Graveney presented the man-of-the-match award for that game at Trent Bridge to the whole team. I loved the symbolism of that; only later would the irony of that award emerge.

• • •

Nowadays it's common to comment on the amount of travel undertaken by the modern player. Journalists love dotting destinations, totting air miles. I swear no team in the 1990s travelled as much as Pakistan, although nobody talked about it because there was no alternative, and there was certainly no notion of skipping a tour. After two months in England, we flew to Canada for a five-match ODI series against India at the Toronto Cricket, Skating and Curling Club, the Sahara Cup; then to Nairobi for a quadrilateral ODI tournament involving Kenya, South Africa and Sri Lanka, the Sameer Cup. Ahead lay Australia and Sharjah as well as our home engagements.

It was in the unlikely setting of the Nairobi Gymkhana that I got my first sight of a new phenomenon. Mushie had picked up an injury, so I requested that the PCB send a replacement leg spinner. I did not even have a name in mind, and when I was introduced to Shahid Afridi, a Pathan teenager from Karachi's Gulshan-e-Iqbal neighbourhood, I was none the wiser. He looked the part in the nets, accurate and quick through the air, so as the session wound up I asked: 'Can you bat?' When he said yes, I told him to pad up, and Waqar and I started bowling off a few paces at him. He smashed them, absolutely smashed them. Next day I padded him up early and got some new balls out for the quicks to bowl at him. He smashed them too. Looks were exchanged. This guy could clearly *bat*. We almost forgot about his leg breaks.

Just then I had a message from Lahore: my father had had a heart attack. He was resting in hospital, but I decided to go home. My parting advice to my locum Saeed Anwar was that Afridi should bat in the top three, and soon after getting home I learnt that he had grasped the opportunity with both hands, reaching three figures in thirty-seven balls, eleven of which he hit for six. Afridi had left Pakistan a leg spinner; he returned an all-rounder.

In some ways, Afridi made me look to my own all-rounder status. Of late, I'd hardly justified it, for which Imran himself had chided me in the pages of *Wisden Cricket Monthly*: 'I've been a bit disappointed with his batting. I batted with him when he made a hundred against Australia in Adelaide, and he looked a great all-rounder. But he hasn't improved, if anything he has gone backwards, and I don't know why.' The simple answer was that now I was captain, something had had to give. The concentration necessary for successful batting requires peace of mind – peace of mind of the kind Pakistani cricket made difficult to achieve. But if I was to set an example, that had to change.

Sheikhupura, 30 kilometres from Lahore, had never hosted a first-class match, let alone a Test, and had rolled out something pitifully slow for the Zimbabweans, who were hardly quick anyway. Still, Grant Flower and Paul Strang peeled off good hundreds, and we managed to get ourselves in a tangle, being 192 in arrears with four wickets in hand when I joined Moin. Strang then picked up my partner to become the first player in seven years to combine a Test century and a five-for – the first, in fact, since me.

That was that. We did not lose another wicket for seven hours and 110 overs, as Saqlain and I added 313. I reached my second Test hundred with a straight six off Strang, and my first Test double hundred with a six over cow corner off Andy Whittall. When I cleared the boundary a ninth time, Ejaz heard the commentators say that I needed two more for the record, and sent Afridi out to tell me. When I hit the eleventh, it went out of the ground beyond long-on, and while Saqlain and I awaited its retrieval we heard the public address announcer confirm that I had surpassed a benchmark set by Wally Hammond at Auckland in 1933.

As Strang tried in desperation to bowl 2 feet outside leg, I swept a twelfth, and I might have gone further had we not lost our last three wickets in a few deliveries. Mind you, few things have made me laugh on a cricket field as much as Waqar, having sat grumpily with his pads on for more than a day, coming out to face Guy Whittall. 'It's reversing a bit,' I told him. 'Look out for the full one.' Waqar was indignant. 'I've been watching for nine hours,' he grunted. 'I know what to do.' Inevitably, he was yorked first ball. I finished with an unbeaten 257, still the tenth-highest score by a Pakistani, having batted for eight hours and ten minutes. And I knew it too, hardly able to walk afterwards due to my lower back, hamstrings, muscles I hardly knew I had that I obviously only used for batting. I recovered just in time to take ten for 106 on a green top in the Second Test in Faisalabad.

At this stage, we were playing good cricket. We dropped our opening game in the Singer Champions Trophy in Sharjah, then won everything else, defending a sub-par total in the final. We then arrived in Australia to participate in the one-day triangular Carlton & United Series, unfancied but confident. We had a bevy of emerging players: the precociously cool Mohammad Wasim, distinctly sharp Mohammad Zahid, and, above all, Afridi, with his six-hitting swagger and jet-propelled quicker ball – so fast that prior to bowling it we would have him signal, so our fine leg could go finer in case of inside edges.

Our weakness was that we lacked a bit of experience in the middle – Saleem had opted out, which eliminated a distraction but cost us in batting quality. When the team was chosen, Majid Khan was typically negative. 'What team have you chosen, Wasim?' he asked. 'You are going to lose.' Fortunately we encountered a home team in flux – almost but not quite ready to move Mark Taylor and Ian Healy on in favour of Adam Gilchrist – which led to some fascinating matches. At Bellerive Oval, for example, I won the toss and batted on a green seamer. Didn't even look at it, just said: 'Yep Mark, we'll bat.' When I got back to the dressing room, Aamir Sohail asked about the pitch. I said: 'Oh yeah, good deck, lots of runs in it.' When the first ball absolutely took off, Sohail stared daggers towards me in the dressing room; I had to laugh. Soon we were three for seven but battled to 149. At the innings break I said: 'We've got enough. A couple of early wickets and we're on the way.' I picked up Taylor from round the wicket coming wide of the crease, got Steve Waugh to drag on, and pinned Michael Bevan behind his shuffle. I then got Ejaz and Mujahid Jamshed to bowl their little dibbly-dobblies, and they picked up Mark Waugh and Stuart Law to help secure a 29-run victory. Even in a dead rubber at the MCG where we were five for 29, we fought Australia to the last: I made 33, took four for 25, and we only lost by three wickets.

I enjoyed the management challenges posed by young players too. Mushtaq Mohammad was our team manager, a very relaxed guy. Our tour manager was the excellent Yawar Saeed. We agreed that there should be no curfews except on the night before a game. On the morning of the first final at the SCG against the West Indies, however, I learnt that Afridi and Saqlain had been out late the night before with another senior player – who, from memory, was Sohail. I scolded them all. Afridi tells the story in his autobiography.

> Here's the thing about Wasim Akram: he is a thorough gentleman. Every time he meets you, the first 90 seconds are nothing but an exchange of pleasantries. He will inquire about you, your family and your health. He is not someone who raises his voice, nor does he ever get straight to business.

But that day, on the morning of the first final, he really gave us an earful. Our only excuse was the late start to the game – it was a day/night match – and that the senior player had said it was okay to step out. But Wasim *bhai* didn't want to hear any of our excuses. He was firm and laid down the law: if we didn't perform that day, there would be no place for us in the team of the future.

Afridi took three for 33, including Lara caught and bowled for zero, and smacked 53 off fifty-four balls. A couple of days later, the West Indies were two for 31 chasing our 165 at the MCG when I took a couple of favourite wickets. I tilted my head to one side, my signal to Moin that I was about to bowl a slower ball, and he crept up a few steps to catch Shivnarine Chanderpaul down the leg side; then I bowled a sharp lifter into Carl Hooper's armpit and had him caught by Afridi at the leg gully I had set. Plans don't always come off. For two to come off consecutively was very rare indeed. We took the finals in straight sets. Few achievements have given me so much satisfaction.

CHAPTER 10

UNDER INVESTIGATION

Wasim ranks among those at the very top of cricket:
a natural athlete, a capable lower-order batsman,
and above all a wonderful fast bowler whose reverse
swing terrorised some of the greatest batters of our
time and some mere mortals like us in the lower order.
I was amazed to find out afterwards that he played so
much of his cricket suffering type 1 diabetes, which
makes his achievements all the more remarkable.

Anil Kumble

In the year after the fiasco of our World Cup quarter-final, Pakistan played as well as anyone in the world, building a plus record against everyone save South Africa. Yet the whispering about fixing kept spreading, and now it was not only about us. An Indian newspaper, *The Pioneer*, had aired the first allegations of links between their players and bookmakers – and, though we did not know it at the time, Mohammad Azharuddin had already introduced Hansie Cronje to the infamous MK Gupta. It was a period during which it was common knowledge that bookmakers called press boxes incessantly, looking for inside knowledge. Who else they were calling in secret was inevitably a source of speculation.

In hindsight, I made one serious mistake – for which I have only myself to blame. Zafar Iqbal was one of my oldest friends, and still went by his childhood nickname of Jojo. He and his elder brother Raja had lived two doors from us in Model Town, and been playmates with my brothers and me. We had stayed close, and Jojo had been a generous and loyal helper; for example, he had done a lot of the organising for my wedding. Huma disliked him and often urged me to keep my distance, but I felt I needed my friends. I was often away from Pakistan, and worried about things at home, particularly after my father was kidnapped.

There are many myths about that incident. It was an amateurish affair. Apparently a rickshaw driver ambushed him at gunpoint as he got out of his car and held him for a day, claiming to have 'lost everything' on a bet. But the kidnapper had no idea what to do next and let him go. My father did not even tell me about it until I returned to Pakistan, by which time justice had taken a standard Pakistani loop: the kidnapper was located, arrested and bailed, then disappeared. Still, it was worrying. And a paradox of my increasing anxiety about whom I could trust was to make me overvalue those I'd known the longest.

I was naive. I was slow to realise that Jojo had become a cricket gambler, then a bookmaker, probably trading on his being 'friends with Wasim': when people lost money, I can imagine it was tempting to blame me. I say this with a heavy heart, although also with an eye on the future. I tell young players now: 'Sometimes childhood friends don't evolve, and you have to see that you've outgrown them. Reserve your respect for people who work hard.' Jojo did not. He was a fun guy, but like a lot of Pakistani men he lived off others, and took rather than gave.

I also showed my trait of stubbornness. I knew I had done nothing wrong – I was angry, in fact, that that World Cup quarter-final loomed ever larger despite my not even having played in it. Had I bowled my overs so slowly as to cause us to be docked an over from our reply? Had I bowled any of the fifteen wides and four no balls we donated to India? Had I thrown my wicket away after sledging an opposition player? Had I dawdled my way through the middle overs of our innings so that we fell way behind the asking rate? No, but the scapegoating continued, amplified by new allegations of malpractice.

At a match in Pakistan, Aamir Sohail had an altercation with Majid Khan over the players' guests using a private box. Sohail retaliated by claiming that bookmakers had tried to influence the outcome of the last Texaco Trophy match of 1996 – the one we had won, where the entire team was awarded the individual award. He and Latif then gave interviews to Delhi's *Outlook* magazine, scattering more allegations. Latif claimed that he had rejected an approach from a bookmaker during that summer's Lord's Test to ensure that our total, nine for 290 overnight, did not reach 300. I had not heard about these approaches at the time, nor had our manager or coach. Why, I wondered. Furthermore, these were games we had won, and fixes that had apparently *not* occurred, so what was the point in raising them so long afterwards? Except maybe to burnish the reputations of the 'whistleblowers'.

The PCB seemed to agree: they suspended Sohail for failing to substantiate his allegations, at least until he offered an 'unconditional apology'. If only they had maintained that attitude to allegations more generally.

•   •   •

All things considered, I was pretty lucky with injury in my career. The exception was my left shoulder. My legs and knees I could harden by running; my back and groin could be strengthened in the gym. But there was nothing much I could do for the shoulder except bowl, and once it started troubling me in 1995 I could never quite shake it off. I strained it again trying to deliver a bouncer in the Singer Akai Cup in Sharjah in April 1997, and had to withdraw from the ensuing short tour of Sri Lanka, where Ramiz Raja stood in as captain for two drawn Tests. Arriving in Manchester, I probably rushed my comeback, and broke down in the first championship match against Nottinghamshire.

Huma and I decided to stay in Altrincham. Lancashire sent me everywhere in search of medical help. I got used to these huge needles being plunged into the shoulder to draw the fluid. Eventually I found a Harley Street specialist, Ian Bayley, who had established a shoulder surgery unit at the Royal National Orthopaedic Hospital in Stanmore, and who examined my shoulder from the inside via a tiny camera. The procedure itself was amazing. Bayley came in from four separate points to shave a loose bone that had burrowed into the ligaments. Lancashire were very good to me: once it was clear I would recover, the committee, of which my former teammate Jack Simmons was chairman, not only voted me a benefit for the following season but appointed me to succeed Winker as captain.

Huma and I were both in doctors' hands that summer: she was expecting our first child. By the time Tahmoor arrived, after a two-day labour on 21 August at Wythenshawe Hospital, my shoulder was sufficiently improved that I could hold him. My mother-in-law arrived from Pakistan to help; the Davis family was also a tremendous support. I was ecstatic about becoming a father, while also having very little idea how to be one – and it was not a good year to be distracted.

In June 1997, Manoj Prabhakar, an Indian all-rounder who had now swerved into politics, made a host of accusations in *Outlook*, including that he had rejected an offer from a teammate to underperform in a match against us in that murky Singer Cup three years earlier. Cricket, he claimed, had 'caved in to the money power'. The Board of Control for Cricket in India appointed a retired Indian chief justice, Yeshwant Chandrachud, to investigate. He interviewed a dozen cricketers, from Gavaskar and Kapil Dev to Tendulkar and Azharuddin, as well as journalists including *Outlook*'s Aniruddha Bahal and *Pioneer*'s Pradeep Magazine. From the players Chandrachud received a chorus of denials, and could find nothing substantial despite acknowledging that 'a large amount of betting took place on cricket in India'. Prabhakar, it would later emerge, was himself compromised: he, among others, had been on Gupta's payroll.

The sight of Indians investigating Indians excited similar demands in Pakistan. The inquiries even crossed over when Rashid Latif met *Outlook*'s Bahal in London, and offered a 'dossier' of information on fixing in Pakistan. One of his allegations was that Saleem was in Azharuddin's orbit, and regularly received calls from India's captain seeking information on behalf of bookmakers. Latif also boasted that he had been taping telephone calls with other Pakistani cricketers. That didn't bother me – I had never had any reason to speak to Latif on the phone – but no doubt chilled others. In the near term, however, no more was learnt, because *Outlook* reportedly declined to pay the sum Latif wanted for his information.

I reunited with the Pakistani team in Toronto when I went to commentate on the Sahara Cup. We had gone backwards. Relaxation had become licence, and there was palpable dissatisfaction with Ramiz's leadership. That tournament is best remembered now for Inzy losing his temper with a spectator who had been heckling him on a loudhailer, calling him '*Aloo*' (potato). When he was out in the field, he called to twelfth man Mohammed Hussain for a bat, which he then brandished as he waded into the crowd.

'What were you doing?' I asked Hussain afterwards.

'Inzy *bhai* asked me for a bat,' he mumbled.

'What could a guy in the field want a bat for?' I said, exasperated. 'If he'd asked you for a knife, would you have got him a knife?' But Hussain just was not very bright.

Ramiz's captaincy did not survive four defeats by India in five completed matches. Saeed Anwar led us in three home ODIs against India as I continued my recovery. I was clearly going to have to listen to what my body was telling me. One unanticipated consequence of my shoulder injury, for example, was that I could no longer return the ball straight: because the surgery had affected the timing of my release – although not the power – I had to aim my throw slightly away from the stumps in order to hit them.

I returned for the Second Test of the three-match series against South Africa to a palpable rift within the PCB about how to address the issue of corruption, reflected in sudden changes of direction. Sohail, who had been on the outer since his clash with Majid, announced: 'I have no intention of playing for Pakistan again. I am totally fed up with them.' He was instantly recalled. With the series on the line for the Third Test in Faisalabad and Waqar also back from injury, Majid then ordered a green top. It looked like paying off. We led the first innings by 69 runs, and only the nightwatchman Pat Symcox and Shaun Pollock really held us up long on the third day. Symcox should never have survived. At one point Mushie bowled him a flipper, which he missed, and it went between off and middle stumps without touching either. I really lost my temper with the groundsman. 'What were you doing?' I shouted at him. 'Don't you even know where to set the stumps?' This poor old guy, he just kept apologising, but there was nothing to be done, and in any case we ended up needing only 142 with all our wickets in hand on the last day. We should have won easily.

Next morning was one of the worst performances I ever witnessed. Sohail carved two boundaries off Donald through point, then picked out the fielder seeking a third, and we lost the next four wickets for eight to Shaun Pollock. I slogged fatally at Symcox, who then got Saqlain and Moin, and we sustained our first Test defeat at the Proteas's hands by 53 runs. It was, of course, later put down as a fix – including by our suggestible and blame-shifting team manager Haroon Rashid. At the time it was viewed, more properly, as a lack of leadership. Saeed Anwar, who'd had a poor series with the bat, paid with his job.

• • •

In the event of a fiasco, who do you turn to? Over Majid's head, I was asked to take over for the seven-match Wills Golden Jubilee Tournament – a quadrangular with Sri Lanka, South Africa and the West Indies and held at Gaddafi Stadium, to mark fifty years of Pakistan's independence. Let's just say that the support was uneven. I soon grasped that Haroon would say whatever he thought expedient in order to protect his job. When I promoted myself ahead of Moin in a game against Sri Lanka so as to keep a left- and right-hander at the wicket, he thought that was a fix as well. Anything out of the ordinary was suspicious – hardly a helpful perspective for the coach of a team like Pakistan. The problem in that series was our historic aversion to chasing, which Faisalabad had not helped. Lahore's evening dew made the ball impossible to grip, swing or spin. Under lights, Aravinda de Silva and Sanath Jayasuriya, wonderful players both, put us to the sword.

In predictably unpredictable fashion, we promptly torched the West Indies. It was not a bad Caribbean team – Courtney Walsh was captain and Brian Lara was at his peak – but we won all three Tests comfortably. Courtney was a superb bowler, a fine captain and a great guy. His blind spot was his batting. At Peshawar, two of Courtney's bats were stolen from the dressing room, which he regarded as such a calamity that he demanded a meeting with the local police commissioner.

'Courtney man, I love you, but use someone else's bat,' I said. 'Your highest score is 1.'

He shook his head solemnly: 'No man, the weight is perfect, the pick-up is perfect, and I have the grip just as I like it.'

The bats were retrieved in time for Courtney to make a pair at Rawalpindi. In the same Test, Lara dropped Sohail when he was 38, allowing him to go on to 160, while Inzy made 177. We won three–nil.

In the Akai Singer Champions Trophy, however, we stumbled against the West Indies, India and England, who had almost by accident arrived at an ideal configuration for Sharjah: long on batting and medium-pacers. Our batters invariably struggled against this kind of bowling. Inzy, in particular, always battled when the pace was off the ball. I was also … well, not injured, but palpably below par. I was hungry but losing weight and conditioning, battling tiredness and headaches. England winning the trophy when they had been expected to make up the numbers triggered the usual set of conspiracy theories and in-house feuds at PCB. My father's kidnapping was belatedly reported, leading to wild rumour-mongering, and I sensed the finger of suspicion. Struggling physically and mentally, I was plunged into despondency. Anticipating that I would be sacked again, I chose to resign the captaincy, went to London to see my shoulder surgeon Ian Bayley, then to Manchester to meet Peter Johnson, an accountant who had agreed to chair my benefit committee. Pakistan went to Bangladesh for the Silver Jubilee Independence Cup under the leadership of what was now Majid's preferred ticket, captain Rashid Latif and vice-captain Aamir Sohail, where they lost the finals 1–2 to India.

While in the UK, I was scrolling teletext when I saw that Pakistan's party for the forthcoming tour of South Africa had been named. I was not in it. There was no public explanation. Internally, it seemed that Majid Khan had finally had his way – anyone mentioned in the context of match-fixing was no longer to be considered for selection. One of the selectors, Zaheer Abbas, disassociated himself from the team; chairman of selectors Salim Altaf stood by the choice. The funny thing was that this was not the worst of my worries.

I was by now feeling very unwell indeed. Weight was falling off me; I had started urinating constantly and copiously; I had never felt weaker. When I returned to Pakistan I played a first-class match for PIA against Allied Bank in Karachi. I dragged myself through fifteen overs, then when I batted went to sweep and strained not one but both hamstrings. I battled to 59, putting on 129 with Moin in two hours, but could not bowl again, and when I got back to Lahore I collapsed in exhaustion. My omission, then, was unnecessary. I would not have been fit to go anyway.

My father was concerned. 'Have you considered diabetes?' he asked. I hardly even knew what it was, but I agreed to take a blood test. The normal human has a blood sugar level of 110; mine was 440.

As I said earlier, I'd always considered myself blessed in my fitness. My diagnosis was a devastating blow. I was barely aware of anyone with diabetes; I certainly was unaware of any athletes with it. When my father took me to see Professor Faisal Masood of Lahore's King Edward Medical College, that was my most pressing question: 'Will I be able to play cricket?'

'Yes,' he said reassuringly. 'But you'll have to manage your sugar levels.'

'What are sugar levels?' I asked.

I clearly had a lot to catch up on. Anyway, Masood explained how whatever you eat and drink turns to glucose which distributes itself round the body according to what it is doing, and how when your pancreas fails to produce enough insulin you need to top it up. He advised me on how to store, carry and administer insulin – and when, because it needed to be used ahead of peak exertion. He gave me advice on diet, around avoiding heavy carbohydrates and oily food in favour of vegetables and salads. Until then, I'd simply eaten everything on my plate. From this point, I would need to be much more careful.

Insulin back then was far less easily portable and usable than today. The bottles and needles were huge, and required sterilisation and freezing. For someone who had tended to take their body for granted, and who had relied on professionals to fix it, the idea that I would have to be my own physician was daunting. I wrestled with it daily. But with Huma's encouragement I began to achieve the level of control necessary for me to resume training. Because, suddenly, I was needed again.

The lifeline came from Khalid Mahmood, whom Nawaz Sharif, re-elected prime minister at Bhutto's expense, had appointed the new chairman of the PCB. Instructed by Sharif to 'fix it', Mahmood came in and made instant changes: he demoted Latif, who was not even sure of his place in the best XI, in favour of Sohail, who had been batting well. He told Majid Khan that simply casting aside every player about whom any suspicion was held was frankly illegal. I'd been removed on the basis of accusations relating to a match I had not even played in. As he had with my leg in London, with the ball at Lord's and the joints in Grenada, Mahmood insisted on proof. Until proof was proffered one way or another, I was to be restored to the colours. Salim Altaf resigned in protest at this 'unconstitutional' move, albeit only temporarily. Meanwhile, I felt grateful to Mahmood but ambivalent.

The truth is that I was less than fully fit, and less than completely popular. With Huma too busy with Tahmoor to come keep me company, I arrived in Durban after a Pakistani victory there to find all the usual cliques and clans pulling in different directions, and I wasn't in any of them. In fact, the leadership clearly regarded me as surplus to requirements. When things went his way, Sohail was arrogant and bombastic; when they didn't, he was petulant and disruptive. Seemingly in protest at my arrival, he resigned in favour of Rashid Latif. We ended up with a team for the Third Test in Port Elizabeth that contained five former captains. It worked as well as you might imagine – we were thumped by 259 runs. I was top scorer in the first innings with 30; Latif made a pair.

One-day cricket did not levy such demands: in the seven-match ODI series, I made 152 at 25.3 and took fifteen wickets at 17. I knew I had lost pace and endurance, so I relied on my smarts. I didn't divulge my diabetes. There was lots of conspiracy theorising about insulin in Pakistan – there still is. I was learning about things like how heat and timing affect your condition, and how it sometimes paid to leave a few sweets with the umpires in case my blood sugar suddenly dropped. It impaired my performances, my mood, even my attempts to socialise with the boys. I'd be out with them and suddenly need to peel off to attend to my personal chemistry. At least, I felt, I was getting on top of it. But I left Africa looking over my shoulder – with good reason.

• • •

In Manchester, the contrast could hardly have been greater. For my last season with Lancashire, I had more or less everything I wanted. I had a supportive coach in Dav Whatmore, and a team including John Crawley and Neil Fairbrother, both averaging over 50, and seamers Peter Martin and Glen Chapple, who took 177 first-class and List A wickets between them. As far as team talks were concerned, I seldom had to say anything more than: 'Let's go out and enjoy ourselves boys.' We were undefeated in the NatWest Trophy, dropped only two AXA League games in seventeen, and were in contention in the championship until the last round. I made my highest score for the county against Notts, 155, smacking five sixes over a 40-metre leg-side boundary. I gave a grateful address to the crowd from the balcony at Old Trafford after we won our final championship match against Hants. It would have been the perfect send-off had Leicestershire not just pulled ahead, but two trophies was a good season's work, and the £100,000 my benefit raised enabled me to pay off the mortgage of our house in Altrincham – after nearly fifteen years of first-class cricket, I finally had a bricks-and-mortar asset to show for it. I wasn't entirely sorry to be done with county cricket: the travel had become a bane and the routine a chore. But my roots in Manchester were now so deep that Huma and I did not consider leaving – and twenty-five years later, I still have not.

It was my homeland now that was problematic. Having realised it could not simply ban players on suspicion of match-fixing, the PCB had set investigations in train. Returning to Lahore, I learnt that a 'fact-finding' committee chaired by Justice Choudhury Ejaz Yousuf had collected another bunch of untested allegations from half-a-dozen current players, the most significant of which for me was an affidavit from Ata-ur-Rehman claiming I had offered him 'a purse of R3–4 lakh for doing a favour' – viz 'to bowl badly' in the last match of that 1994 ODI series in New Zealand, in line with 'arrangements' made by Saleem Malik and Ejaz Ahmed. There was no proof of this, only his word. Nobody pointed out that Ejaz was not actually on that tour. Nobody thought it strange that Ata-ur-Rehman had waited more than four years to share this knowledge, and had played many games alongside me without protest. Yousuf recommended that Saleem, Ejaz and myself be 'kept away from the Pakistan team and be not considered for selection' pending a fully-fledged commission of inquiry that would conduct public hearings in Lahore. It was to be overseen by Justice Malik Mohammad Qayyum, a distinguished jurist, assisted by PCB legal adviser Ali Sibtain Fazli. There seemed a determination, particularly intense in Majid, to push me out once and for all, and to advance a bunch of fresh, seemingly untainted faces for Sohail to lead – including, it was rumoured, Majid's son Basid, Pakistan's under-nineteen captain.

The Pakistani team was then on its way to Toronto for another instalment of the Sahara Cup. With Saqlain I was finishing the county season, but I was there, as it were, in spirit. Sohail's attitude to me at the time has been succinctly described in the autobiography of Shahid Afridi, who reported a mid-pitch conference after Afridi had struck some early boundaries. 'I know you've fixed this match with Wasim Akram,' Sohail said. 'I know what you're up to Afridi.' After Afridi had made a century, Sohail struck a more conciliatory note: 'Stay on my side. Join me. I will connect you with the right people. I can help you run Pakistan cricket.' First paranoid intimidation; second oily grooming; throughout, total cowardice, because I was not present to respond.

What was most depressing about the scenario was that, because Pakistanis position themselves relative to where they perceive power lies, and it was assumed that my detractors were on top while I was away, I returned home to find myself isolated. I could feel it and, frankly, I shut down. I stayed home, feeling numb, saying nothing. Having never cultivated journalists as adeptly as Sohail or Rashid Latif, I had no real notion of whom to turn to. Huma asked Ahsan Chishty to come to Pakistan, but he could hardly prise a word from me. 'People who claimed to be my friends now won't take my calls,' I said. 'People whose offices I would walk straight into now keep me waiting indefinitely.' He suggested we go see his father's friend Zafar Altaf, a former board chairman. Tea was served, pleasantries were exchanged, but I had not the slightest idea how to broach the topic. Apparently I did not utter a word for twenty minutes and we left.

Much of this period, I must confess, is a blank to me. It is like a trauma I have completely repressed. Only recently have I had the nerve to revisit it. For this book, Ahsan reminded me of a story I had buried. I went to see my father. My father, I have said, was a man of very few words, on all of which I hung. While I visited, I asked Ahsan to stay in the car. Twenty minutes later, I came out, got in the passenger's seat, and sat staring ahead.

'What did he say?' asked Ahsan.

'He gave me the name of a solicitor,' I replied. Then I exploded: 'How many people do I have to tell I've done nothing? How many?!'

When even your father is wondering, you feel truly alone.

At last I did get some effective help. My English lawyer Naynesh Desai chased down Ata-ur-Rehman, by now in Newcastle and engaged to an English woman: Ata admitted that he had been cajoled into providing the affidavit by Aamir Sohail. Would he be prepared to swear to that? Yes, he told Naynesh, on two conditions: that he be provided with a return air fare to London, and a shawarma from Edgware Road. Naynesh gladly obliged: his office was just nearby said takeaway strip. Ata duly came in, dictated the story, enjoyed his shawarma while the statement was typed up, then went through it line by line with his fiancée until he was happy. Naynesh sent it to Pakistan to be notarised.

Khawaja Tariq Rahim, a former governor of Punjab, then offered his services pro bono as a legal representative. It meant, at least, that I would not have to walk alone into the dark-pink brick buildings of Lahore's High Court, where a black-clad Qayyum presided, a portrait of Jinnah on the wall behind him. The tone of the commission was sour from the start. The first witness was Sarfraz Nawaz, a great cricketer in his day, but a politician predisposed to wild allegations and assertions, such as that Dean Jones had been forced to retire because of match-fixing (nonsense) and that Imran Khan should be stoned to death as an adulterer (weird). Next was Fareshteh Gati Aslam, a journalist from the *News* who had gained a degree of notoriety by regurgitating allegations initiated by Rashid Latif and Aamir Sohail, with minimal proof beyond them: she thereby lumped me in with Saleem Malik, blackened by the Australians, and also Ejaz Ahmed, disliked because he was close to us both. Such witnesses got a lot more attention than Yawar Saeed, who said he believed me completely clean, and Arif Ali Abbasi, who said he had never seen any proof of fixing.

I sat mostly on my own while the rest of the team gathered on the other side of the court. It was like I was contagious or radioactive. It's not, I think now, that they were unsympathetic so much as scared, and there was safety in numbers. Periodically, someone in the court would come up and ask for an autograph. Then, as I drove home, people would throw themselves at my car and hold evening paper headlines up against my windscreen. The stress was intense, and it exacerbated my diabetes as well as my depression. When we hosted Australia for the First Test at Rawalpindi, Sohail led a team coached by Javed, who had little regard for him, and which included me, Saleem, Saqlain, Mushie, Saeed and Inzy – all of us under accusation. How was that meant to work? I bowled swiftly in my first spell, dismissing Mark Taylor and Justin Langer in consecutive balls. But after that I struggled, as did we all, and we succumbed by an innings. The day after, bizarrely, Taylor and Mark Waugh joined us in court in Lahore to recount their unsavoury experiences of Saleem, who had top-scored against them the day before. Life could hardly get any stranger.

The next day it was the turn of Sohail, who had been so voluble with the press, but who now said that he had 'no personal knowledge of match-fixing', even though 'we were constantly being told that some of the players were involved'. What was he up to now? Pretending to be a leader? Rather than accuse me outright of corruption in the quarter-final, he now said simply that my absence had been demoralising: 'The morale fell. The atmosphere was as if we had already lost the match.' Isn't morale a leader's responsibility? Why had he so failed to discharge it? Would it not have been a good deal worse for morale had I played while unfit and broken down or underperformed? How did his stupid shot when in complete command affect morale? Even Qayyum looked underwhelmed. He excused Sohail with a note of contempt: 'Now go and practise. For what good it will do you.' To inquire further into the Bangalore quarter-final, Dan Kiesel was called, and gave the only possible answer: my fitness or otherwise could only be confirmed by me. 'He was in pain and it was for him to decide,' Dan testified.

I did supply confirmation when I next took the stand. Again, I had to repeat how I had been injured. Again, I had to state that I'd never offered Ata anything. I testified about my father's kidnapping; the inquiry also took evidence from the investigating officer, who confirmed that the miscreant had not been a fixer or a bookmaker.

'You appear to be very unpopular among your teammates,' Qayyum said at one point. 'Why?'

My anger with Majid Khan boiled over: 'Majid's attitude to me has always been antagonistic. On no occasion has he ever appreciated me or congratulated me, even when we won the series against England and the West Indies. The board have never helped me respond to these wild allegations and I have been left on my own. What am I and my family going through? That doesn't seem to matter.'

The only questions that really concerned me were about Jojo. I had to admit I did not know, as was alleged, whether he was a bookmaker. Perhaps I'd been naive. I was not so unworldly that I did not know that people bet on cricket in Pakistan. When Jojo and his brother appeared after Waqar, I have to confess, it shook me: Jojo looked evasive, and I began seeing him in a different light. There were also rumours that my brother Nadeem was a gambler. It did not emerge that our relationship had, for various reasons, rather cooled. Perhaps he had also taken my name in vain. I honestly did not know.

Yet the real problem with the inquiry was that it became a matter of one word against another. The witnesses veered between the extremes of Saleem Malik, who just went on protesting his innocence, and Haroon Rashid, for whom anything beyond the limits of his imagination had to be somehow corrupt. Haroon, for instance, accused Saqlain of deliberately giving away runs in a game, when all that had happened was that a ball change had rendered Saqlain unable to maintain his grip. It was typical of the kind of casual smear tossed around without any consideration of the danger to the reputation of an individual, by people who either wanted to shift blame or curry favour. In the middle of it all, accompanied by his twin brother and a personal bodyguard, appeared the hapless Ata-ur-Rehman, trying to back away from his bogus allegation against me. Most effusive was, inevitably, Rashid Latif, now unconstrained by being in the team. One of his allegations against me was that I 'used a mobile phone freely'. He flourished his tape-recorded conversations with Ata, Saeed Anwar, Basit Ali and others, although he greatly decreased their probative value by conceding he had edited them – Qayyum ended up relying little on their content.

Having lost the series to Australia, we next lost to Zimbabwe, succumbing on a green top in Peshawar. Nobody was going to fault my effort. I took five for 53 and three for 47, then top-scored in the second innings with 31. But by now we were in total disarray, barely capable of talking to one another. The captain probably saw the writing on the wall and resigned, although two rain-affected draws under Moin's leadership meant that we lost another series. Sohail now took the opportunity to go back to Qayyum and give further evidence – suddenly he produced an affidavit from Ata saying that I had pressured him to withdraw his allegation against me. Let's just say that it did little for Ata's credibility.

My counsel Khawaja Tariq Rahim ended up putting it well: no inquiry could have set a standard of proof low enough to draw conclusions from what he called an abundance of 'hearsay evidence, tainted with ulterior motives and malafide intentions, beset with contradictions' that were 'indicative of the sheer lack of credibility of the persons making the depositions'. There was factual carelessness, such as Ata's original affidavit implicating the absent Ejaz. There was idle inference, like Latif basing allegations on mobile phone use. There was wavering consistency, including Sohail's initial guardedness and later talkativeness. There were strategic leaks – an interim report was shown to certain journalists at the Commonwealth Games. Lacking, too, was completeness in the initial allegations. Not until December 1998 was it

Witnesses: Mushtaq Ahmed and Inzamam-ul-Haq arrive to testify in the Qayyum inquiry.

MARK RAY

revealed that both Mark Waugh and Shane Warne had received money from a bookmaker for 'pitch and weather information' before their fateful encounters with Saleem Malik. That did not help their credibility either.

At that point, the inquiry had been effectively winding up. With confirmation that cover-ups were not confined to Pakistan, it effectively had to restart, and moved to Melbourne for a week of hearings in January 1999. Shane Warne was examined; Mark Waugh was examined again. By now, however, I was far away. I was about to head to India. And I was, again, captain of my country.

CHAPTER 11

MISSION TO INDIA

Wasim was a real inspiration for fast bowlers all over the world and especially in the Subcontinent. His career coincided with the advent of better-quality television production and the growth of TV sets, and his skills reached so many kids who aspired to bowl like him. When he was bowling, you were captivated. Easily one of the most skilful bowlers I have played against and a tough competitor, but always had a smile on his face and exuded joy and confidence both on and off the field. Pleasure to have both played against him and interacted with him.

Rahul Dravid

I was an international cricketer for almost twenty years, and played 104 Tests and 356 one-day internationals. Only 5 per cent of these matches were in India. Perhaps I should consider myself lucky to have played so many. Politics, never absent during my career, now precludes the possibility of Pakistan playing cricket in India almost completely. But I go on thinking that a miraculous thaw is possible. After all, it was in 1998 that India detonated five nuclear devices at Pokhran, and Pakistan six nuclear devices in the Chaghai Hills. Yet barely six months later, India's cricketers were involved in some of the most stirring Tests of all time.

My role came almost as a shock. Eventually, on 3 January 1999, despite the best efforts of Aamir Sohail and Majid Khan, the PCB executive council led by Khalid Mahmood appointed me skipper, with Moin as my vice-captain. The Qayyum inquiry was still in progress, but nothing of substance had emerged, Ata having made a fool of himself, and Ali Fazli having publicly stated: 'Everyone is considered innocent until and unless proved guilty.' His discovery of this principle was belated but welcome.

A squad of twenty-three gathered at Gaddafi Stadium, where I watched them with coach Javed and chairman of selectors Wasim Bari. We were particularly taken with a broad-shouldered 23-year-old from Rawalpindi who had been around our squad for the previous year. Shoaib Akhtar had taken only seventeen costly wickets in seven Tests, being basically in competition for Waqar's spot with the speedy Mohammad Zahid and Mohammad Akram. But he had added a yard and grown up a little – he had the eagerness and humility of a young cricketer on the rise.

The other player who caught the eye was Shahid Afridi, who we now saw as having red ball potential. When we named him in the fifteen-man squad, Imran said: 'I've got one suggestion for you. Have Shahid Afridi open with Saeed Anwar.' He pointed to the disruptive effect of a left–right combination, and the impact of early boundaries, how they broke up fields, challenged lengths. That meant there was no place for Sohail, but frankly we were better off without him.

The tour remained in doubt until the very last moment. Some did not think the games should be taking place at all. Hindu nationalists stamped their feet as always. Shiv Sena leader Bal Thackeray said that 'Hindus should rise up against the Pakistan cricket team'. I aimed for a note of cordiality: 'We are going there to better the relations between the two countries, and I hope the Indian government will not allow a handful of people to deprive cricket lovers of some action and tension-packed cricket.' Not until 14 February did Indian prime minister Atal Bihari Vajpayee announce that the visit would go ahead; not for another week did we get our itinerary. The expectation as we took our forty-minute flight from Lahore to Delhi was tremendous, almost oppressive. India was in the process of building an impressive unit under Mohammad Azharuddin. Sachin Tendulkar, playing his first Tests against us as an adult, was now flanked by Rahul Dravid and Sourav Ganguly. Javagal Srinath swung the ball both ways at pace, Anil Kumble never stopped gnawing at your patience, and Nayan Mongia was a keeper who could bat. They would take a lot of beating.

My approach among colleagues was to accentuate the positives. The pressure would be on the hosts. We were now to avoid Mumbai, the stronghold of Shiv Sena, which had attacked the headquarters of the Board of Control for Cricket in India at Wankhede Stadium, breaking windows, trashing files and damaging historic trophies. Saboteurs also dug up the pitch in Delhi in an attempt to foil the Test there, while a rickshaw driver burned himself to death in protest at our presence on Indian soil. Imagine dealing with that, among your own countrymen.

Kudos to the BCCI and their boss Jagmohan Dalmiya. They bent over backwards to make us feel comfortable and secure. There were no customs or security checks when we arrived at Indira Gandhi Airport. There were two buses when we left the airport: one a decoy full of armed security going via major thoroughfares, the other ferrying us through backstreets to our hotel, where we were the only guests. Military units were posted at nearby buildings when we came out and returned from training and play. We never felt in a moment's danger.

Interest in the series was overwhelming. There were 300 media representatives at the first press conference with Javed, my manager Shaharyar Khan, and his PCB assistant Muin Munir. We were felicitated by home minister LK Advani, who it turned out had spent his first fifteen years in Karachi. We played a warm-up match at Gwalior against India A. The veteran Saleem Malik and new cap Yousuf Youhana made stylish centuries; I made 40 and took five for 55. Then, as we departed, we found our route to the airport thronged by well-wishers four- and five-deep on each side of the road. Just ordinary people – clerks and students, shopkeepers and road sweepers – who'd waited in the sun for us for two hours. Gwalior was where Nathuram Godse had hatched his plan to assassinate Mahatma Gandhi, so this was a poignant reminder of sport's transcendent status in the public mind.

Next we were bound for Chennai – located to the south, perhaps bearing fewer wounds of partition, it was judged the likeliest location for a calm First Test. No chances were to be taken with nationalist excesses. Indian flags, we learnt, would be banned at venues. No spectator was permitted to wear black, traditionally a colour of protest. Commandos would become a regular presence in our dressing room; likewise cameramen from Channel 4, who were making what turned out to be an excellent documentary, *A Bat and Ball War*. I got on well with Shaharyar, a former Pakistani foreign secretary. He was a master of diplomatic niceties; he also happened to be a diabetic. For all the trauma of the preceding year, the team, absent the barrack-room lawyers Aamir Sohail and Rashid Latif, was cohesive, united by the common cause.

Javed as coach always required taking the rough with the smooth. At his best, he was fantastic, hardworking and knowledgeable. He made a massive contribution to that tour by stressing fielding and catching, involving himself in the drills. But that was in a sense his problem – he was at heart a player, and part of him still ached to be out there. He could also play favourites. Now he took a set against Afridi, perhaps aware that our apprentice opener had been promoted by Imran. The day before we played the First Test at Chidambaram Stadium, he would not let Afridi bat in the nets, and I had to insist on Afridi's selection ahead of Asif Mujtaba.

Javed may have felt justified when we slumped to five for 91 just after lunch on an excellent batting pitch under a typical blazing sun. Moin put on 63 with young Yousuf Youhana, and 60 with me, but India was 190 in arrears with all ten wickets in hand at the close. On the second morning, fortunately, we surged back. I disposed of both openers. Then, apparently determined to assert himself against Saqlain, as he had against Warne a year earlier, Tendulkar came down the wicket to his third ball, and miscued a doosra to point. India were four for 125 at lunch, and though Dravid and Ganguly held us up in the afternoon, we kept India's lead to 16 runs.

Afridi now played the innings of his life: 141 in five hours with twenty-one fours and three sixes. Inzamam helped him add 97, and Saleem 106. The ascendancy, nonetheless, would not stop veering. In the last session of the third day, eight wickets fell in twenty-seven overs. On the last day, India needed 231, with eight wickets remaining. Though Tendulkar was clearly troubled by a bad back, it was equally apparent we would not get so lucky with him a second time.

I am bound to say that we enjoyed all the good fortune going round on the last day. I bowled twenty-six no balls in the match in forty-two overs. Not one of them coincided with a dismissal. The umpires, Steve Dunne and VK Ramaswamy, colluded in a shocking decision against Ganguly, the ball effectively hitting the ground twice as Moin came forward to accept a rebound off the silly point fielder – I did not realise how bad the call was until I later saw the replay. And Tendulkar was incredible. To that point, nobody in the world had played Saqlain with confidence. Tendulkar read his variations with ease, slapping his off-break, paddling his doosra, and defending as though he had all the time in the world. How were we going to get him out?

Frankly, we set ourselves to break through at the other end – a process I started with a ball I'm still proud of. Rahul Dravid was a wonderful player. He set himself to bat for eternity. I'd bowled him two coming back and hit his pads, perilously close to lbw but with a glint of inside edge. Thinking he'd expect a third inducker, I switched it round for the away swinger. It pitched leg, and hit the outside of off stump with a tiny click, so I knew I had bowled him before I saw the evidence. At lunch India were five for 86. Around the Channel 4 cameras in the dressing room we were buoyant, the five wickets we needed considerably simpler than our hosts' quest for 185. Our silver-tongued manager was going around saying: 'Remember to be sportsmanlike in victory.'

Except that the ball after lunch would not reverse, and Tendulkar inspired Mongia to an epic resistance. We could not break through. The overs ticked away, and their target grew nearer. At tea, our dressing room mood was subdued. Just afterwards, Moin failed to stump Tendulkar, who proceeded to his eighteenth Test century soon after in a 16-run Saqlain over. I could see the heads slumping round me and made a point of urging everyone on. 'One wicket and the match is ours!' I shouted over the noise of the crowd, clapping my hands. 'One wicket is all it takes!' I'm not sure anyone else believed it, but I did. With 95 needed, Waqar and I grabbed at the new ball, only to give away 33 in five overs. Then Mongia got overexcited, took an almighty slog at me, and holed out to Waqar in the covers.

That sharpened the contest. It was Tendulkar vs Pakistan. He was wincing with pain, but that made him all the more dangerous – in a hurry to win, he would play all his strokes. I brought Saqlain back for the left-handed Sunil Joshi but we could hardly get near him, so effectively did Tendulkar commandeer the strike. When we did get a look, Joshi hit a straight six. I must have had half a dozen fielders on the boundary when I came over to Saqlain with India needing only 17 to win. 'What should I do?' he asked.

Tendulkar was flinging the bat so hard, I could think of only one option: 'Hang a doosra out slow and wide of off stump.'

Saqlain looked miserable. 'But he'll hit me for six,' he protested.

'We just have to try something different,' I said. 'Don't worry about it. If there's any blame to take, I will take it.' I patted him on the back and tried to smile.

Saqlain didn't get the line quite right but he got the length and the pace. Tendulkar came down the pitch, lost his shape, and skewed the ball into the off side where I was the only fielder in the ring. There cannot be too many fielders in history who've felt exactly as I did in that moment, knowing that everyone in one country was willing me to catch what everyone in another country was willing me to drop. 'Shape up!' I told myself. 'Balance! Eye on the ball! You've caught a million of these at practice!' I put my hands up, fingers to the sky, and took the ball in front of my eyes. Tendulkar's masterpiece, spread over six and three-quarter hours, was complete, and now both ends were open.

Next over I hit Kumble on the pads with consecutive balls. They were both out, frankly – well, I thought so anyway. As they tended to in those days, the umpire turned the first down and gave the second. Joshi shovelled the next ball back to Saqlain, who forced Srinath to play on in his next over.

I had been told that the Chennai crowd had a reputation for sportsmanship, but what happened next I still find very moving. Somehow, in our euphoria, we suddenly thought of taking a victory lap. 'Should we?' I asked Shaharyar. 'Go ahead,' he said. 'You will be making history.' So it was that the 40,000 locals still in the stadium took it into their hearts to applaud us all the way. Pakistan and India had played a 12-run Test and they had borne witness. They had seen one of the great Test hundreds, Tendulkar's 136; one of the great Test spells, Saqlain's ten for 187; and only the second result in a Test match involving our countries in sixteen years. They were applauding not just us but cricket.

Were we on the brink of something special? We flew to Delhi, where the BCCI had drafted a security cordon of 10,000 police augmented by snake charmers, in case Shiv Sena made good a threat to release cobras in Feroz Shah Kotla. Huma was waiting for me with Tahmoor at the Taj Land's End. The Indian crowd were waiting too. After we lost the toss, they barracked Inzy something fearful, harking back to his temperamental outburst in Toronto by chanting 'Aloo!' When we batted, I could see the steam coming out of his ears.

'Take it easy,' I told him. 'You'll get yourself out.'

Inzy looked back grimly. 'If 44,000 people call you a potato all day,' he said, 'you're going to get upset.'

He did his best. We all did. But on a surface that turned from the first day, in a match where Saqlain took another ten wickets, Anil Kumble went one better in taking ten in an innings. An *innings* – I still cannot quite believe it. He was a wonderful bowler, never let up, never stopped trying. Switched after five exploratory overs to the Pavilion End where the Indian Arani Jayaprakash was standing, he proved all but unplayable, getting the ball to fizz and steeple as we poked and prodded powerlessly. After Afridi and Saeed Anwar had put on 101 for the first wicket, we fell apart.

The end was a reprise of eighteen months earlier in Sheikhupura. I hung in for an hour and a half, utterly determined to thwart Kumble's record; the Indians were just as determined to bring it about, to the extent of Srinath bowling so wide of off stump that last man Waqar could not reach the ball. 'You just hold up an end,' I told Waqar at the end of the over. 'He's not getting me out.' Next ball I nudged straight to short leg. Waqar stared at me all the way off. Azharuddin and I posed soberly with the trophy, each perhaps a little relieved: as I knew from Bangalore three years earlier, life would have been sour for the loser.

Administrators, meanwhile, were getting ambitious. Originally, a three-Test series had been planned. Now the Third Test was turned into the opening match of the 'Asian Test Championship' – a pan-Asian, four-Test festival also featuring Sri Lanka, with two independent umpires standing in each match and a bonus-point system based on run and wicket totals. For the opening fixture, Eden Gardens brimmed to its 100,000 capacity. I'd not seen a ground so full since the World Cup final seven years earlier, and our start was even more inauspicious. We had picked an extra batter in Wajahatullah Wasti, but he was one of the six to fall in the first hour for 31. It was left to Moin to lead our rebuilding, first with Saleem, then with me, so that we wrung out a batting bonus point. India were halfway to our total with nine wickets in hand just after lunch on the second day when our other change for the match was vindicated.

Waqar had managed only two wickets in the two preceding Tests. Javed and I could no longer ignore the fact that Shoaib was not just marginally but massively faster. I did not like decisions like this – I knew they smarted. Waqar was hurt. He wished Shoaib well, but he would not speak to me for about a year afterwards. Still, this was better than the opposite, and the selectors' intuition was now justified. In the second over of his third spell, Shoaib knocked out Dravid's leg stump and Tendulkar's middle stump with consecutive reverse-swinging yorkers. I've watched them many times since and I'm not sure anyone on earth could have played them, so late in flight do they tail. The Kolkata crowd was utterly disoriented. They had roared for Tendulkar as he had walked out, always so serene and composed; they'd kept up their roar all the way to Shoaib's delivery stride; then, confusion, bafflement, and a silence so deep you could hear the cries from our dressing room: '*Zinbadad!*'; '*Allah-o-Akbar!*' Shoaib went down on his knees in celebration, and we hugged each other in disbelief.

We were back in it. I returned to pick up Azharuddin and Sadagoppan Ramesh, and we removed their last five for 18 in fifty-three balls to limit our deficit to 38. Our second innings was then a duel between Srinath and Saeed Anwar. Srinath may have been a better fast bowler than the venerable Kapil Dev – he was tireless, persistent, and hit the bat hard. My only criticism of Saeed is that with his talent he should have been Pakistan's Brian Lara – he was casual about his fitness, a reluctant worker, and a shallow thinker about the game. But only Inzy in my time rivalled him for sweetness of timing. Srinath took eight for 86 but could not disturb Saeed, who carried his bat for 188.

I yielded the first over to Shoaib in the second innings, just as Imran had done for me: this kid was incredible, and his exuberance and confidence suggested he knew it. But India started their chase for 279 well, Ramesh adding 108 with VVS Laxman. Dravid and Tendulkar then seemed to be settling when the latter punched me wide of mid-on and came jogging back for a third. Moin's brother Nadeem, the substitute fielder, was retrieving rather than chasing, and Shoaib sauntered up from mid-off to prevent overthrows as the return came in. You could not have choreographed what ensued. Tendulkar and Shoaib were both watching the throw. Anticipating that the return would bounce, Shoaib took a couple of steps back into the runner's path as Tendulkar groped for the crease. The ball unexpectedly hit the stumps. At first it looked like one of those moments when the bails fall to no effect, but then I sensed that Tendulkar was agitated, and that the crowd was uneasy. We huddled in the middle while the decision was referred to third umpire KT Francis, with a dawning sense that this could be a turning point in the Test, although we did not anticipate how great.

When the lights showed three reds, the six-figure Kolkata crowd was thunderstruck. Tendulkar's disgruntled body language magnified the discontent; apparently he went straight to Francis's quarters to watch the replay. Azharuddin emerged slowly as if waiting to see how things unfolded. This was not the usual noise of an Indian crowd, excited and passionate; it had a jagged edge, accompanied by makeshift projectiles. Dravid played out the rest of my over, but when Shoaib walked to his position at deep fine leg he was pelted with bottles.

Naturally I was worried. Could I guarantee the safety of my players? Could I ensure the integrity of the match? That very day, Vajpayee was on his way to Lahore: his famous bus *yatra*, ahead of signing the peace-restoring Lahore Declaration. Nothing in a captaincy manual prepares you for such moments. We withdrew towards the centre while attempts were made to restore order. Finally, umpires Steve Bucknor and David Orchard called an early tea, whereupon Dalmiya prevailed on Tendulkar to come out and pacify the crowd, and a message blazed across the big screen: 'Calcutta loves cricket. Please respect Eden's traditions.' Eden's traditions, though, were part of the problem. There was obviously concern at the prospect of a sequel to the riot that had concluded India's 1996 World Cup.

During the break I was approached by the match referee, Cammie Smith, with Sunil Gavaskar. 'Wasim, we think you should recall Sachin,' said Sunny. 'People will love you in India.'

Sunny knew how partisan the Kolkata crowd could be – he'd once refused to play a Test here because he had been so badly barracked the previous time. But I had my own fans to worry about. 'Sunny *bhai*, they might love me in India, but they'll hate me in Pakistan!' I said. 'Anyway, it's not my decision. The umpire's given him out. It's too late for me to withdraw the appeal. Play has continued. We all know it's an accident, but cricket's full of accidents. It's not up to captains to rectify them.' This, I found out, was also the opinion of the on-field umpires, and the neutral cricket commentators, Ian Chappell and Michael Holding.

Still, I wasn't unsympathetic to the ground authorities' predicament. I could feel the discontent simmering, especially when Shoaib had Dravid caught off his gloves and trapped Mongia lbw. Our flamboyant young fast bowler had become a scourge, a magnet of controversy, a focus of annoyance. Kumble stuck it out with Ganguly to see India through to the last day, on which India would need 65 with four wickets left. That night, police surrounded our dressing room and our bus in a protective cordon, but there were no incidents.

That the last day might prove short did not discourage 65,000 passionate Bengalis from turning up. I opened with Shoaib. We decided we would concede Ganguly the single and try to get at Kumble. I posted a single floating slip, Azhar Mahmood, and got a little lucky. A ball reversed away, Ganguly drove on the up, and Azhar took a wonderful catch to his left at full stretch. In my next over I nicked off Srinath, whereupon Shoaib removed Kumble. With each wicket the mood in the stands soured further, until missiles were seized and fires lit. The edgy police chief decided he could take no more: he took the unprecedented decision to clear the stadium. With twenty-six balls bowled in the morning, we were called off the field, and the police used their lathis zealously. I guess if you have to make provision for cobras, then spectators don't pose an undue challenge, although we were confined to our dressing room for a tense three hours. Personally I never felt in any particular danger. I thought that disappointment was the overriding sentiment rather than hostility. I was, however, concerned for the result. It was an unearthly feeling when we re-entered the empty stadium in pursuit of the last wicket, which Shoaib took with his first ball back, bowling Venkatesh Prasad. Remarks in the presentation ceremony echoed round the back of stands that in the match had housed nearly half a million souls. Javed likened it, accurately, to a 'ghost town'.

We now returned to Lahore to host Sri Lanka on a lifeless surface, of which young Wasti took advantage with a brace of hundreds. The game also proved unexpectedly memorable for me. Having left the bulk of the bowling to the spinners, I slipped off the ground for a rest. I had just lit one of my very occasional cigarettes when a message came from Moin in the middle – the ball had suddenly started reversing. I was sceptical: the ball had gone gun-barrel straight for two and a half days, and Romesh Kaluwitharana had moved to an accomplished century. But Moin was right. He took the catch as my first ball darted away from Kalu. My next two, inswingers, bowled Niroshan Bandaratilleke, round his legs, and Pramodya Wickramasinghe, through the gate. Not even Shane Warne's hat-trick four years earlier had followed so closely on a cigarette. I'm not sure now that I didn't overstep on at least one occasion – having been a little stiff, I felt myself stretching. But I'm not complaining.

By virtue of Sri Lanka having played a high-scoring draw with India in Colombo, we faced them again in a final in Dhaka in Bangladesh – something of an anticlimax, especially when Ejaz and Inzy put on 367 for the third wicket in reply to their 231, and we had time for a burst at them late on the third day. It was one of those occasions a bowler relishes, when he knows time is short but opportunity long – every ball can, and must, count. With the last two deliveries of my opening over, I bounced out Avishka Gunawardene and knocked Chaminda Vaas's stumps askew. When I had the ball again for my second over, I held it for the inswinger, but must have altered my action slightly because it carried on. Mahela Jayawardene ended up chasing something on the line of fifth stump and parrying to Wasti at second slip. Hat-tricks in consecutive Tests! I ran out Marvan Attapattu the next morning to speed our championship triumph by an innings and 175 runs.

I still have Vaas's splintered stump, one of my favourite cricket souvenirs, from one of my favourite cricket experiences. I hope another Pakistani captain gets an opportunity like mine. For all their occasional excesses, there is simply no cricket public like India's, and no cricket relationship like Pakistan's with India.

CHAPTER 12

A CUP FORFEITED

Cricket is a team sport, but everything goes back to the rivalry of batter and bowler, and in Wasim Akram every batter had a wonderful rival – when you play against someone of that calibre, it lifts your game as well, and the experience stays with you forever. Wasim was a master. He made the ball talk. His run-up was so natural. Unlike most fast bowlers, he didn't need to measure his steps; he could just start from anywhere and still be as effective. He ran through the crease so quickly you hardly had time to set yourself up. When I first faced him, I'd never encountered anyone like Wasim. Every game we played against each other I remember, and every time we meet now it is in warm friendship.

Sachin Tendulkar

As the 1999 World Cup approached, I couldn't help feeling that it was our time. With Shahid Afridi exuding power at the top, Yousuf Youhana offering silky strokes in the middle, and Azhar Mahmood enhancing our all-round balance, we had renewed ourselves as a one-day side since 1996. As our lead-in to England, we won a Pepsi Cup in India, Azhar taking five for 38 in the final, and a Coca-Cola Cup in the UAE, where I started the final by trapping Ramesh and Dravid lbw in the first four balls. Shoaib finished the latter tournament with an Opel for player of the series, and his confidence was booming.

My sole source of concern was the old bane of fixing, which even when it was merely rumoured rather than evidenced was unsettling. In general, I took the attitude that players should now be wise to inducements. I remember during our stay in Dubai, I was introduced to a wealthy businessman who pushed a Bulgari watch across the table to me. 'I want you to have this because you are a great player,' he said. I pushed the timepiece back. 'Thanks, but I'll buy one myself one day,' I said, then got up and left – later, incidentally, I *did* buy the same watch. I trusted that by now my players knew to take the same attitude.

One game in the Coca-Cola Cup, however, had ramifications. Batting in daylight at Sharjah, England recovered from five for 86 to post 206. I came in at the innings break to find Javed gabbling about the match being fixed – he claimed he had had a tip-off, from somebody who ought to know, that Saleem, Mahmood, Afridi, Moin and Inzy were in on the scam. 'Get a Qur'an!' he demanded.

'What do you mean get a Qur'an?' I asked.

'Get the players to put their hands on the Qur'an and swear the match is not fixed!' Javed thundered.

'Are you crazy?' I shouted back. 'What are you on about? Just sit down before you upset everyone.'

Javed still had a phone in his hand, and thrust it at me. 'Talk to the guy!' he shouted.

I took the phone, and a voice said: 'The match is fixed.'

'I don't think so,' I said sharply – a fix needed a captain's involvement, and I was damn sure I wasn't in on anything. But by the time I handed the phone back, the word was out: the coach believed a fix was in. Javed was an intimidating presence, and grew wilder still when a Qur'an could not be found. He started loudly issuing explicit instructions to each player before they went in. A middling target like 206 requires only a couple of partnerships, but the atmosphere grew tenser and tenser and we simply could not build anything. Finally, as the ball nibbled around under lights, we succumbed to our own tentativeness, losing five wickets for six runs in four overs.

By the end of that tournament, the rift between Javed and the players could not be healed. His exit was specifically about his always demanding an equal share of prize money, as though he was still a player. It was not a big deal to me: as captain, I was well paid. But for youngsters dependent on distributions from a prize pool, it was unfair. Much as I revered him, I did not stop Javed when he walked away.

When Majid Khan was subsequently not appointed to a new term as PCB CEO, I almost burst into applause.

I now had a freer hand. When Khalid asked for my view on coaches for the World Cup, I called together Mushtaq Mohammad and Richard Pybus, a young technical analyst from South Africa recommended to me by an English friend. With our team manager Zafar Altaf, we had, I thought, the right balance of calm heads and analytical expertise. We planned the campaign with an eye to our capabilities. It would be a bowler's World Cup. It was early in the English season, and the small white Dukes ball would swing sharply. As we were a brittle batting side, we thought our best chance was to repeat the policy so successful in the 1996–97 Carlton & United Series, which was to bat first where possible. We liked the look of Abdul Razzaq, a nineteen-year-old seam-bowling all-rounder from Lahore with a sound defensive technique, and decided to deploy him as a kind of third opener in the event Afridi did not come off in the opening berth. It remedied our 1996 weakness by providing a fifth bowler and extended our batting to number nine. In fact, I'm not sure we ever had a better World Cup line-up than this, with Saeed Anwar in peak form and Shoaib bowling very fast – and, at the back of my mind, I craved the chance to emulate Imran by leading us to the cup.

We showed how the plan might work against the West Indies at Bristol, where I batted first on an overcast day on which I suspect most captains would have bowled. We slipped to four for 42, but Lara kept bowling Ambrose, Walsh and Merv Dillon to shut us out for good, and we recovered against their lesser bowlers via numbers six, seven and eight: Yousuf Youhana, Azhar Mahmood and myself. I hit four fours and two sixes in 43 off twenty-nine balls, and we set them 230 to win. Shoaib bowled a furious spell, so fast that Sherwin Campbell's attempted hook flew over third man for six before he was bowled all over the place. Only Chanderpaul held us up, Mahmood and Razzaq sharing six wickets with their medium-pacers. We were then four for 58 against Scotland at Chester-le-Street before Youhana, Moin and I put on 203 for the last two wickets, and Shoaib and I bundled out their first five for 19.

Australia sent us in on a grey morning at Headingley, but Razzaq showed his maturity, Inzy his touch and Moin his sharp finishing skills as we made eight for 275, including 40 from Glenn McGrath's last three overs. There was a wonderful, noisy crowd, festooned with Pakistani flags and orchestrated by silver-bearded spectator Abdul Jalil, and they exploded when I bowled Gilchrist with the third ball of the Aussies' reply. Steve Waugh's team fought hard as always: they were four for 214 with nine overs remaining. But Shoaib yorked Waugh with a rocket, and I came back to get Michael Bevan, Damien Martyn and McGrath to complete a 10-run win. Moin's two catches that day should not be forgotten: he went wide to his right to accept Mark Waugh's edge one-handed, then sprang from behind the stumps to collect Darren Lehmann's miscued sweep.

Suddenly, we were red-hot. Everyone wanted to board our bandwagon. Nawaz Sharif began calling me every other day, with comments on our previous game and urgings for our next. And at Derby, everything about the formula clicked: Inzy came in perfectly platformed – three for 128 with twenty-two overs left – and flailed an unbeaten 73 off sixty-one balls. Shoaib struck twice in his opening spell, Azhar and Saqlain strangled them through the middle, and we had the game in hand long before it was won, guaranteeing that we would progress to the Super Six. We were playing with confidence – maybe even overconfidence. Because at Northampton, I departed from our successful policy, left out Razzaq to give Waqar a game, and sent Bangladesh in. We had not lost, they had not won, and we might even get an early finish and enhance our run rate – as Australia later did against Bangladesh.

The rest is history, and in some eyes mystery. Azhar, who'd been so good, was abruptly quite bad, going wicketless at seven an over, and their nine for 223 was exactly the kind of score we struggled to chase. Khaled Mahmud's medium-pacers swung wickedly, and Inzy sold Saeed down the river before playing across a straight one himself. Only Azhar and I, putting on a painstaking 55 in seventy-eight balls, could cobble a partnership together, before I made the mistake of pushing and running, then holed out sweeping. We bowled twenty-eight wides; in our defence, they bowled twenty-one.

Our 62-run defeat was exactly the kind of loss that sometimes trips up a team that has been travelling well, the XI with nothing to gain succumbing to the team with nothing to lose – or so I tried to rationalise it. Imran rang. 'You've been well beaten,' he said. 'Make sure to praise them.' So I commented at the end about taking pleasure in the success of 'our Muslim brothers'. It turned out that I had added a gaffe to a debacle – it sounded like I did not care. I was also soon to be unwell. In the next few days, I picked up a throat infection that worsened into a fever, and had it not been so important I would not have played our opening Super Six game at Trent Bridge. I wasn't about to allow another Bangalore 1996.

We were still strongly positioned, because of points achieved against other qualifiers, which carried over into the Six. But to this climactic stage of the World Cup, we made a poor start. I reverted to batting first against South Africa, but we were tentative, almost haunted. Only Moin played with any freedom, having come in with fifteen overs to go and our scoring rate at 3.3. Shoaib, Azhar and I had the Proteas five for 58 after twenty overs, but Jacques Kallis got set, Lance Klusener carved us up, and we lost by three wickets with an over to spare.

Next we faced India. Since Vajpayee's visit, Pakistan had controversially seized the heights above Kargil, touching off a shooting match in disputed Kashmir, and threatening our non-shooting match at Old Trafford. Frankly, a bilateral fixture would never have gone ahead; that we were in an ICC event of which we were both prior winners made things possible – just. It helped that I had built a good rapport with Azharuddin, and that some of our guys had formed friendships with their counterparts. Perhaps it was also just as well that it was not a tense or close match – the packed crowd, 90 per cent South Asian, made lots of noise but not much trouble. Sensing our diffidence in chasing, Azha batted first and made 59 in a score of 220, which was too much for us. We had won nine of our previous one-day internationals against India, but maintained our record of never beating them in a World Cup as we fell 47 runs short. That same day, in Kargil, six Pakistani soldiers and three Indian officers were killed.

Nawaz Sharif had been telling me of his plans to fly to England for the Lord's final; when next we spoke he was sounding equivocal. But the team was still in good shape. At the Oval we faced Zimbabwe, who had been playing great cricket: Heath Streak was hooping the Dukes, and the classy left-hander Neil Johnson had won three man-of-the-match awards. I was relieved to win the toss, Saeed made a fine 103, and Afridi provided us with a finishing burst to set them 272 to win. Razzaq, Azhar and Saqlain, who took a hat-trick, did the rest, despite Johnson's 54. Our carryover points now propelled us into the semi-final against New Zealand.

New Zealand's seam bowlers had been unexpectedly effective in the World Cup, while Stephen Fleming had been batting fluently and captaining shrewdly – he caused me some concern straight away by deciding to set us a target. I need not have worried. Shoaib got Nathan Astle and I got Craig McMillan at the top, Shoaib came back to bowl Fleming with a sublime yorker, and I stopped Adam Parore with one of my own. Saeed unrolled his second consecutive century, putting on 194 for the first wicket with Wajahatullah Wasti, and after our roller-coaster campaign we found ourselves in the World Cup final – for Moin, Inzy, Ejaz and myself, a second.

That first final seven years earlier had seemed like a divine gift. We had fought our way back from nowhere. Now we had had to come back from somewhere, from something like early favouritism, following our four consecutive wins, burdened all the while. We could struggle under such pressure. It had been our undoing in 1996. At practice the day before the final, Lord's seemed full of Pakistani politicians and PCB officials – not Nawaz, too shrewd, but enough to make a nuisance of themselves at practice and in our dressing room, which they insisted on occupying.

That evening, nonetheless, I thought there was an air of confidence around us. Yousuf Youhana was now carrying a hamstring injury, but we had Razzaq back to provide steadiness at number three, extending our batting to number nine in case of early losses. We had matchwinners in Saeed and Shoaib, experience in Moin and Inzy. We had an extra day's rest after our undemanding semi, while Australia had played an exhausting semi against South Africa. We had, above all, a plan. At the team dinner, the strong consensus was that we should bat first if possible – we were more conscious of our failure against Bangladesh than our success against New Zealand. I was pleased next morning to win the toss. Only Australia, in 1996, had failed to win a World Cup final after putting runs on the board.

What I'll always remember about that morning is how quickly everything seemed to dissolve after we lost the early wicket of Wasti to a fine Mark Waugh slips catch. There was a ridiculous number of officials in the small Lord's dressing room – so many that neither Mushtaq nor Pybus could find places on the balcony. Saeed had hit three scintillating early boundaries, then at the end of the fifth over signalled that he needed a new grip – the fact that he, as an experienced professional cricketer, had not had three bats ready to go on perhaps the biggest day of his career simply beggars belief. Yousuf then ran out not with a bat but with a handful of grips and a grip cone. It takes a long time to get to the middle at Lord's – you must tramp down two flights of stairs and hurry through the Long Room – so the interruption was interminable, even before Yousuf got out there. Saeed then must have spent at least five minutes fiddling with the bat, breaking his flow, his rhythm and his concentration.

I was furious. I laid into Yousuf as he came back in – meekly he said that he had never changed a grip before. I was in the midst of dressing him down when Saeed aimed an airy drive at his next ball and dragged on. We then went thirteen balls without scoring. McGrath's opening spell was 6–3–6–1. Steve Waugh caught Razzaq driving at

Tom Moody and we were three for 67 after twenty. Then he threw the ball to Shane Warne, who bowled his nine overs consecutively – I was the last of his four wickets, slogging as we ran out of batting. Next over we were done: all out 132 in, frankly, ideal batting conditions.

Australia were excellent. They were guaranteed excellence by the presence of McGrath and Warne. They next showed us how to chase. Shoaib and I bowled fast, but Gilchrist hit us faster, slapping his way to 54 in thirty-six balls. I had Ricky Ponting caught behind, but the game was over by 4.30 pm – at 59.1 overs, with only four-and-a-half hours' play, the shortest World Cup final of all, and the most one-sided.

We were stunned. I was shattered. As against Bangladesh, I tried a gracious concession speech. Asked whether we had let our fans down, I claimed: 'No, I'm not disappointed in any way. We didn't let our supporters down. Australia played better cricket on the day ... They bowled well and they fielded well and they were mentally tough. We had a bad day.' Again I may have struck the wrong note, and it was not really what I was feeling inside. I don't think I ever looked on an opposing captain with such envy as I looked on Steve Waugh as he held the trophy aloft. We all knew that Waugh had his differences with Warne. But Australians above all love winning games of cricket; in Pakistan, as I've said, winning is nice, but losing will always be useful to some. I knew that my detractors would take advantage of the defeat. I knew that my supporters would pay. Watching television a few days later, Khalid Mahmood found out that president Rafiq Tarar had sacked him as chairman of the PCB. Mushtaq and Pybus lost their jobs. Poor Inzy had his house stoned. I was burned in effigy in Lahore.

Not that I was there. I had not planned to return to Pakistan straight away in any case, having signed to play some games with Smethwick CC in the Birmingham League – both Mushtaq and Steve Waugh had played there, and a Pakistani businessman not only paid me handsomely but lent me his Porsche to commute from Manchester. Truth be told, I was grieving a little. Although we were led by Asif Din, a former Warwickshire player, the standard was poor, and hitting sixes over 30-metre boundaries was unfulfilling. I actually wanted to get back to Pakistan, where we had a busy schedule up to and including a tour of Australia.

But now I was again under scrutiny. Tarar appointed two new figures to head an ad-hoc committee of the PCB: Mujeeb-ur-Rehman, whose brother Saifur headed the government's anti-corruption bureau Ehtesab, and Majid Khan's cousin Javed Zaman, whose son was married to Majid's daughter. They suspended me, Ejaz and Saleem Malik on suspicion of unspecified 'immoral and unethical activities'. They asked Ali Sibtain Fazli to produce a detailed summary of Qayyum's inquiry, which also held new hearings – specifically to address the Pepsi Cup match against England, now the subject of florid allegations by Javed Miandad.

The World Cup final was now felt to be terribly suspicious. Why had I batted first on a 'seaming pitch'? For one thing, it was a good batting wicket, on which Steve Waugh said he would have batted first, and estimated a par score to be 260. For another thing, we had followed the policy of batting on winning the toss for the whole cup, losing only when we departed it. Why had we got out to Shane Warne? Maybe because he was the best bowler in the world. Why had we lost to Australia? Maybe because they were the best team around.

So I withdrew from my contract with Smethwick to return to Lahore, where I was summoned by Ehtesab. The Ehtesab Cell was scarcely an integrity body at all. It had huge powers but, I discovered, limited expertise. I travelled to Islamabad at my own expense, staying at the Islamabad Club, and for four entire days was questioned by a brigadier who knew so little about cricket that I had to explain to him the difference between a red ball and a white ball. I was allowed no representation. I had to surrender all my financial records, all my bank accounts and tax returns. They accessed my parents' accounts, those of my brothers and my friends. And they found … nothing. To save face, they had to say that I had slightly underpaid some taxes, which I promptly made good. Ehtesab then called in Shoaib and Ejaz, to similarly ridiculous effect.

I also made a final appearance before Justice Qayyum, testifying that I held no suspicion about the Coca-Cola Cup game against England. It was, in other words, another completely pointless exercise that did nothing but damage to innocent reputations, brought about by our chronic national immaturity – the brittle Pakistani arrogance that expects victory and can only explain defeat by claiming a conspiracy. We had had an amazing year – we'd won the Asian Test Championship and two one-day tournaments, then finished runner-up in a third. But because we did not win every game, because sometimes other teams outplayed us, we had to be crooks.

At least there were now no grounds to replace me as captain, so the new guard at the PCB changed their tune. When I returned to Manchester, I received a call from Mujeeb-ur-Rehman, who many thought was an entitled brat. He had unveiled all manner of stupid ideas to rebrand

Pakistani cricket, including a new logo resembling Nike swooshes that nobody liked but everyone nodded at because he was the new pooh-bah. Now he told me he was coming to London, and that I should come shopping with him in Bond Street – I could hardly say no, and suffered through one of the more excruciating days of my life. I was not expected to pay for him, except in the sense that he was essentially buying me, proceeding to convene a press conference at the Pakistan High Commission where I was publicly reinstated as captain for the forthcoming DMC Trophy in Toronto. The clamour for change was satisfied by a new coach, Wasim Raja, and new selectors: Wasim's brother Ramiz, Naushad Ali and Abdur Raquib. They recalled, after his tireless lobbying, the zombie figure of Aamir Sohail.

The eruption of the Kargil War in Kashmir had by now reopened the rift with India: the DMC Trophy became instead three one-day internationals against the West Indies, which we won handily. I actually liked Wasim Raja. He was good company and widely experienced. Unfortunately he could not hold his liquor – three drinks and he was a different man. On the plane on the way home, he got involved in an altercation for flouting the no-smoking signs, and did not have his contract renewed. I persuaded Mujeeb to rehire Pybus – energetic, a good organiser and a low-key personality – for our forthcoming Coca-Cola Champions Trophy. But the biggest personnel change was just around the corner.

• • •

On 30 September 1999, at his fortieth hearing, Qayyum finally heard from the last of his seventy witnesses. The report was more or less prepared already. Its presentation to the PCB on 12 October would normally have been huge news but for a huger event: a military coup that seized control of Pakistan from the Sharif government, following the army's growing disillusionment with the Kargil War.

It was now by no means clear who was in charge at the PCB, although at least we knew who wasn't: Mujeeb was arrested. The chief of the armed forces, General Pervez Musharraf, became ex officio the patron of the PCB – the post once held by his military predecessor General Zia. Zia had got rid of his predecessor Ali Bhutto, Benazir's father, during an England tour of Pakistan; this time we were in Sharjah. For a team that can crumble under negligible pressure, Pakistani teams can actually thrive in turmoil. We went unbeaten in the Coca-Cola Sharjah Cup, blitzing the West Indies and Sri Lanka.

For me, too, the outcome of the coup was not unfavourable. For interim PCB chairman, Rafiq Tarar nominated Zafar Altaf, who held his own clear-out: his Qayyum work done, Fazli left. The report then rather sat there, the subject of rumour and insinuation, awaiting a permanent chairman and CEO. People focused, momentarily at least, on the cricket: our three Tests in Australia would be the first ever broadcast live in Pakistan, on PTV.

Our tour, however, was poorly structured. In a year in which we had played twenty-nine one-day internationals since our last Test, we warmed up with just a fifty-over match against Western Australia and a four-day match against Queensland before meeting Australia at the Gabba. Fitness standards had slipped during the turnover of coaches, to the extent that Inzy looked almost sylph-like. Shoaib in particular wasn't ready. Over him a further cloud hovered:

during the game at the WACA, it emerged, he had been videoed in action on the instruction of the local umpiring director, Rick Evans, who'd sent the footage to the ACB. It was noted that one of the match officials, Ross Emerson, had no-balled Muttiah Muralitharan the previous season, and Australian umpires of that era were not only poor but pushy and high-handed, overeager to assert themselves. We reassured ourselves that nobody had ever questioned Shoaib's action. But equally, Murali had gone unchallenged everywhere but Australia.

Thanks to Inzy and Youhana, we actually held our own at the Gabba on the first day after being sent in. Moin played a spirited hand on the second morning to guide us to 367. But over the next two days, our lack of tough recent cricket told, for there was no tougher cricket than in Australia in the Waugh–Warne years. Slater and Mark Waugh ground out hundreds, Gilchrist made a dashing 81 and Warne a hearty 86. Saeed's 171-run fourth-wicket partnership with Youhana in the second innings was our only real encouragement as we went down by ten wickets. When we lost Saeed cheaply in the Second Test at Bellerive Oval after being sent in, and Ejaz soon after, we looked to be sliding quickly out of the series.

In demanding conditions, we rallied. Mohammad Wasim, a skilful player, played his best innings since a century on debut two years earlier; Azhar and I hung around later to drag us to 222. Australia then lost their last nine wickets for 55 in twenty overs, mainly to Saqlain, whose doosra they were facing for the first time in a Test – always a teasing challenge. I hardly saw a Pakistani team bat better than we did in our second innings, with Inzy crafting a wonderful 118 in 191 balls, supported by Saeed and Ejaz. We seemed to have discovered our Test match rhythm, after a year of white ball fits and starts, and set Australia 369 to win in the fourth innings. When I trapped Ponting for his third consecutive nought, the hosts were five for 126.

With Justin Langer and Adam Gilchrist at the crease, Australia began the last day needing 181 for victory, with the bookies quoting 9 to 1 – pretty telling in a two-horse race. Still, I had my own problems. Waqar had rolled an ankle, Shoaib was still not quite fit, and the surface was this very dark soil I had never seen before: though scuffed on one side, the ball was neither reverse-swinging nor carrying. I was conscious, too, of how quickly Gilchrist could score. He had taken us apart in the World Cup final. He disposed unfailingly of the bad ball and could really hurt you if you let him. My defensiveness in that first hour let the Australians settle, so that they were well established by the time I reached for the second new ball.

Mind you, the match would have been over by lunch had it not been for one of the worst umpiring decisions I ever saw. At five for 237, Langer drove at a wide one from me, got an almost deafening edge, and amazed us by remaining at the wicket; we were even more amazed when Queenslander Peter Parker gave him not out. To use the Aussie vernacular, Langer 'fucking smashed it' – and he knew it. We then failed to put it behind us. Gilchrist made a telling observation about us in his autobiography: 'They [Pakistan] were a real team, if you like. When they were going well, they were exuberant, laughing, talking non-stop, all encouraging each other. But we knew that when they turned, they turned together, and it wouldn't take much before they were pointing fingers and gesturing at each other ... Before long we'd hear bowlers complaining about the fielders, or gesturing at the captain if they were hit for a boundary.' Imagine being that captain.

Shoaib came on and bowled a fiery spell, but the Australians played Saqlain well, working out that he turned his doosra more than his off-break. With every over that Langer survived, we grew more aggrieved – the big screen made a point of showing the replay over and over again so that the snicko could be studied. With every over, Gilchrist grew more dominant. The latter reached his century just before lunch, with 92 still needed; the former followed just after, when there were 59 to get. The countdown was agonising, especially as we were not generating chances, let alone wickets. And so for the second time I lost a series in Australia – an experience so disappointing I could not drag myself to the presentations.

Now we were broken: we went down in Perth by an innings and 20 runs in three days. Here we again left out Waqar in favour of the young Mohammad Akram – in hindsight a mistake, and one that further antagonised Waqar. We should probably have given Shoaib a break, especially as there emerged further newspaper reports that his action had been filmed, along with pro-forma denials of anything untoward. But before we returned for the CUB Series, we clearly had work to do. Unfortunately, we were not best placed to do it.

CHAPTER 13

GENERAL DISARRAY

Wasim was one of the greatest fast bowlers I have
ever seen – alongside Malcolm Marshall, probably the
hardest to face. He had it all: pace, left-arm angle from
over or round, quick arm action with reverse swing,
and could hit you on the foot or on the head with no
discernible change in action. Then we had to try to get
him out as well, and he usually smashed it everywhere!
Fantastic all-rounder – one of the all-time greats.

Nasser Hussain

At home, change was afoot. As chairman of the PCB, Musharraf had appointed his friend Lt Gen Tauqir Zia, who had been director-general of military operations in the Kargil War, then succeeded Musharraf as corps commander in the prestigious I Strike Corps. That caused the usual spill of positions: Pybus was out, replaced by Intikhab Alam; Yawar Saeed was succeeded as manager by Brigadier Mohammed Nasir Ahmed and as a director by Brigadier Munawar Ahmad Rana. All of a sudden there were medals everywhere, but none earned in cricket counted, and to me Tauqir took an instant dislike. He was a bully, barrel-chested, with a booming voice, a misplaced confidence in his judgement, and a marked preference for his cronies.

Among other things, Tauqir adored Shoaib, both of them hailing from the Pindi Club. At first this had advantages. When we returned to Australia, we found that the ICC had imposed, without warning, consultation or even real reason, a bowling ban on Shoaib. Tauqir went straight to the top, petitioning the BCCI's Jagmohan Dalmiya, now chairman of the ICC, to commute the sentence – an agreement was reached, frankly ridiculous, that Shoaib would not bowl bouncers for the series. The super-fast full ball with which he dismissed Steve Waugh in the opening game of the CUB Series at the Gabba, where he bowled a matchwinning spell, was the perfect retort. We proceeded to play surprisingly well, and advanced to the finals at India's expense.

But I could see the writing on the wall now. Tauqir called in Javed and Ramiz Raja as consultants. He listened to the malcontented Sohail and Rashid Latif. His brigadier proxy in Australia, Mohammed Nasir Ahmed, was throwing his weight around also, at least until I confronted him. In the last round-robin match at the MCG, I wanted to rest Razzaq, who had a niggle. Next I knew he was on the field as a substitute. 'What are you doing here?' I asked.

'The brigadier told me,' he said meekly.

So I took our manager aside. 'You might be a brigadier,' I told him, 'but this is not a war and I am the captain. Leave the cricket to me.' Oddly enough, he took it like a man, and we got on fine from that point: as a manager he was actually very organised and good company.

His boss Tauqir, however, was not. When we went down 0–2 in the finals, I knew my days were numbered. On our return to Pakistan, Tauqir was petitioned night and day by my rivals, such as Waqar and Saeed. He indulged Shoaib, permitting him to employ his own medical personnel and to travel separately from the rest of the team. He would later promote his son Junaid, who enjoyed a rapid rise to international cricket. I'd been down this road before. A few years earlier I might have dug in; now I was approaching thirty-four and could see the end, if not of cricket then at least of the captaincy. Nobody told me, of course. I learnt second-hand that I had been replaced by Saeed, who proceeded to lead us to defeat in Test and one-day international series in Sri Lanka. Intikhab's comeback proved a brief one, as Javed wormed his way back into the coach's role again. Our one gain of the tour was Younis

Khan, a 22-year-old right-hander from Peshawar, who made a century on debut at Rawalpindi, where we added 145 for the ninth wicket. Humble, hardworking, a straight arrow – I would take a lot of pleasure in his success.

My time was passing. As if to reinforce that fact, I broke down in the same game. Huma urged me to think about what to do after cricket, and I agreed to try some commentating in the English summer. But my problems were about to be dwarfed by cricket's. The short-lived Saeed experiment was succeeded by a longer-term Moin project. Our keeper became captain for the Coca-Cola Sharjah Cup in March 2000, which we won, defeating South Africa in the final. Moin's counterpart Hansie Cronje made 79 in seventy-three balls for the losing cause.

I had never known Hansie well, while respecting his leathery toughness. He looked every inch the South African cricketer – competitive, fit, a little dour – and seemed set for a long career. Little did anyone suspect it, but we had just seen his final international innings. A week later, as South Africa prepared to host Australia for a three-match one-day series, it emerged that Hansie had been in the pay of the representative of an Indian cricket betting syndicate, Sanjeev Chawla. Their communications, in which several other South African teammates were named, had been intercepted as part of a routine phone tap by India's Central Bureau of Investigation. This radically shifted conceptions of match-fixing. No longer was it a murky Eastern bazaar. It appeared to be a global shopping mall where cricketers were for sale.

When the news about Cronje emerged, I was in the West Indies, where Moin, with the good brigadier as manager, was leading us in a triangular one-day series also involving

Zimbabwe. It stirred interest in the Qayyum inquiry, the report of which was still in Tauqir's bottom drawer. The chairman tried to deflect: he stated publicly that the report had found no evidence of 'planned match-fixing'. Qayyum retorted, also publicly, that there were indeed 'members of the current team against whom punishment is recommended'. Newspapers duly bandied names about, including mine. The *News of the World* published a classic tabloid sting where, posing as potential cricket gamblers, they cajoled Saleem Malik into boasting that 'when you've got the main players in your hand, you'll have to be really unlucky to lose'.

With Cricket South Africa foreshadowing the King Commission to look into Cronje's malfeasance, and India's CBI burrowing deeper into Chawla's links to cricket, there came pressure on the PCB to reveal all – they did so, with their usual perfect timing, the day before we were due to play the Third Test against the West Indies at St John's, Antigua. Life bans were imposed on Saleem Malik and Ata-ur-Rehman, who had 'prima facie perjured himself' in accusing me of trying to bribe him in the Christchurch ODI. Fines were imposed of R1–3 lakh on Waqar, Inzy, Akram Raza, Saeed Anwar, Mushie and … on me.

I did not read Qayyum's report at the time. It had nothing to tell me – I knew I was innocent. I finally sat down with it for this book, and it was even more shocking than I had imagined. It is schizophrenic. It deplores the tendency to explain every setback by corruption:

When they react to losses, the public should be more tolerant
in its criticism and remember that cricket is still a game of
chance and the players are indeed human still. The other

team is there to play too and the Pakistan team is not that invincible, at least not all of the time, that if they lose or fail to come from behind there must be something amiss.

But in the next breath it implicitly endorses the idea that fixing is routine, condoning and even commending the most sweeping defamations. Of Rashid Latif, for instance, Qayyum says:

> Rashid Latif has stated in his statement that the whole team in New Zealand other than Asif Mujtaba and possibly Aamir Sohail was involved in match-fixing. In other matches too, different people have made allegations against a substantial part of the team. However, this commission finds *no evidence to support this*. Most of the allegations, beyond those against three or four individuals, appear *conjecture or based on hearsay* … Nevertheless, his persistence in pursuing this matter needs to be appreciated [my italics].

What? Rashid could make repeated and uncorroborated allegations against an entire team, and it was a *good thing*? Good would have meant evidence. Good would have been proof. Good would have been trying to find a legitimate channel for exposing the alleged dishonesty, rather than self-dramatisingly leaking to journalists every five minutes. Elsewhere, in fact, Qayyum recommended that 'players be forbidden to speak to the press', and the 'PCB should actively take to defending its players, present and past, and not allow anyone to defame them'. But hadn't they just endorsed Rashid doing exactly that?

Speaking of defamation, what about the great defamer himself, Aamir Sohail? Qayyum has a bob each way on 'the allegation that Aamir Sohail induced Ata to make the statement against Wasim Akram':

> While this commission is minded to disbelieve anything
> Ata-ur-Rehman says in light of the number of times he has
> changed his statement, it must still consider whether Aamir
> Sohail could have influenced Ata into making a false first
> affidavit. Even if it appears unlikely, there is a chance that
> Aamir Sohail did. This introduces some doubt in my mind
> about Ata's first affidavit.

So it should have, especially as Sohail had the wider ambition of blaming my absence for his disastrous mishandling of the World Cup quarter-final. As Qayyum observes, Sohail wavered in his attitudes every bit as much as Ata, his willing tool:

> Aamir Sohail by his subsequent actions ironically seems to
> clear Wasim Akram. When Sohail later became the captain of
> the Pakistan team, he played Wasim under him. Even recently
> Sohail agreed to play under the man he said is likely to be
> crooked. In all of this Aamir Sohail gives some credence to
> Ata's statements that Aamir Sohail put him up to making
> the first affidavit and that it was false. Moreover, it needs
> be noted that when Aamir Sohail appeared initially before
> this Commission he was the Captain of Pakistan and had
> nothing substantial to say. This was despite his making a lot of
> allegations in the press. Even Ata-ur-Rehman talks of this in
> his taped conversation with Rashid Latif. Thereafter, once he
> had left the captaincy he came back on 19.12.98 to the court
> with several allegations. All of this damages Aamir Sohail's
> credibility and gives some credence to Ata's second statement.

I should say it does. But against Sohail, no action. On the contrary, having been left out of the team to the West Indies, he transitioned the following year to become the PCB's chief selector – bad behaviour rewarded.

As for me, I was struck by what Qayyum says in relation to the chief charge, that I offered Ata money to bowl badly in the Christchurch ODI:

> The first allegation was prima facie the strongest against
> Wasim Akram. However, having considered the entire
> evidence, on record, this commission has come to the
> conclusion that Ata-ur-Rehman in view of his retraction
> from his earlier statement and various subsequent statements
> cannot be believed with any degree of certainty. His
> statement cannot be made the basis of holding Wasim Akram
> guilty of the offence of match-fixing. Ata's first story was that
> compelling that if Ata-ur-Rehman had not retracted from his
> earlier statement and if his statement had stood the test of
> cross-examination, then perhaps this commission might have
> held Wasim Akram guilty of fixing the Christchurch one-day
> match. But in the present scenario, this is not possible.

The two assertions do not reconcile. How can a statement be 'compelling' if it 'cannot be believed'? Just because something sounds exciting does not make it less false. And just because something is couched in legal language does not make it more sensible. Like this:

> The evidence against Wasim Akram has not come up to
> the requisite level, primarily because of Ata-ur-Rehman's
> perjuring himself. This Commission is willing to give him
> the benefit of doubt. However, there has been some evidence

to cast doubt on his integrity. As such, this Commission recommends that he be removed from the captaincy of the Pakistan Cricket Team and a person of impeccable character be appointed. Moreover, he should be censured, kept under watch and his finances should be investigated.

Why? I was the victim of someone Qayyum deemed a perjurer, whose perjuries there was reason to believe had been engineered by another. My finances had already been investigated by Ehtesab. Yet somehow *I* deserved to be censured, fined, and barred from the captaincy? How did any of that make sense?

Some years later, in an interview, Qayyum professed a 'soft corner' for me, inferring he'd treated me gently out of admiration for my cricket. But in the end, the worst defamations of me came not from Rashid Latif nor Aamir Sohail nor even Ata-ur-Rehman. They were contained in Qayyum's report, which penalised me on evidence whose dubiousness it acknowledged, which debased my achievements by giving official endorsement to the stain of 'fixer'. Because nobody at the time read the report in detail – not even me. They were interested only in the penalties, and worked backwards from them to guess at guilt.

After reading Qayyum, the only regret I now really harbour is my association with Jojo. I let him get close, and I can see now that he probably used that for his own ends. Huma warned me. Ahsan warned me. I was, and remain, a stubborn man. I wanted to be loyal. It was a mistake. Perhaps it coloured the judge's impressions of me. But I was guilty only of finding it hard to let go of relations so long-lasting, at a time when it seemed almost impossible to distinguish between friend and foe, even in my own dressing room.

The sense of injustice I felt on the release of Qayyum's report immediately began to gnaw at me. What could I do? The only avenue open to me was to perform. The next day, with what felt like the eyes of the world on me, now officially censured as a player and disbarred as a captain, I started the Test match against the West Indies – an erratic team by this point, while containing some outstanding players in Walsh, Ambrose, Chanderpaul and their captain Jimmy Adams. Walsh bowled splendidly to hurry us out for 269 despite Youhana's unbeaten 103. Then I threw myself into the fightback – for Pakistan, for Moin, and for myself, angrily taking six for 61.

Finally, we set them 216 to win. I got both openers. I came back to break the stand between Adams and Wavell Hinds. I trapped Ramnaresh Sarwan, bowled Reon King, caught Franklyn Rose, and had Adams caught behind – only to have Billy Doctrove turn it down. For years teams would file reports on umpires to the ICC, with West Indians among the worst. Steve Bucknor was virtually blind by the time his career ended. Doctrove was nearly as bad. He next turned down a short-leg catch offered by Walsh that was so obvious we hardly bothered appealing.

Still, as Adams and Walsh held us at bay, we did ourselves no favours. Twice Saqlain bungled run-outs, on the second occasion with both batters at the same end. And somehow I could not get a look at Walsh, for whom one ball would have been enough. Adams took everything, including the leg bye that clinched the West Indies's one-wicket win. I'd taken eleven for 110 off 56.2 overs, hung in two and half hours to score 26 and 24, taken two catches, and still finished on the losing side. It was like my fate with Qayyum in a way: no matter how hard I tried, I was still defeated.

For the damage was done, and nothing could repair my reputation. Two days later it was announced that I would not be commentating for Channel 4. Naynesh Desai persuaded them to say it was a joint decision: 'After consultations with Channel 4, Wasim Akram has decided that it would be inappropriate to be part of the commentary team this summer and has asked to be released from his contract in order to concentrate on his playing career.' Nobody was fooled, least of all me. I was a pariah, and I would have to get used to it.

• • •

For a period under Moin, we played good cricket. As I've said, he was a fighter – also, I think, the most selfless Pakistani player I ever saw, setting an example by sacrificing everything for the team. We travelled from the West Indies to Bangladesh, where Dhaka was hosting its first Asia Cup, which we sailed through unbeaten. On we went to Sri Lanka, where I was man of the match in both Tests.

Sri Lanka was never an easy destination. It was always crucifyingly hot. Murali was always turning the ball miles. There was always a mediocre local umpire. We got ourselves into trouble in our first innings at the Sinhalese Sports Club, slumping to nine for 176 chasing 273. I put on 90 for the last wicket with Arshad Khan, who contributed nine. Then, despite being so tired I could not change my boots, I went out and took five for 45. These included my 400th Test wicket, Russell Arnold, while I also took the catch that gave Waqar his 300th, although at the time we still had little to say to each other.

Knocking off the winning runs with Younis Khan was very satisfying. So was my hundred at Galle, off eighty-nine balls with eight fours and six sixes, to speed a win by an innings and 163 runs. I was then rather bemused on returning home to be confronted by Tauqir Zia. 'You're too old,' he told me baldly. 'You should retire.' It's true I'd just turned thirty-four. But in the previous eighteen months, I'd averaged 30 with the bat and 23 with the ball in fifteen Tests. The years were clocking up, but I knew my game, and in Moin as captain I had full confidence.

Still, I was not so naive I did not realise that politics were at issue. The lobbyists were at work. In July 2000, Rashid Latif gave an interview to the *Sunday Telegraph* in which he claimed to have been offered £15,000 to ensure Pakistan were bowled out for under 300 in the 1996 Lord's Test. And who knows? Maybe he had. But had he told me, his captain, at the time? No. Had he reported it to his coach or manager? No. Had he told Qayyum? No. Amazingly, these stories only ever came out when Rashid wanted attention, and English newspapers lapped them up as eagerly as their Pakistani counterparts. Look at the 'cheating Pakis'! They always were and they always will be!

Also hard at work ingratiating himself with Tauqir was Waqar, who in September led us in a tournament in Singapore, the Godrej Singapore Challenge. As if in synch, I began struggling with my fitness, returning with a number of niggles from the ICC Knockout in Nairobi, where we lost in the semi-final. It was as though having been told so regularly I was old, I had started believing it. My body was following my mind; my morale was following my reputation. When England landed in Lahore to commence a tour of three Tests and three one-day internationals, Huma and I invited my Lancashire colleague Athers for dinner: he saw the armed guard at our door as an emblem of the strain I was under, with Huma now expecting our second child.

Another old county colleague, Andrew Flintoff, was clearly emerging as a powerful all-rounder: he made 84 off sixty balls against us as England won the first ODI at National Stadium. I had a forgettable time. For my 100th Test, I was presented with a gold plaque by Javed, who had been there for almost all of them, as player, captain and coach. What a genius; what a rogue. In the ensuing draw on a very flat Faisalabad pitch, however, I picked up a solitary wicket, Graham Thorpe lbw. I was then ruled out of what should have been my 101st Test when I suffered an injury in the nets at Karachi before the toss. On the last day I left early, so convinced was I that the match was destined for a draw; in fact, in near darkness, England won a famous helter-skelter victory. Moin, who had clashed with Tauqir in that match over the paltry matter of a few extra free tickets, was further undermined. Huma and I, meanwhile, returned to Manchester wondering about our futures, both personal and professional.

Though we were often apart, Huma had been my rock throughout this period. I was the classic cricketer, always coming and going, always preparing for or recovering from a tour if I wasn't on one. She was always future-focused. Sometimes it was as though she could see round corners. When our son Akbar was ready to be born early in the new year, she announced: 'I have been looking into this. There is always the chance that the UK will leave the European Union. It is too late for Tahmoor. But we must ensure that Akbar will always be guaranteed a European passport.' A friend of ours, an eye surgeon, recommended a maternity hospital in north-western Ireland, so we took the car ferry from Holyhead to Dublin, then flew to Sligo, where my in-laws arrived as I headed back to Pakistan.

Again, Tauqir insisted I play a first-class match in order to justify my inclusion for the forthcoming tour of New Zealand. Frankly, it felt like he was willing me to fail. In fact, in the Quaid-e-Azam Trophy final for Lahore Blues against Karachi Whites, I took nine for 103 off 44.5 overs. I learnt I had become a father for the second time at the subsequent training camp. Was I completely with it when we headed south? I could feel the pressure on my captain. Waqar's ambition, Tauqir's interventions, Javed's unpredictability and ongoing tribulations over Shoaib's action were all combining against Moin. I also learnt that I could no longer override my body, plus the general pointlessness of fitness tests – I strained my side in the one-day internationals and had to miss the three-Test series.

Before I left for home, there was a classic Pakistani fiasco when Tauqir wanted to replace Saqlain for bowling badly in the fourth one-day international. The players stood firm – temporarily anyway. After taking soundings, Moin told Tauqir that he would refuse to lead the team if the decision was not reversed. 'Very well,' Tauqir replied. 'I'm bringing everyone home.' Overnight, Tauqir realised that this might not be a proportional response, and both Saqlain and the replacement were allowed to stay. But when Moin was ruled out of the Third Test with an injury, Inzy was appointed as his locum, and Waqar as his successor for the ARY Gold Cup in Sharjah. When Waqar's team was chosen for our tour of England, in fact, the irrepressible Rashid Latif turned up as keeper in Moin's stead. Tauqir made clear his reluctance to include me by setting a preposterous succession of fitness tests – all of which I passed.

Javed, at least, was out, though firing shots as ever, claiming in his resignation that the one-day series in New Zealand had been fixed. Still, I was pleased to see the return of Pybus and, despite my forebodings, it proved an enjoyable if short tour. Now that he had what he wanted, Waqar captained well, and we squared the two-Test series. At my old home ground of Old Trafford, I ran Thorpe out to precipitate an England collapse of eight for 75, and got the unfortunate Nick Knight lbw with a delivery that not only hit him way too high but was a huge undetected no ball too. Sometimes you get lucky …

After the NatWest Series, I finally had a chance to spend some time with my budding household in Altrincham. We were now five: Huma and I, the two boys, and our indispensable live-in helper, Muhammad Abbas, who'd been with us five years as a driver, handyman, cleaner and now assistant child-carer. I would be seeing more of this, I knew. Huma was encouraging me all the time to think past cricket. It would not always be there. It might not always define me. I had responsibilities that extended beyond bowling and batting. She was right, of course: nothing surpasses the importance of family. This was reinforced for me when we played the second Asian Test Championship in August. While we were beating Bangladesh at Multan, Saeed Anwar's three-year-old daughter Bismah, who had suffered a long-term illness, died suddenly. In the Test he had made a brilliant century. But what consolation was that for such a loss? Saeed's grief turned him towards Allah – he joined Inzy, Mushie and others in becoming increasingly devout. I was an observant Muslim. I had read the Qur'an three times in Arabic. I joined in attending Friday prayers on tour. But being Muslim could be complicated – even more so after September 11, one of whose many immediate consequences for cricket was the cancellation of an anticipated New Zealand tour of Pakistan.

So I kept up playing. I was not going to give them any excuse not to pick me. I took eleven wickets at nine in two games for PIA in the PCB Patron's Trophy; I took six wickets at 10 as Pakistan won the Khaleej Times Trophy in Sharjah; I even volunteered to play in the Hong Kong Sixes, which basically consisted of batters trying to belt sixes out of tiny Kowloon Stadium – we beat South Africa in the final; I took 5–0–27–3 for the tournament. Actually I loved the heady carnival atmosphere, the partying, the wealth. These moments, however, were in their way deluding. They made it harder for me to accept that time was running out. In Australia and England, they understand retirement. For a leading player, it is an organised and deliberate process, in which you receive ample advice and support. In Pakistan, the game tends to retire you rather than the other way around. It just happens.

On 9 January 2002, Waqar threw me the new ball at Bangabandhu National Stadium in Dhaka, and I bowled two exploratory overs at the Bangladeshi openers, Mehrab Hossain and Al Sahariar. My second ball, to Sahariar, was a no ball; my sixteenth, to Hossain, went to the boundary. I pulled up in my follow-through, clutching a hamstring where I had felt a familiar burn. I knew enough of injuries by then to realise it was serious – so serious, in fact, that although I did not know it at the time, I had bowled my 22,627th and last Test delivery. No ceremony. No farewell. It just … happened.

• • •

It was hardly Pakistan's biggest problem at that moment. New Zealand arrived on their rescheduled tour, only for it to be abandoned when a bomb exploded near the visitors' hotel in Karachi. It would be eighteen months until we hosted our next Test – the day after tomorrow, of course, a longer exile lurked. So I played on, perhaps more from habit than anything else. In the One-Day National Tournament, I took fifteen wickets at 13, suggesting I still had value in white ball cricket. And in what would prove to be my last year as an international cricketer, I played no fewer than thirty-two matches, in Pakistan, the UAE, Australia, South Africa, Zimbabwe, Kenya and Morocco, taking fifty-five wickets at 20.4 and scoring 345 runs at 20.3. I still had some days when it all clicked. In a game mostly notable for being indoors in Melbourne, part of the Docklands Challenge, I dismissed Adam Gilchrist caught behind and Ricky Ponting caught and bowled with the first two deliveries of the match. The near-term objective was the chance of a fourth World Cup appearance and a second victory.

The former proved within reach; I realised almost as soon as we arrived in South Africa that the latter was never going to happen. We had a solid coaching staff, Pybus having returned after a brief tenure by Mudassar Nazar, reinforced by the excellent Australian Daryl Foster. We had a good squad and some handy reinforcements: on our coach ride into Johannesburg, Saeed, in his new devout avatar, seized the bus microphone and announced that we were bound to win the cup because 'Allah would send down his angels to ensure victory'. But Waqar was by now not in our best XI. He was captain because of Tauqir, and Tauqir was a nuisance. Shoaib, for example, took it into his head to contact Tauqir directly with a request that he be joined by his own doctor,

Tauseef Razzaq. Our manager Shaharyar Khan, who was unaware of the request before Tauqir's acquiescence, pointed out that the squad already had a doctor (Riaz Ahmed), a trainer (Dennis Waight), a psychologist (Amir Saleem) and an analyst (Sikander Bakht). But Dr Razzaq came regardless.

Frankly, Tauqir did not seem able to help himself. Immediately before our opening match, against Australia at Wanderers, we were summoned for a team meeting to be addressed by the PCB chairman. A pep talk, we assumed, as we gathered in a conference room around a speakerphone. 'Good luck for your important game tomorrow,' Tauqir began, before his tone darkened, and he started barking commands and admonitions. 'So if you don't win,' he finished, 'I have proof that you are match-fixers.' Players blanched; I saw our coaches' eyes bug.

Next morning, I picked up Gilchrist, Matthew Hayden and Damien Martyn in a seven-over opening spell, but we had repeated the mistake of 1996 in leaving out Saqlain and trying to cobble together our fifth bowler from part-timers. Andrew Symonds, probably the last Aussie picked, made 143 not out in 125 balls. I was then our top scorer, with 33 off thirty-one balls, by which stage the match was already lost. We were mauled by India, who took 143 off 18.4 overs from Waqar and Shoaib, and even by England, where Shoaib went at seven an over.

Our swiftest bowler might have provided us with the spark we needed, but Shoaib was all over the place. He is a fun guy, a real character, generous and open. But during this cup he became completely mesmerised by the speed guns, in use for the first time at an ICC event – he was like the vain man who cannot tear himself away from a mirror.

I wasn't much bothered to be clocking 135 kilometres per hour; he was hell-bent on 161.3 kilometres per hour – breaking through the 100-miles-per-hour barrier. When he touched it bowling the last ball of his second over to England's Knight, he blew kisses to the Cape Town crowd. 'Fuck off down to third man,' I told him. 'We've got a game to win.' People remember the ball; they forget that Knight hooked Shoaib for six in his next over, and that Ashley Giles later straight-drove him for six. *Ashley Giles*! So much for the miraculous Dr Razzaq.

In the end we beat only the Netherlands and Namibia, which enabled me to secure my 500th ODI wicket but not much else. After a delayed start on 4 March 2003, we were three for 73 against Zimbabwe at Bulawayo's Queens Sports Club when the rain began to fall, and fall, and fall. What goes around comes around. In 1992, we had benefited from the lack of reserve days, which saved us from a crucial defeat against England. Now we suffered because of it. The no result saw us eliminated. And me.

CHAPTER 14

BATTLING MY DEMONS

Wasim's craft with the cricket ball was akin to the mystique that the great Ben Hogan effected with his golf swing. Great golfers still talk about Hogan. Great cricketers still marvel at the wonder of Wasim. But allied to Wasim's mastery of the game is an affectionate personality that enables him to wear the cloak of greatness with extraordinary humility. He is generous in all the ways that you would expect from a close friend, showing the same fallibilities we all recognise in each other. A special person. A friend.

Alan Wilkins

I never formally retired from international cricket; rather, I had to accept that playing on was futile. Tauqir already hated my guts, but two appointments after the World Cup made my exit certain: Aamir Sohail wormed his way into the role of chief selector, and Rashid Latif was appointed captain. I was one of those excluded from the team for the Sharjah Trophy, along with Waqar, Shoaib, Saeed and Inzy. Pybus again lost his job to Javed. All were eventually received back into the fold. From the PCB, I would receive no further contact.

My international debuts had been unspectacular; my international exits even less so. I was involved in my farewell Test for five overs; in my last ODI, I did not even take the field. Part of me could not accept it ending this way. I accepted an offer to play for Hampshire from their likeable president Rod Bransgrove, hoping to make a case for further international white ball honours: my old Lancashire teammate John Crawley was captain, and it was the first summer of a new format, T20, of which I liked the look. 'I'm probably not going to play any more Test cricket,' I told the county's head of cricket Paul Terry. 'So maybe not too much bowling in the County Championship, eh?' My first day at New Road I bowled twenty-six overs, and ended up walking like a duck. I did enjoy my five-match glance at T20, taking eight wickets at 15. But with Huma and the boys in Lahore, I was rattling around a five-bedroom rental in Southampton, which unlike cosmopolitan Manchester I found small and quiet. The Rose Bowl was a twenty-minute drive away, but beyond the dressing room I made few friends.

On 13 May 2003, I gave an interview to Sky's Charles Colville, tipping my hand. I was looking to life after cricket: 'My future is somewhere else after September. Maybe I will be working in television or coaching. There are no regrets. There have been ups and downs but I would not have changed it for anything else.' In fact, although I had no complaints about my treatment at Hants, and had developed a strong regard for Bransgrove and Terry, I regretted having signed. Two months later I finished a National League match at the Rose Bowl against Notts on the losing side, found a phone box, rang Huma and said: 'I don't think I can do this any more.' Bransgrove was very understanding, but I insisted on paying the county back, as I felt I had let them down.

I returned home, where Pakistan under Rashid Latif were managing to lose a one-day series 3–2 against South Africa after having won the first two games. At the final presentation, I was felicitated by my sponsor Pepsi, which presented me with a Honda City and a trophy. I still cherish the memory of that evening – it was the nearest I ever came to an official farewell. Tauqir, who was meant to have spoken, cried off at the last moment; Sohail and Latif looked on sourly. Regime change was in the offing: within four months, all three were gone, succeeded respectively by Shaharyar Khan, Wasim Bari and Inzy. Javed departed a final time in June 2004, replaced by Bob Woolmer.

Pepsi's gifts were generous and meaningful. I was not, in fact, hugely well off. My father had bought me a farmhouse, and I owned our home in Altrincham and two plots of land, but I had only about $25,000 in liquid assets – not much for nearly two decades at the top of my sport. And though I might feel I was done with the old, I was not quite ready for the new. I was lucky it came looking. In November 2003, ESPN Star signed me as a commentator for more than I had been earning as a cricketer, and my first assignment was in Australia, where India were touring.

I had done dribs and drabs of commentary work over the years. It had not come naturally, and it didn't now. I struggled with the hours – commentators arrive earlier than players, work through breaks, and can never switch entirely off. A player can burn off a late night in the field; a commentator, in air-conditioned inertia, has no such outlet. I had been an intuitive cricketer, not given to verbalising my game, and found it hard to initiate conversation. Fortunately my colleagues – old friends Ravi Shastri and Sunny Gavaskar, professional broadcasters such as Alan Wilkins and Harsha Bhogle, and producers like Hugh Bevan and Ray Hume – looked after me like good teammates. They got me talking by asking questions, and provided regular feedback and helpful suggestions. One from Alan I have not forgotten: 'When you start, always have an end in mind.' By March 2004, when Pakistan toured India, I was feeling more comfortable about my job.

In October I started more of a passion project. I became a brand ambassador for the Swiss drug giant Roche, promoting Accu-Chek, a blood glucose measurement system for diabetics. I toured first Pakistan then later India and Australia, spreading awareness of the disease and its treatment. Although it was widespread, due to worsening obesity levels, there was – and remains – tremendous ignorance and fear of diabetes in the Subcontinent. I was, I thought, a good advertisement for the fully-lived life despite the disease: I had taken almost 250 international wickets post my diagnosis and fathered two children. My relationships with Roche and the Danish company Novo Nordisk, whose speciality is insulin pens, are two I greatly value.

It was no longer, however, a life with an on-field component into which I could plough my energies. I did not miss the endless politics, the cynicism, the deceit – all the things that had stood in cricket's way. But when Pakistan went to India in March 2005 and India to Pakistan in January 2006, it felt strange to be looking on. I was a big name, a big presence. And I had big problems.

• • •

Many will read this book with an eye to the controversies around ball tampering, match-fixing and throwing. In some ways they are easier for me to discuss because I have nothing to hide. The part of my story that's hardest to share has nothing to do with cricket, but if I'm to be honest I must go ahead: I was for a long time neither a good husband to Huma nor a good father to Tahmoor and Akbar. I was the classic Punjabi male parent: I turned up occasionally scattering gifts but left the burden of child-rearing to my wife. In fact, the boys probably saw more of Muhammad Abbas, our valued family helper, than they did of me.

I simply had no idea what to do, coupled with the fact that I had developed the traits of selfishness and laziness endemic to athletes, so used to having things done for them, so used to being the most important person in every room. I liked to indulge myself; I liked to party. Huma had never really enjoyed the cricket circus. She did not like watching. She did not fit in with other wives. She was a smart, brave, independent woman. She had toured out of love for me. Now she remained at home out of love for the boys. Having seen the impact of cricket on her husband, I suspect she subtly steered them away from the game – they never, in fact, developed any interest in cricket, which I'm not unhappy about.

That left me to my own devices more and more. I was travelling a lot, appearing on talk shows, doing commercials – notably for Unilever, Rexona's Date with Fate campaign, and for Mobilink, a 4G provider. I even judged *Ek Khiladi Ek Haseena*, a reality dance competition in India. I'd had a long acquaintance with celebrity and television: as far back as 1990, I'd been on the celebrity edition of *The Krypton Factor* in the UK, with Steve Ovett and Steve Coogan. But this was a lot more intense. The culture of fame in South Asia is all consuming, seductive and corrupting. You can go to ten parties a night, and some do. And it took its toll on me. My devices turned into vices. Worst of all, I developed a dependence on cocaine. It started innocuously enough when I was offered a line at a party in England, but my use grew steadily more serious, to the point that I felt I needed it to function. It made me volatile. It made me deceptive. Huma, I know, was often lonely in this time, in Manchester and in Lahore. She would talk of her desire to move to Karachi, to be nearer her parents and siblings. I was reluctant. Why? Partly because I liked going to Karachi on my own, pretending it was work when it was actually about partying, often for days at a time.

Much as I dislike having to admit it now, it was far harder to admit it then – for, needless to say, Huma eventually found me out, discovering a packet of cocaine in my wallet. She responded as a wife and a mother would, but also as a clinician. 'I know you're doing drugs,' she said. 'You need help.' I agreed. It was getting out of hand. I couldn't control it. One line would become two, two would become four; four would become a gram, a gram would become two. I could not sleep. I could not eat. I grew inattentive to my diabetes, which caused me headaches and mood swings. Like a lot of addicts, part of me welcomed discovery: the secrecy had been exhausting. I agreed to enter a rehabilitation program. Huma told Ahsan: 'I hope he doesn't run away. I want my Wasim back.'

I tried. Goodness knows, I tried. Movies conjure up an image of rehab as a caring, nurturing environment. This facility in Lahore was brutal: a bare building with five cells, a meeting room and a kitchen. The doctor was a complete con man who worked primarily on manipulating families rather than treating patients, on separating relatives from money rather than users from drugs – he was charging more than 2 lakh rupees a week.

I was informed initially that I would be there for a month; after two days, this mandatory minimum stay was lengthened to three months. The treatment was essentially sedation, with fistfuls of tablets to take in the morning and evening, coupled with lectures and prayer. I felt lethargic. I gained weight. For an hour a day I wandered round our little exercise yard like a zombie. From there I could see my father's office, although he had no idea where I was. Otherwise I had nothing to do but stew.

I did not see Huma, Tahmoor and Akbar for a month. When they visited I screamed at my wife: 'I've got to get out of here. I have to work. I have to call my boss. They'll fire me!'

The doctor stood there triumphantly. 'I told you he would do this!' he gloated.

I tried to keep my side of the bargain. I remained another seven weeks, until even Huma could see that the doctor was a scam artist. But I felt embittered. On the day I got out I rang Ahsan, who knew where I had been but whom Huma had asked to pretend otherwise. 'Where have you been?' I cried down the phone. 'You don't care about me.'

Once out I tried to keep calm, to get centred. Shah Rukh Khan offered me an attractive job as the bowling coach at Kolkata Knight Riders – my first senior coaching role anywhere. When Ahsan came over a couple of months later, Huma said to him: 'Wasim seems better, but I'm not sure.'

She was right: try as I might, part of me was still smouldering about the indignity of what I'd been put through. My pride was hurt, and the lure of my former lifestyle remained. I briefly contemplated divorce. I settled for heading to the 2009 Champions Trophy where, out from under Huma's daily scrutiny, I started using again.

· · ·

I'm aware this will shock some people. I'm aware it will disappoint them. Top athletes are meant to be better than this, although the public is simultaneously well aware that they're not. Hellraisers like George Best and John Daly have exerted a perverse allure. Football fans were transfixed by the fall of Diego Maradona; golf lovers are fascinated by Tiger Woods's battle back to competitiveness. I don't compare myself to them. My dalliance with drugs came after my playing days were over, and that may be the key to understanding it, whether as a substitute for the adrenaline rush of competition, which I sorely missed, or to take advantage of the opportunity, which I had never had. It is the retired sportsman's dilemma: what, after a life of utter focus, sacrifice and denial, do you suddenly do with all this freedom? A truism I certainly learnt is that only a tiny minority escape the clutches of their addiction the first time they try. I learnt it to my cost.

While I was away enjoying a taste of my former ways, Huma, Tahmoor and Akbar in Lahore developed bad throats. We still don't really know why. It followed a dental appointment, where Huma may have picked up an infection. Anyway, the boys got better, Huma did not. I left the Champions Trophy to attend the KKR bowlers' camp in Gurgaon, but while I was there her condition worsened.

Eventually, on 6 October 2009, Huma was admitted to the National Hospital in Defence, where she was diagnosed with infective endocarditis. As it was clear from our conversations that she was getting no better, I resolved to return to Lahore. When I arrived I was shocked at her decline, and equally by the doctors' inability to provide a straight answer to a straight question. Finally, it was decided to move her to the Doctors Hospital in case her heart valve needed replacing, although inevitably there were further tests and scans to be done. In one instance, I was advised, the said scanner was actually in the basement of a doctor's house a mile away. Our bill would eventually exceed US$200,000.

Nothing appeared to be happening. The medicos seemed inattentive to everything except making sure we were charged for everything. I was anxious, and so was Huma. I remember her stroking my newly grown beard at her bedside. 'If something happens to me, what will happen to my boys?' she asked.

'Babe,' I replied soothingly, 'nothing is going to happen to you. And I'm here to look after the boys.' She just smiled because she knew there was no way that I, the classic Punjabi hands-off dad, could look after anyone.

We were getting nowhere; we had to get somewhere. A friend in Singapore urged me to take her there, in particular to the Mount Elizabeth Hospital, via air ambulance. The cost was astronomical, more than US$100,000, but it seemed the only way to get rigorous attention. There was not even a doctor available to examine Huma when we left for the airport on 20 October with my brother-in-law.

Our Hope Air Ambulance had been airborne for about half an hour when Huma suddenly said: 'Where is my husband?'

I took her hand. 'I'm here my baby,' I said.

With that, Huma's eyes closed, but presently she grew restless and distressed. The emergency medical crew on the plane administered intravenous diazepam, whereupon she was seized by a cardiac arrest. The medicos rushed into action, worked on resuscitating her for half an hour, and finally restored a tiny pulse. So we flew on for Chennai, where arrangements were made to get her to Apollo Hospital. I was so stressed I was calling friends, talking through my fear that Huma would not make it. Harvey says that I rang him but he could not understand a word I was saying.

When we landed at Chennai International Airport, we had none of the relevant permissions; we had no visas.

Indian authorities waived the requirements. The Apollo waived all payment. I'll never forget their kindness.

It was to no avail. Huma had suffered a severe brain-stem injury and required assistance to breathe. She held on desperately. So did I. But on 26 October she died. She was forty-two.

• • •

Parts of Huma's death still baffle me. The posthumous diagnosis was a rare fungal infection called mucormycosis, which the doctors in Pakistan had failed to recognise, and to which Huma was susceptible because of a congenital heart defect. I was upset about this. Months of angry back-and-forth ensued between me and the Pakistani medical and dental communities. A government inquiry suggested negligence, and recommended the cancellation of twenty-two medical licences; doctors threatened countersuits. None of it brought Huma back. All that could be returned to Lahore was her body, for which Sony's Vivek Khushalani kindly lent me his plane.

The worst part of this period was the mourning, which in Pakistan has reached extravagance on a par with weddings. Islam's main death ritual is the Janazah, a largely silent prayer involving an imam, and ending with takbirs and taslim. It has become surrounded, thanks less to religion than to custom, by a forty-day period of mandatory hospitality. One must offer refreshment to every visitor who comes to condole, and in this case that ran to thousands of people, from the president and prime minister downwards. We had to erect marquees in our garden under which to lay out enormous quantities of food and drink – I'll be eternally grateful to my friends Ramzan Sheikh and Fareed Bajwa, who took on the task of catering. We also had to remain earnest through some of the more ridiculous visitors. A senior superintendent of police, for instance, arrived and promptly went to the bathroom, where he remained for fifteen minutes. 'Has he come down with diarrhoea?' Ahsan wondered. Presently the door opened, followed by a huge waft of dope. He spoke unintelligible nonsense for a few minutes then left.

It was horrifying and purifying. Huma's last selfless, unconscious act was curing me of my drug problem. That way of life was over, and I have never looked back. She was right about something else too: I had no idea how to look after my boys. A lot of the responsibility fell on Muhammad, a wonderful man with four children of his own, who never stops working except, five times daily, to pray. I owe him an enormous amount. But there is no substitute for a father in the lives of boys, and, I regret to say, I hardly knew where to begin, although one step I did take was to start again in Karachi. Huma had always wanted us to live there, to be closer to her family. In her honour I finally did so, and I've made that my home base in Pakistan ever since.

· · ·

Over the years I have had my problems with kin. I suppose everyone does, although my difficulties have largely concerned money. When someone is successful in Pakistan, they readily become a kind of family bank, or financial arranger. Huma had always been the steadying influence, in all our lives. Now she was gone, I was bereft, with Tahmoor thirteen and Akbar eight. The media had a field day linking me up with a procession of beautiful women, including, for a time, my fellow judge on *Ek Khiladi Ek Haseena*, Sushmita Sen. The truth is I was far from ready for anything serious. I was mourning; from time to time, it feels like I still am. The irony is that my second wife and I had already met. We just didn't know it.

On 22 December 2007, I was having dinner at the Beach Hotel in Brighton, in Melbourne, with some business acquaintances and my Singaporean friend Ali Zahid. Our host had asked along two female acquaintances in public relations, including 26-year-old Shaniera Thompson. 'There'll be some cricket guys there,' Shaniera was told, although she was none the wiser: she had no interest in the game. Still, like the professional woman she was, Shaniera handed me her card. Later I texted her saying that it had been nice to meet. Our paths crossed a couple of other times on my visit: seated across the table from one another at a dinner at Southbank, we laughed a lot, which is a solid start to any friendship. 'I'm kind of a big deal at home,' I hinted at one point. She paid no attention. She thought Pakistan was in India.

We maintained our text exchanges over the next couple of years, and she went to work for the business I had invested in, which unfortunately went bad. But until I returned to Australia at the end of 2009, partly to sort that out, we did not meet again. I was by now a widower, a very confused widower, unsure of how to start again, unsure some days if I even wanted to. Shaniera is a lively, motivated person with a huge heart. I enjoyed her company, her irreverence, although she had her first taste of my reputation one night after we had dinner in Southbank. We were walking towards a cab rank to get taxis home when I suddenly said: 'You'd better go the other way.' I had spotted a posse of South Asian cab drivers rushing towards me shouting: 'Wasim *bhai*! Wasim *bhai*!' She took the hint.

I was a day-to-day proposition at the time. Some days I could face; other days I really struggled with my burdens. I was about to go to the under-nineteen World Cup in New Zealand in January 2010, and I was dreading it: the further separation from my boys; the additional work, in which my interest was dwindling. On the spur of the moment, I asked Shaniera if she would like to come with me for a few days, just as a friend – I would book her a separate room, and we would just hang out. She agreed. It was an excellent decision, on my part at least. Like a lot of my countrymen, I start the day slowly, and I have a tendency to cocoon in hotel rooms. Shaniera would not let me. She got me up early every morning, got me to come running with her, to read the papers over breakfast, to seize the day. I gradually felt able to confide in her about what I was feeling – how heartbroken I was about Huma, how afraid I felt for Tahmoor and Akbar, and about my capacity to look after them. Shaniera was always, always positive, like the best possible friend. When I kissed her on our last day together, it was warm but chaste. 'When will I see you again?' I asked.

I next suggested she join me during the Indian Premier League, after my stint with Kolkata Knight Riders. She agreed to come for eight days, when we were based at the Trident in Delhi. It drew her a little into my world. She remembers a man throwing himself through our car window ('Wasim *bhai*!') in his excitement at seeing me; she remembers a night we wanted to dine in the hotel restaurant, which was officially closed, but which they opened because it was me, and laid on a string quartet; we both still joke about her asking for a glass of champagne at one stage, and the waiter opening a $1000 bottle because it was assumed I could afford it. Fame in South Asia, I had to explain, requires precautions. I asked Shaniera, who was wide-eyed about being in India for the first time, if she wanted to take in the Taj Mahal. When she expressed interest, I sent her off to Agra with a driver and a packed lunch – there was no way I could risk the crowds.

We had to be discreet too. Because a well-known cricketer in the company of a beautiful woman naturally excites media curiosity, we were careful not to be photographed together. 'Don't google me!' I would warn Shaniera. Maybe Australian newspapers are more reliable, but 99 per cent of what's published in the celebrity world of India and Pakistan is either false or distorted. Besides, I was far from ready for another relationship. I did not want to get married again, I did not want another set of in-laws, and I thought that the boys, who were at the American School in Karachi, were too young to accept another mother figure. But I also enjoyed Shaniera's company, so I next invited her to the 2010 Champions Trophy in South Africa. It had some sad associations for me: I had been here a year earlier when Huma had been ill. Shaniera was sympathetic but would not let me brood. One day she decided we should go to a safari park. Why? Well, we were in Africa, weren't we? I had to admit that while I had been to Africa many, many times, seldom had I strayed beyond hotels and cricket grounds. In the nicest possible way, Shaniera was not going to accept that.

Between times, however, I was a mess. There were days I could not get out of bed. There were days when all I could do was cry. I was forty-four – an age where you're meant to know your life's purpose and to be on a path to fulfilling it. I was famous and financially secure – conditions which are assumed to insulate you from sorrow and yearning. And with Shaniera, I really did not know what I was doing. In Pakistan, love follows marriage rather than the other way round. My relationship with Huma had been an exception; I was terribly unsure how to follow it. Still, I wanted Shaniera to meet my boys, and suggested we unite around Christmas and New Year in Singapore, where I was catching up with my friend Ali.

In hindsight, this was probably the turning point in our relationship. Shaniera loved Tahmoor and Akbar on sight, and they loved her playfulness, energy and spirit. We went to Sentosa. We went to the zoo. We went shopping. She played Nerf wars with the boys in the hotel room. She played *Survivor Pakistan* with them in a tropical downpour. One day on the Skytrain, I saw Akbar holding Shaniera's hand. It was a very intense moment. Because of the boys, and out of respect for her, I still booked Shaniera her own room. But it was around this time I started to wonder about her as a life partner. She came with me to Sri Lanka six weeks after that, where we celebrated her birthday, 20 March, with the boys.

Looking back, this must have been very awkward for Shaniera. She could work only intermittently – she had to sell her car and move back in with her parents, who were understandably confused about the status of our relationship. She regularly found herself in challenging situations, including being bitten by a rabid dog while running on a beach in Galle. But she never complained, and she fitted increasingly well into all our lives, so much so that she joined us in Altrincham for the 2011 English cricket season.

Shaniera was like Huma in some ways, not in others. For instance, she also liked going to Dunham Massey, but rather than driving she worked out that we could walk there through the woods. She enjoyed activities: taking the boys fishing in the nearby canal, putting up tents in the backyard, getting them to talk over the dinner table, walking after dinner to prise them away from their games consoles. She embraced, and was embraced by, my wonderful neighbours, the Davis family. At the end of the summer, Pam said to me: 'Don't bring anyone else. We like Shaniera and we're not doing this again. You'd be mad not to snap her up.'

It was time, I thought finally, to take a big step. When we reunited in Dubai at year's end, I sprang a surprise. We were at dinner gazing towards the Burj Khalifa when I said: 'We're going to Pakistan tomorrow.' I wanted to share my homeland with her. I knew it would be a shock. Shaniera says that she can be an anxious person, and Pakistan does not allow for anxiety. You must plunge right in. But it was time. Fortunately she embraced the country just as she embraced everything else, and for much of 2012 we were together, including for a few weeks at the IPL, where KKR, now under Gautam Gambhir, were the form side. When the season got to the sharp end, she left me to it, returning to Pakistan: she watched the final, where KKR beat Chennai Super Kings, with Huma's mother. Later in the year, Shaniera took Akbar to meet her family in Australia, where they made him hugely welcome, like he was one of their own.

Now the only obstacle to our future was, frankly, me. It had been more than three years since Huma's death. But mourning has its own timetable. You never know when it has run its course. You never know if it will relent at all. I could still be morose. I could still be self-involved. In the summer of 2012–13, I came to Australia to commentate, and Shaniera followed me to Brisbane and Adelaide. It was not much fun for her. Commentary can be exhausting. She would be waiting in the evenings, only for me to be tired and a bit irritable from the demands of the day. Then, when she did not come to Sydney, I went out, had a late night, failed to call her until 3 pm the next day, and she told me off in no uncertain terms.

Maybe it was a last hesitation. I was wondering whether the commitment was right for both of us, given the differences in our circumstances, cultures, ages, and probably expectations also. I left Australia with our relationship in some doubt. It did not help that Indian media around the same time reported a Chinese whisper, quickly scotched, that I was marrying Sushmita Sen. Anyway, when I was reunited with Tahmoor and Akbar in Pakistan, I could tell that they were crestfallen by Shaniera's absence. I knew she would be missing them. I was also missing her. That was all it took. I rang and told her: 'I don't want to do this alone. And I don't want to do this without you.'

CHAPTER 15

A NEW BEGINNING

Wasim Akram is one of the true greats of world cricket and one of the main men that young left-arm bowlers look up to. I have been extremely fortunate to have spent some time with Wasim, to hear his thoughts on left-arm swing bowling and his mindset in regards to the art of bowling. He's a true legend whose wisdom and popularity continues ever strong in cricket circles.

Mitchell Starc

So Shaniera returned to Pakistan, where I had built a new house in Defence. We have regarded it as home ever since. She threw herself at once into learning the culture and the language of my country, into understanding the issues and challenges besetting its people. I introduced her to my friends, including to Imran in Islamabad. Being the Australian partner of a prominent Pakistani has some unique demands, including of modesty: Shaniera, for example, had to go through her Twitter and Facebook time lines eliminating any photographs of her in skirts or on the beach. We were conscious that at some stage the relationship would become public; it happened a little sooner than we had hoped.

At the end of May 2013, we landed in Lahore after the IPL. Shaniera was the first to notice evidence of activity in the airport. 'Someone important must be arriving,' she said. 'Maybe a politician.' We were confronted as we exited customs by a wall of press and television cameras. Maybe fifty newspapers and news channels had reporters there, their spotlights dazzling. Had a cordon of Rangers not formed around us to part the crowd, we might not have made it through. On television, Shaniera saw women gesticulating angrily: that Wasim had chosen an Australian partner was an insult to Pakistani womanhood.

Good call: me, Shaniera and my parents on our impromptu wedding day.

Lahore a couple of days later was even crazier. Our flight details had been leaked and the crowd ran into the thousands. Talking heads on television were debating the rightfulness of our relationship, claiming that it was against Islam for us not to be married – this was not something lightly ignored. The Australian attitude was a little more relaxed.

'Yes, Waz, you can marry Shaniera, on one condition,' said her father Tony, a man I warmed to straight away.

'Of course Tony, what's that?' I asked anxiously.

'You can't support anyone but St Kilda,' he replied.

So that's how Shane Warne and I ended up with something else in common. But it felt like I should tie the knot sooner rather than later, so I broached the topic with Shaniera in as casual a way as I could.

'Hey baba,' I said on the phone from my father's house in Model Town. 'Did you bring that nice salwar kameez with you? Because, ummm, I thought we, errrr, might get married today ...'

We'd agreed we did not want a big wedding. No matter where we held it, it would be impractical for the friends and family of at least one of us to come. But, well, yes, I gave my bride only a couple of hours' notice, in which time she was rushed to a salon, Nabila's, for a Pakistani wedding makeover.

Shaniera arrived for the ceremony at my father's house caked in 7 inches of make-up. It was incredibly hot. The electricity had failed, depriving us of air conditioning. There were only ten people present, although my nieces had happily strewn rose petals on the floor, and the moulvi led us smoothly through the vows.

Shaniera was anxious; I was anxious. The first thing I said to her when we were alone in the car, of which she reminds me from time to time, was: 'Don't go psycho on me.' My excuse is that it was a huge step. We had climbed a mountain. We had a further mountain to climb. Still, at least we would be climbing it together.

• • •

The 2014 IPL proved memorable for me for several reasons. First of all, KKR won nine consecutive games to take out the tournament, with Manish Pandey making an unforgettable 94 off fifty balls in the final. But the personal developments were, for me, more momentous.

While the league was on, my father died, on 30 April after a long illness, and I flew from Abu Dhabi to Lahore to bury him. He was, still, my hero. There was nothing slick or fancy about my father. He understood his duties as a paternal provider, and he discharged them, honourably, without complaint. His approval meant a lot to me. Ahsan recalls one time when we went to pay our respects to him. I was at the top of my game. I had just won a man-of-the-series award or some such, and Ahsan thinks that maybe I was expecting my father to say something. He didn't. It was all very civil and courteous and we went on our way. Still, I don't remember feeling disappointed. That was how he approached life. He never got carried away with anything. At maintaining such an even temper, I have not been as good, but I have always had his example in mind.

Also during the league, Shaniera conceived. It was soon after learning this news that we paid our reminiscent visit to Mozang. Our child, we knew, would grow up under circumstances that were very different to ours. She would be much more fortunate materially; she would face a far more troubled world. Ten days before her birth, the Taliban stormed an army-run school in Peshawar and murdered 150 people, including 134 children, in an almost unimaginable storm of viciousness. Pakistan was plunged into mourning, and we with them. We called our newborn Aiyla, an Arabic name for moonlight, with the idea of a little light shining through the gloom.

We needed it, to be honest. There were periods where life in Pakistan was extremely challenging. I was in Lahore in 2009 when gunmen attacked the Sri Lankan team bus, which set our cricket back so far. In 2015, there was an upsurge in violence as paramilitaries sought to curb the influence of the Mohajir Qaumi Movement in Karachi, and its fugitive chieftain Altaf Hussein was sentenced to jail in absentia. Two mothers whom Shaniera knew were shot; most of our other friends were victims of gun crime; there were regular 'bomb days' which prevented the boys going to school and closed the mobile network. Everyone was on edge. In August, I was driving to a fast bowling camp at National Stadium when I cut another guy off in traffic. He stopped his car and approached brandishing a revolver, then fired a shot into the air. 'I'm Wasim Akram!' I exclaimed. 'If anything happens to me, you'll be in big trouble!' It wasn't exactly original, but it didn't look like he would be satisfied with a selfie: he studied my PCB tracksuit, lowered his gun and went back to his car. Noting his licence plate, I actually filed a case against him. It turned out he was a retired army major now in corporate security, and I was persuaded by some contacts in the military to let the matter go. That's Pakistan.

The situation in India was every bit as bad, maybe even worse. When I captained Pakistan in India in January 1999, Shiv Sena had been regarded as crackpots; a decade and a half on, their views were mainstream. When they attacked the headquarters of the BCCI during India's one-day series against South Africa in October 2015, in protest against umpire Aleem Dar officiating and Shoaib and I commentating, it became clear that we could not be protected. We were staying in the same hotel as Shaharyar Khan, who was in his second term as PCB chairman, and had come to lobby the BCCI to restart bilateral cricket. Shiv Sena achieved their aim of preventing this – we had to hurriedly leave the country.

Perhaps this had long been coming. By the end of my time at KKR, Pakistanis could arrive and exit India only via Delhi and Mumbai. I missed Tahmoor's graduation because I could not fly from Kolkata to Dubai. There were two kinds of visa, of which I had slightly the better kind, which did not require me to report to the police daily; otherwise you arrived on a par with a criminal on bail. I would have liked to continue at KKR. I respected Gautam Gambhir, a good captain. Over the years I had worked with a host of Indian pacers, ranging from Ishant Sharma and Mohammad Shami to Umesh Yadav and Jaydev Unadkat. We had access to international stars like Sunil Narine, Brett Lee, Jacques Kallis and the young Pat Cummins. Shah Rukh Khan, a humble man with a big heart and an open hand, was a great owner, Venky Mysore an astute CEO. But just as the government had excommunicated Pakistani players, so it had made life impossible for Pakistani coaches. The friendships of my playing days, incidentally, have all survived. In November 2015 I played with Sachin, Sourav Ganguly, Viru Sehwag and VVS Laxman in the Cricket All-Star Series in the US, which Warnie helped organise; in June 2016, my great pal Ravi Shastri, now India's coach, was a guest at my fiftieth birthday in Phuket, Thailand. But while I love their country, in which I have at least as many friends as in Pakistan, it feels like I may never visit it again. The daily hatred on social media saddens and baffles me. It's horrendous that it has come to this when the two nations have so much in common, not least cricket.

• • •

I tried to look on the positive side of this forced change. I had really enjoyed the camaraderie of broadcasting. But by the time my relationship with ESPN Star ended, following the News Corporation takeover in 2013, commentary had become a bit of a chore, and when you're bored the public can tell. I spread my wings in August 2016 and hosted Geo's

The Sportsman Show, an interview program whose guests ranged from Waqar and Moin to the squash immortal Jahangir Khan and the tennis pro Aisam-ul-Haq Qureshi. I followed this with *Geo Khelo,* a game show co-hosted with Shoaib, broadcast over two and a half hours every night during Ramadan.

I started leveraging my name more. On turning fifty, I launched the first in a range of colognes in partnership with the lifestyle brand Junaid Jamshed. It is called 414, for the number of Test wickets I took, and comes in a gift box shaped like a red six-stitcher; it has since been complemented by 502, named for my number of one-day wickets, and sold in a white gift box. MS Dhoni had, in many respects, led the field in this market. My 'Scent of Sultan' has since inspired Afridi to produce his own range, in bottles shaped like a cricket bat.

Simultaneously, I started moving more heavily into advertisements – more lucrative than commentary, and more fun. I renewed my acquaintance with Pepsi, shooting an advertisement for Lay's with Lionel Messi. I joined up with Ufone – our commercial spoofing *The Shawshank Redemption,* filmed in Bangkok, was one of the funniest I have ever done. I became the face of Procter & Gamble's Ariel laundry detergent. In March 2019, the government of my old friend Imran Khan awarded me the Hilal-e-Imtiaz, the nation's second-highest civilian honour – a humbling distinction. But last year I was at Lahore airport when a little boy saw me, came up and sang me the Ariel jingle. Perhaps that is true fame.

There was a new game in town, too. With the arrival of the Pakistan Super League, I became involved with Islamabad United, and helped my old friend Dean Jones coach them to the inaugural title. In August 2017, I became cricket operations manager at a new franchise, the Multan Sultans, coached by another former opponent, Tom Moody. The margins in T20 are fine, and the results are volatile. Subsequently, I became president of the Karachi Kings, who won in 2021 and then finished last in 2022. At the time of writing, I'm not sure if I will be back. I may have contributed what I can.

Besides, there are other things to do, and nobody lives forever. The last two years have seen the deaths of five great Australian cricketers: Alan Davidson, Rod Marsh, Dean Jones, Shane Warne and Andrew Symonds. I met the first; I saw the second; I tried like hell to get the last three out, and enjoyed their friendships afterwards. Only Davo, a delightful man with whom I had an animated conversation about left-arm pace bowling during the Bellerive Test in 1999, lived to a ripe old age; Symonds was ten years my junior. The passings were jolting for those of us who were contemporaries. How could we lose Warnie? I could not sleep the night after, remembering the fun we had had just recently in the US. But there's no escaping it: my generation are closer to the end than the beginning.

• • •

It's a truism that the game of cricket has changed completely since I started playing, although perhaps it might be more interesting to reflect on those things that have not changed. The simple fact of the matter is that the most reliable means of developing robust and versatile cricketers is four-day cricket. That's it. End of story. If you can play four-day cricket, you can do anything, from T20 to Test cricket.

A player who comes via the T20 path alone will, I think, find it far harder to broaden their game. David Warner is still the exception that proves the rule. So it is self-defeating that administrators, whether in Pakistan or England, Australia or South Africa, now so neglect four-day cricket. If you're used to batting for ten minutes, you'll never be able to bat for an hour; if you're used to bowling four overs, you'll never get through twenty. It only works the other way round.

T20 has had other impacts too. It fascinates me that a skill in my time so rare, left-arm pace bowling, has become so widespread. The only such bowler I can remember from growing up was India's Karsan Ghavri – not a bad player, I thought, given that he could toss up some slow ones also. When I was first round the Pakistan squad, there was only Azeem Hafeez and Saleem Jaffar. Nowadays everyone has a left-arm quick. I've enjoyed working with the likes of Mitchell Starc and Shaheen Shah Afridi; Mohammed Amir might have been the best of all but for falling among thieves in 2010. This century there's been Chaminda Vaas, Zaheer Khan, Ashish Nehra, Mitchell Johnson; now you have Trent Boult, Mustafizur Rahman, Sam Curran, David Willey, Sheldon Cottrell, Thangarasu Natarajan, Tymal Mills, Khaleel Ahmed and many others.

With the passing of time, of course, comes some perspective. Even out of some of the really desperate situations I faced in my career, the heat has now gone. Am I happy about my years in cricket? Not about everything, but I am satisfied – that I did my best, tried my hardest, loved the game, and played to win while staying on the right side of a sportsmanlike line. About the setbacks and scandals, I no longer harbour any particular bitterness. Pakistanis are notorious for pulling themselves apart; I'm not sure they get enough credit for putting themselves back together. Some readers will probably reach the end of this book wondering how a team so often angry among themselves was so successful. The answer is that my countrymen fall in as readily as they fall out. A number of the players who sat away from me in that courtroom in 1998 and would not even exchange glances with me have reached out since then seeking favours, looking for jobs – and, frankly, I have helped them where it's been possible. I could catch up with Waqar, Moin, Ejaz, Inzy, Shoaib, Saeed, Yousuf and others tomorrow and it would be like old times. Pakistan during my career had many fine players and many great days. I'd do it all again.

Sometimes in our expectations of cricketers, I think, we forget of whom our national teams are composed: ambitious and driven young men, fiercely competitive, sometimes immature, often unworldly, doing their damnedest to get the better of others very much like them, burdened by expectation, acclaimed in success, reviled in failure. Pakistani cricketers are often poorly educated – I should know, as I was. Pakistani cricketers can find it difficult to distinguish friend from enemy – I should know, as I at times failed to do so. It is an environment that breeds temperamental, insecure, inconsistent teams. There remains no players' association in Pakistan. Competent player managers are few. Opportunities to play abroad are restricted. The PCB is still beholden to the government and still operates a monopoly. Players still get a day to sign their contracts, and are discouraged from getting outside advice. All these things existed in my time, for sure; it is appalling that the same conditions still apply. But authoritarianism and micromanagement run deep in my country. During the recent series with Australia, Ramiz Raja as chairman of the board was dictating the commentary rosters. It's a wonder he wasn't giving Babar Azam the batting order too.

What I'm happiest about, however, is my future, as it is reflected in the children that Shaniera has done so much to help me raise. I have two beautiful boys, with great values, who work hard and take care. Tahmoor graduated from Allegheny College, a liberal arts college in Pennsylvania, and is now pursuing his masters at Wayne in Michigan. Akbar is looking to restart college after the dire disruption of COVID. An education is the greatest gift you can give any child. I always told my boys that I would support them in whatever they did, but that they needed first to study, and they have made me very proud. Plus we now have Aiyla's future to look forward to. Shaniera and I were right in that the world she's growing up in has proved very different to the one we were raised in, and like every family we've been buffeted by the challenges of these last few years. But now our world is expanding again, as is Aiyla's understanding of it. Recently she came to me and said insistently: 'Daddy, show me your TikTok.'

'Aiyla!' I protested. 'You're seven!'

She asked nicely about my social media accounts, so I showed her some tweets. 'Six million followers!' she exclaimed. Then she looked at me curiously. I could hear the cogs in her mind turning. Who was this man, her dad? What was his story? Where did he come from? What did he do that justified so many likes? This is for her then, and for you.

STATISTICS
WASIM AKRAM

Compiled by Ric Finlay

TEST MATCHES (104)

Batting

Inns	NO	Runs	Ave	HS	100s	50s	Ct
147	19	2898	22.64	257*	3	7	44

Bowling

Balls	Mdns	Runs	Wkts	Ave	best	5wl	10wM
22,627	871	9779	414	23.62	7-119	25	5

FIRST-CLASS (257)

Batting

Inns	NO	Runs	Ave	HS	100s	50s	Ct
355	40	7161	22.73	257*	7	24	97

Bowling

Balls	Mdns	Runs	Wkts	Ave	best	5wl	10wM
50,278	1965	22,549	1042	21.64	8-30	70	16

ONE-DAY INTERNATIONAL (356)

Batting

Inns	NO	Runs	Ave	HS	100s	50s	ct
280	55	3717	16.52	86	-	6	88

Bowling

Balls	Mdns	Runs	Wkts	Ave	best	5wl
18,186	236	11,812	502	23.53	5.15	6

LIST A (594)

Batting

Inns	NO	Runs	Ave	HS	100s	50s	ct
467	97	6993	18.90	89*	-	17	147

Bowling

Balls	Mdns	Runs	Wkts	Ave	best	5wl
29,719	387	19,303	881	21.91	5-10	12

T20 (5)

Batting

Inns	NO	Runs	Ave	HS	100s	50s	ct
5	1	55	13.75	24	-	-	-

Bowling

Balls	Mdns	Runs	Wkts	Ave	best	5wl
114	1	121	8	15.12	2-19	-

*Not out

Wasim Akram in Test Matches

BATTING

By Series

Series	v.	in	M	Inn	NO	Runs	Ave	HS	100s	50s	0s	ct	st
1984-85	NZ	NZ	2	4	3	9	9.00	8*	0	0	1	0	0
1985-86	SL	Pak	3	2	1	9	9.00	5*	0	0	0	1	0
1985-86	SL	SL	3	4	0	30	7.50	19	0	0	2	0	0
1986-87	WI	Pak	2	4	0	67	16.75	66	0	1	2	0	0
1986-87	Ind	Ind	5	6	1	89	17.80	62	0	1	1	2	0
1987	Eng	Eng	5	4	0	80	20.00	43	0	0	0	4	0
1987-88	Eng	Pak	2	2	0	77	38.50	40	0	0	0	0	0
1987-88	WI	WI	3	5	1	49	12.25	38	0	0	1	1	0
1989-90	Ind	Pak	4	3	0	58	19.33	30	0	0	1	1	0
1989-90	Aus	Aus	3	5	0	197	39.40	123	1	1	0	2	0
1990-91	NZ	Pak	2	2	0	29	14.50	28	0	0	0	1	0
1990-91	WI	Pak	3	5	1	72	18.00	38	0	0	1	0	0
1991-92	SL	Pak	3	3	1	87	43.50	54	0	1	0	0	0
1992	Eng	Eng	4	7	1	118	19.67	45*	0	0	1	0	0
1992-93	NZ	NZ	1	2	0	42	21.00	27	0	0	0	0	0
1992-93	WI	WI	3	5	0	44	8.80	29	0	0	1	4	0

Series	v.	in	M	Inn	NO	Runs	Ave	HS	100s	50s	0s	ct	st
1993-94	Zim	Pak	2	3	1	42	21.00	16*	0	0	0	1	0
1993-94	NZ	NZ	3	3	0	57	19.00	35	0	0	0	0	0
1994-95	SL	SL	2	2	0	49	24.50	37	0	0	0	2	0
1994-95	Aus	Pak	2	4	1	93	31.00	45*	0	0	0	1	0
1994-95	RSA	RSA	1	2	0	52	26.00	41	0	0	0	0	0
1994-95	Zim	Zim	3	5	0	51	10.20	27	0	0	1	1	0
1995-96	SL	Pak	2	3	0	64	21.33	36	0	0	0	2	0
1995-96	Aus	Aus	3	6	0	68	11.33	33	0	0	0	2	0
1995-96	NZ	NZ	1	2	0	21	10.50	19	0	0	0	0	0
1996	Eng	Eng	3	5	1	98	24.50	40	0	0	0	1	0
1996-97	Zim	Pak	2	2	1	292	292.00	257*	1	0	0	2	0
1997-98	RSA	Pak	2	2	0	11	5.50	9	0	0	0	0	0
1997-98	WI	Pak	3	3	0	16	5.33	11	0	0	1	2	0
1997-98	RSA	RSA	1	2	1	35	35.00	30*	0	0	0	0	0
1997-98	Zim	Zim	1	2	1	12	12.00	12*	0	0	1	0	0
1998-99	Aus	Pak	2	3	0	50	16.67	35	0	0	1	1	0
1998-99	Zim	Pak	2	3	0	43	14.33	31	0	0	0	1	0
1998-99	Ind	Ind	3	6	0	130	21.67	38	0	0	0	3	0
1998-99	SL	Pak	1	2	0	21	10.50	17	0	0	0	0	0
1998-99	SL	Ban	1	1	0	8	8.00	8	0	0	0	1	0
1999-00	Aus	Aus	3	6	1	154	30.80	52	0	1	0	1	0
1999-00	SL	Pak	1	2	0	79	39.50	79	0	1	1	0	0
1999-00	WI	WI	3	5	0	108	21.60	42	0	0	1	3	0
1999-00	SL	SL	3	3	1	198	99.00	100	1	1	0	3	0
2000-01	Eng	Pak	2	3	1	6	3.00	4*	0	0	0	1	0
2001	Eng	Eng	2	4	1	83	27.67	36	0	0	0	0	0
2001-02	Ban	Pak	1	0	0	0	–	dnb	0	0	0	0	0
Total			**104**	**147**	**19**	**2898**	**22.64**	**257***	**3**	**7**	**17**	**44**	**0**

* Not out

By Opposition

Against	M	Inn	NO	Runs	Ave	HS	100s	50s	0s	ct	st
Australia	13	24	2	562	25.55	123	1	2	1	7	0
Bangladesh	2	0	0	0	–	dnb	0	0	0	0	0
England	18	25	4	462	22.00	45*	0	0	1	6	0
India	12	15	1	277	19.79	62	0	1	2	6	0
New Zealand	9	13	3	158	15.80	35	0	0	1	1	0
South Africa	4	6	1	98	19.60	41	0	0	0	0	0
Sri Lanka	19	22	3	545	28.68	100	1	3	3	9	0
West Indies	17	27	2	356	14.24	66	0	1	7	10	0
Zimbabwe	10	15	3	440	36.67	257*	1	0	2	5	0
Total	**104**	**147**	**19**	**2898**	**22.64**	**257***	**3**	**7**	**17**	**44**	**0**

Test Match Centuries

Score	for	v.	Season	Venue	Bat Position	BF
257*	Pak	Zim	1996-97	Sheikhupura	8	370
123	Pak	Aus	1989-90	Adelaide	7	195
100	Pak	SL	1999-00	Galle	8	89

BOWLING

By Series

Series	v.	in	M	balls	mdns	runs	wkts	Ave	best	5wI	10wM
1984-85	NZ	NZ	2	562	21	233	12	19.42	5-56	2	1
1985-86	SL	Pak	3	623	31	251	8	31.38	2-17	0	0
1985-86	SL	SL	3	585	35	204	8	25.50	4-55	0	0
1986-87	WI	Pak	2	222	5	112	6	18.67	6-91	1	0
1986-87	Ind	Ind	5	956	31	413	13	31.77	5-96	1	0
1987	Eng	Eng	5	1084	38	464	16	29.00	4-111	0	0
1987-88	Eng	Pak	2	241	7	102	2	51.00	2-64	0	0
1987-88	WI	WI	3	702	22	319	11	29.00	4-73	0	0
1989-90	Ind	Pak	4	1228	50	551	18	30.61	5-101	1	0
1989-90	Aus	Aus	3	814	37	318	17	18.71	6-62	3	1
1990-91	NZ	Pak	2	473	24	162	10	16.20	4-44	0	0
1990-91	WI	Pak	3	636	12	298	21	14.19	5-28	1	0
1991-92	SL	Pak	3	510	21	211	6	35.17	3-71	0	0
1992	Eng	Eng	4	1013	36	462	21	22.00	6-67	2	0
1992-93	NZ	NZ	1	318	13	111	8	13.88	5-45	1	0
1992-93	WI	WI	3	649	17	358	9	39.78	4-75	0	0
1993-94	Zim	Pak	2	458	14	203	11	18.45	5-65	1	0
1993-94	NZ	NZ	3	958	41	431	25	17.24	7-119	2	1
1994-95	SL	SL	2	452	24	175	13	13.46	5-43	1	0
1994-95	Aus	Pak	2	425	10	200	9	22.22	5-63	1	0
1994-95	RSA	RSA	1	354	15	166	4	41.50	2-53	0	0
1994-95	Zim	Zim	3	794	31	313	13	24.08	5-43	1	0
1995-96	SL	Pak	2	258	12	110	9	12.22	5-55	1	0
1995-96	Aus	Aus	3	736	32	273	14	19.50	4-50	0	0
1995-96	NZ	NZ	1	215	7	84	5	16.80	5-53	1	0
1996	Eng	Eng	3	768	29	350	11	31.82	3-67	0	0
1996-97	Zim	Pak	2	430	21	180	11	16.36	6-48	1	1
1997-98	RSA	Pak	2	240	9	114	6	19.00	4-42	0	0
1997-98	WI	Pak	3	643	30	294	17	17.29	4-42	0	0
1997-98	RSA	RSA	1	252	11	107	3	35.67	3-70	0	0
1997-98	Zim	Zim	1	323	14	137	4	34.25	3-70	0	0
1998-99	Aus	Pak	2	474	10	222	5	44.40	3-111	0	0
1998-99	Zim	Pak	2	396	17	163	8	20.38	5-52	1	0

Series	v.	in	M	balls	mdns	runs	wkts	Ave	best	5wl	10wM
1998–99	Ind	Ind	3	744	23	335	14	23.93	3-43	0	0
1998–99	SL	Pak	1	134	4	69	5	13.80	4-30	0	0
1998–99	SL	Ban	1	126	2	78	5	15.60	3-33	0	0
1999–00	Aus	Aus	3	541	13	275	5	55.00	2-87	0	0
1999–00	SL	Pak	1	13	0	8	0	-	0-8	0	0
1999–00	WI	WI	3	698	35	264	15	17.60	6-61	2	1
1999–00	SL	SL	3	573	23	234	9	26.00	5-45	1	0
2000–01	Eng	Pak	2	354	20	123	2	61.50	1-1	0	0
2001	Eng	Eng	2	522	20	247	5	49.40	2-59	0	0
2001–02	Ban	Pak	1	114	3	49	0	-	0-17	0	0
2001–02	Ban	Ban	1	16	1	5	0	-	0-5	0	0
Total			**104**	**22,627**	**871**	**9778**	**414**	**23.62**	**7-119**	**25**	**5**

By Opposition

Against	M	balls	mdns	runs	wkts	Ave	best	5wl	10wM
Australia	13	2990	102	1288	50	25.76	6-62	4	1
Bangladesh	2	130	4	54	0	-	0-5	0	0
England	18	3982	150	1748	57	30.67	6-67	2	0
India	12	2928	104	1299	45	28.87	5-96	2	0
New Zealand	9	2526	106	1021	60	17.02	7-119	6	2
South Africa	4	846	35	387	13	29.77	4-42	0	0
Sri Lanka	19	3274	152	1340	63	21.27	5-43	3	0
West Indies	17	3550	121	1645	79	20.82	6-61	4	1
Zimbabwe	10	2401	97	996	47	21.19	6-48	4	1
Total	**104**	**22,627**	**871**	**9778**	**414**	**23.62**	**7-119**	**25**	**5**

By Calendar Year

Year	M	balls	mdns	runs	wkts	Ave	best	5wl	10wM
1985	5	1185	52	484	20	24.20	5-56	2	1
1986	5	807	40	316	14	22.57	6-91	1	0
1987	12	2281	76	979	31	31.58	5-96	1	0
1988	3	702	22	319	11	29.00	4-73	0	0
1989	4	1228	50	551	18	30.61	5-101	1	0
1990	8	1923	73	778	48	16.21	6-62	4	1
1991	2	270	11	78	1	78.00	1-31	0	0
1992	5	1253	46	595	26	22.88	6-67	2	0
1993	6	1425	44	672	28	24.00	5-45	2	0
1994	7	1835	75	806	47	17.15	7-119	4	1
1995	10	2357	97	946	45	21.02	5-43	3	0
1996	5	1198	50	530	22	24.09	6-48	1	1
1997	5	883	39	408	23	17.74	4-42	0	0
1998	6	1445	52	629	20	31.45	5-52	1	0
1999	8	1545	42	757	29	26.10	4-30	0	0

Year	M	balls	mdns	runs	wkts	Ave	best	5wl	10wM
2000	9	1638	78	629	26	24.19	6-61	3	1
2001	3	636	23	296	5	59.20	2-59	0	0
2002	1	16	1	5	0	-	0-5	0	0
Total	104	22,627	871	9778	414	23.62	7-119	25	5

Mode of Dismissal

Against	M	balls	wkts	bowled	ct	ct wkt	ct field	c&b	hit wkt	LBW	stpd
Australia	13	2990	50	13	25	9	15	1	0	12	0
Bangladesh	2	130	0	0	0	0	0	0	0	0	0
England	18	3982	57	18	28	10	17	1	0	11	0
India	12	2928	45	13	14	7	7	0	0	18	0
New Zealand	9	2526	60	13	31	13	18	0	0	16	0
South Africa	4	846	13	3	9	4	5	0	0	1	0
Sri Lanka	19	3274	63	14	36	12	23	1	0	13	0
West Indies	17	3550	79	16	30	9	19	2	0	33	0
Zimbabwe	10	2401	47	11	20	5	15	0	0	16	0
Total	104	22,627	414	101	193	69	119	5	0	120	0

PAKISTAN TEST CAREER BOWLING

Player	M	balls	mdns	runs	wkts	Ave	best	5wl	10wM
Wasim Akram	104	22,627	871	9778	414	23.62	7-119	25	5
Waqar Younis	87	16,224	517	8788	373	23.56	7-76	22	5
Imran Khan	88	19,458	727	8258	362	22.81	8-58	23	6
Danish Kaneria	61	17,697	516	9082	261	34.80	7-77	15	2
Abdul Qadir	67	17,126	608	7742	236	32.81	9-56	15	5

PAKISTAN TEST CAPTAINS

Player	M	W	L	D	%W/P	%L/P	%DT/P	W:L	toss	%toss	span (d)
Misbah-ul-Haq	56	26	19	11	46.43	33.93	19.64	1.37 :1	29	51.79	2376
Imran Khan	48	14	8	26	29.17	16.67	54.17	1.75 :1	25	52.08	3450
Javed Miandad	34	14	6	14	41.18	17.65	41.18	2.33 :1	12	35.29	4697
Inzamam-ul-Haq	31	11	11	9	35.48	35.48	29.03	1.00 :1	16	51.61	2134
Wasim Akram	25	12	8	5	48.00	32.00	20.00	1.50 :1	8	32.00	2418

COMPARATIVE STATISTICS IN TEST MATCHES

Batting summary	Inn	NO	Runs	Ave	HS	100s	50s
In matches at home	51	7	1116	25.36	257*	1	3
In matches away	96	12	1782	21.21	123	2	4
In the 1st innings	94	11	1888	22.75	257*	2	3
In the 2nd innings	53	8	1010	22.44	123	1	4
For a winning team	54	6	1137	23.69	100	1	3
For a losing team	54	6	786	16.38	79	0	2
Drawn or no result	39	7	975	30.47	257*	2	2

* Not out

Bowling summary	Balls	Md	RC	W	Ave	best	10M	5I
In matches at home	7872	300	3422	154	22.22	6/48	1	8
In matches away	14,755	571	6356	260	24.45	7/119	4	17
In the 1st Innings	14,460	558	6221	242	25.71	6/48	0	13
In the 2nd Innings	8167	312	3557	172	20.68	7/119	0	12
For a winning team	8944	355	3901	211	18.49	7/119	2	13
For a losing team	6209	235	2692	109	24.70	6/61	3	7
Drawn or no result	7474	281	3185	94	33.88	5/28	0	5

BEST BOWLING IN AN INNINGS IN TESTS

w	RC	for	v.	Season	Venue
7	119	Pak	NZ	1993-94	Wellington
6	43	Pak	NZ	1993-94	Auckland
6	48	Pak	Zim	1996-97	Faisalabad
6	61	Pak	WI	1999-00	St. John's
6	62	Pak	Aus	1989-90	Melbourne
6	67	Pak	Eng	1992	The Oval
6	91	Pak	WI	1986-87	Faisalabad
5	28	Pak	WI	1990-91	Lahore
5	43	Pak	SL	1994-95	Colombo (PSS)
5	43	Pak	Zim	1994-95	Bulawayo
5	45	Pak	SL	2000	Colombo (SSC)
5	45	Pak	NZ	1992-93	Hamilton
5	49	Pak	WI	1999-00	St. John's
5	52	Pak	Zim	1998-99	Peshawar
5	53	Pak	NZ	1995-96	Christchurch
5	55	Pak	SL	1995-96	Peshawar
5	56	Pak	NZ	1984-85	Dunedin
5	63	Pak	Aus	1994-95	Karachi
5	65	Pak	Zim	1993-94	Rawalpindi
5	72	Pak	NZ	1984-85	Dunedin
5	96	Pak	Ind	1986-87	Kolkata
5	98	Pak	Aus	1989-90	Melbourne
5	100	Pak	Aus	1989-90	Adelaide
5	101	Pak	Ind	1989-90	Sialkot
5	128	Pak	Eng	1992	Old Trafford

BEST BOWLING IN A MATCH IN TESTS

w	RC	v.	Season	Venue
11	110	WI	1999-00	St. John's
11	160	Aus	1989-90	Melbourne
11	179	NZ	1993-94	Wellington

w	RC	v.	Season	Venue
10	106	Zim	1996–97	Faisalabad
10	128	NZ	1984–85	Dunedin
9	89	WI	1990–91	Lahore
9	93	NZ	1993–94	Auckland
9	103	Eng	1992	The Oval

RESULTS WITH AND WITHOUT WASIM AKRAM IN TESTS

	M	W	L	D	%W/P	%L/P	%DT/P
Pak without Wasim Akram	27	7	5	15	25.93	18.52	55.56
with Wasim Akram	104	41	27	36	39.42	25.96	34.62

Wasim Akram – First-Class Record – Season by Season

Batting

Season	M	Inn	NO	runs	HS	Ave	100	50s	ct
1984-85	6	8	5	36	12*	12.00	0	0	3
1985-86	11	10	1	56	19*	6.22	0	0	5
1986-87	8	11	2	157	66	17.44	0	2	3
1987	14	11	2	245	59*	27.22	0	1	7
1987-88	6	9	2	198	56	28.29	0	1	1
1988	10	18	2	496	116*	31.00	1	3	2
1988-89	1	2	0	25	19	12.50	0	0	1
1989	13	20	3	350	49	20.59	0	0	3
1989-90	7	8	0	255	123	31.88	1	1	3
1990	8	11	0	135	32	12.27	0	0	0
1990-91	5	7	1	101	38	16.83	0	0	1
1991	14	19	2	471	122	27.71	1	1	5
1991-92	5	6	1	157	54	31.40	0	1	0
1992	14	18	3	299	45*	19.93	0	0	5
1992-93	8	12	0	127	29	10.58	0	0	7
1993	13	21	0	516	117	24.57	1	1	3
1993-94	6	7	1	114	35	19.00	0	0	1
1994	9	13	0	322	98	24.77	0	2	2
1994-95	7	11	1	196	45*	19.60	0	0	3
1995	14	22	3	423	61	22.26	0	4	1
1995-96	7	12	0	153	36	12.75	0	0	2
1996	7	9	1	211	68	26.38	0	1	4
1996-97	3	4	1	321	257*	107.00	1	0	2
1997	1	2	0	16	13	8.00	0	0	1
1997-98	9	10	2	133	59	16.63	0	1	3
1998	13	18	1	531	155	31.24	1	2	8

Season	M	Inn	NO	runs	HS	Ave	100	50s	ct
1998-99	10	17	0	298	40	17.53	0	0	7
1999-00	8	15	2	368	79	28.31	0	2	4
2000	3	3	1	198	100	99.00	1	1	3
2000-01	3	5	1	35	23	8.75	0	0	2
2001	5	6	1	93	36	18.60	0	0	2
2001-02	4	3	0	70	40	23.33	0	0	1
2003	5	7	1	55	23	9.17	0	0	0
Total	**257**	**355**	**40**	**7161**	**257***	**22.73**	**7**	**24**	**95**

* Not out

Bowling

Season	M	balls	mdns	runs	W	BB	Ave	5i	10m	SR
1984-85	6	1274	51	545	26	7-50	20.96	3	1	49.00
1985-86	11	1917	96	786	24	4-55	32.75	0	0	79.88
1986-87	8	1328	40	599	20	6-91	29.95	2	0	66.40
1987	14	2364	82	1095	39	6-34	28.08	2	0	60.62
1987-88	6	1003	30	452	14	4-73	32.29	0	0	71.64
1988	10	1750	76	666	31	7-53	21.48	2	0	56.45
1988-89	1	202	8	73	5	4-40	14.60	0	0	40.40
1989	13	2797	103	1117	63	7-42	17.73	7	2	44.40
1989-90	7	2042	87	869	35	6-62	24.83	4	1	58.34
1990	8	1224	44	640	16	3-76	40.00	0	0	76.50
1990-91	5	1109	36	460	31	5-28	14.84	1	0	35.77
1991	14	2577	99	1251	56	6-66	22.34	7	1	46.02
1991-92	5	773	36	284	13	5-47	21.85	1	0	59.46
1992	14	2999	127	1330	82	6-32	16.22	7	2	36.57
1992-93	8	1710	53	833	35	6-53	23.80	2	1	48.86
1993	13	2456	93	1137	59	8-68	19.27	5	1	41.63
1993-94	6	1638	69	689	40	7-119	17.23	3	1	40.95
1994	9	1894	74	905	46	8-30	19.67	4	1	41.17
1994-95	7	1789	71	746	31	5-43	24.06	2	0	57.71
1995	14	3109	108	1598	81	7-52	19.73	7	3	38.38
1995-96	7	1437	58	569	34	5-53	16.74	2	0	42.26
1996	7	1631	67	787	32	5-58	24.59	1	0	50.97
1996-97	3	490	25	214	13	6-48	16.46	1	1	37.69
1997	1	216	10	86	3	3-74	28.67	0	0	72.00
1997-98	9	1644	77	708	35	4-42	20.23	0	0	46.97
1998	13	2015	75	1025	48	5-56	21.35	1	0	41.98
1998-99	10	1979	59	939	43	5-52	21.84	2	0	46.02
1999-00	8	1410	49	638	21	6-61	30.38	2	1	67.14
2000	3	573	23	234	9	5-45	26.00	1	0	63.67
2000-01	3	623	34	226	11	6-36	20.55	1	0	56.64
2001	5	918	44	385	15	4-18	25.67	0	0	61.20

Season	M	balls	mdns	runs	W	BB	Ave	5i	10m	SR
2001-02	4	382	16	160	11	4-39	14.55	0	0	34.73
2003	5	1005	44	503	20	3-31	25.15	0	0	50.25
Total	257	50,278	1964	22,549	1042	8-30	21.64	70	16	48.25

Wasim Akram in ODIs

BATTING

By Calendar Year

Year	M	Inn	NO	runs	HS	Ave	ScRt	100s	50s	0s	ct
1984	1	0	0	0	dnb	-	-	0	0	0	0
1985	14	5	2	11	9	3.67	61.11	0	0	1	2
1986	17	9	1	68	24	8.50	93.15	0	0	0	3
1987	24	18	3	200	48*	13.33	111.73	0	0	2	3
1988	12	11	2	70	18	7.78	73.68	0	0	1	5
1989	18	16	3	145	37	11.15	104.32	0	0	3	4
1990	13	11	3	282	86	35.25	105.62	0	1	0	2
1991	8	8	0	66	19	8.25	86.84	0	0	2	2
1992	27	24	6	274	36	15.22	83.28	0	0	1	6
1993	26	22	5	287	39*	16.88	97.95	0	0	4	3
1994	21	13	1	150	33	12.50	63.83	0	0	3	3
1995	12	11	2	193	50	21.44	84.28	0	1	1	5
1996	26	21	4	338	66*	19.88	107.99	0	2	2	12
1997	19	17	2	146	33	9.73	64.32	0	0	1	9
1998	16	14	2	278	57	23.17	97.89	0	1	0	3
1999	27	21	3	360	79	20.00	100.56	0	1	1	16
2000	30	23	4	388	42*	20.42	67.01	0	0	2	5
2001	12	10	3	103	28*	14.71	82.40	0	0	1	2
2002	27	21	7	287	49*	20.50	91.11	0	0	3	3
2003	6	5	2	71	33	23.67	102.90	0	0	0	0
Total	356	280	55	3717	86	16.52	88.44	0	6	28	88

* Not out

By Opponents

Against	M	Inn	NO	runs	HS	Ave	ScRt	100s	50s	0s	ct	st
Australia	49	45	5	806	86	20.15	89.86	0	1	4	8	0
Bangladesh	6	2	1	59	30*	59.00	78.67	0	0	0	1	0
England	32	25	4	222	34	10.57	77.89	0	0	3	6	0
India	48	38	8	425	50	14.17	91.79	0	1	1	14	0

Against	M	Inn	NO	runs	HS	Ave	ScRt	100s	50s	0s	ct	st
Kenya	2	0	0	0	dnb	-	-	0	0	0	0	0
Namibia	1	1	1	20	20*	-	142.86	0	0	0	0	0
Netherlands	2	1	0	1	1	1.00	25.00	0	0	0	0	0
New Zealand	38	30	7	459	66*	19.96	91.62	0	2	3	10	0
Scotland	1	1	1	37	37*	-	194.74	0	0	0	0	0
South Africa	24	22	5	345	57	20.29	79.31	0	1	1	1	0
Sri Lanka	59	46	8	674	79	17.74	102.90	0	1	5	18	0
United Arab Emirates	2	0	0	0	dnb	-	-	0	0	0	1	0
West Indies	64	51	9	498	43	11.86	73.78	0	0	9	18	0
Zimbabwe	28	18	6	171	38	14.25	95.00	0	0	2	11	0
Total	**356**	**280**	**55**	**3717**	**86**	**16.52**	**88.44**	**0**	**6**	**28**	**88**	**0**

* Not out

BOWLING

By Calendar Year

Year	M	balls	mdns	runs	wkts	best	5WM	Ave	SR	R/6bO
1984	1	24	0	31	0	0-31	0	-	-	7.75
1985	14	608	7	399	17	5-21	1	23.47	35.76	3.94
1986	17	768	22	392	23	4-19	0	17.04	33.39	3.06
1987	24	1350	18	891	31	3-25	0	28.74	43.55	3.96
1988	12	617	5	418	16	3-37	0	26.13	38.56	4.06
1989	18	852	7	571	30	5-38	1	19.03	28.40	4.02
1990	13	722	10	419	16	3-45	0	26.19	45.13	3.48
1991	8	411	5	309	10	3-27	0	30.90	41.10	4.51
1992	27	1461	17	930	43	5-19	1	21.63	33.98	3.82
1993	26	1372	13	850	45	5-15	2	18.89	30.49	3.72
1994	21	1160	18	682	31	4-23	0	22.00	37.42	3.53
1995	12	673	3	389	20	3-18	0	19.45	33.65	3.47
1996	26	1267	17	885	33	4-35	0	26.82	38.39	4.19
1997	19	969	13	593	26	4-25	0	22.81	37.27	3.67
1998	16	858	5	628	22	4-43	0	28.55	39.00	4.39
1999	27	1333	18	845	33	4-40	0	25.61	40.39	3.80
2000	30	1514	28	1055	36	3-10	0	29.31	42.06	4.18
2001	12	584	8	356	14	3-19	0	25.43	41.71	3.66
2002	27	1358	18	968	44	4-22	0	22.00	30.86	4.28
2003	6	285	4	201	12	5-28	1	16.75	23.75	4.23
Total	**356**	**18,186**	**236**	**11,812**	**502**	**5-15**	**6**	**23.53**	**36.23**	**3.90**

Modes of Dismissal

Against	M	balls	wkts	bowled	caught	ct wkt	ct field	c&b	hit wkt	LBW
Australia	49	2612	67	28	27	13	12	2	1	11
Bangladesh	6	258	9	3	5	1	4	0	0	1
England	32	1650	32	13	16	8	7	1	0	3
India	48	2425	60	19	27	8	18	1	1	13
Kenya	2	84	5	1	2	1	1	0	0	2
Namibia	1	54	5	0	1	1	0	0	0	4
Netherlands	2	111	3	1	1	1	0	0	0	1
New Zealand	38	1873	64	18	34	15	18	1	0	12
Scotland	1	47	3	3	0	0	0	0	0	0
South Africa	24	1341	35	14	14	5	8	1	0	7
Sri Lanka	59	3029	92	30	40	15	23	2	0	22
United Arab Emirates	2	102	5	3	2	0	2	0	0	0
West Indies	64	3304	89	32	44	14	27	3	1	12
Zimbabwe	28	1296	33	11	18	11	6	1	0	4
Total	**356**	**18,186**	**502**	**176**	**231**	**93**	**126**	**12**	**3**	**92**

Dismissals by Batting Position

Bat position	Op	#3	#4	#5	#6	#7	#8	#9	#10	#11	avPos
Number	173	56	40	34	44	28	49	33	26	19	4.73

Pakistan ODI Captains

Player	M	W	L	D	T	%W/P	%L/P	W:L	toss	%toss	span (d)
Imran Khan	139	75	59	4	1	53.96	42.45	1.27 :1	73	52.52	3540
Wasim Akram	**109**	**66**	**41**	**0**	**2**	**60.55**	**37.61**	**1.61 :1**	**59**	**54.13**	**2560**
Inzamam-ul-Haq	87	51	33	3	0	58.62	37.93	1.55 :1	49	56.32	1573
Misbah-ul-Haq	87	45	39	1	2	51.72	44.83	1.15 :1	37	42.53	2453
Javed Miandad	62	26	33	2	1	41.94	53.23	0.79 :1	29	46.77	4438
Waqar Younis	62	37	23	2	0	59.68	37.10	1.61 :1	33	53.23	3407
Sarfraz Ahmed	50	28	20	2	0	56.00	40.00	1.40 :1	20	40.00	1459

Comparative Statistics in ODIs

Batting summary	Inn	NO	Runs	Ave	HS	100s	50s
In matches at home	48	7	660	16.10	66*	0	2
In matches away	233	48	3057	16.52	86	0	4
Batting 1st	176	34	2374	16.72	86	0	5
Batting 2nd	105	21	1343	15.99	79	0	1

Batting summary	Inn	NO	Runs	Ave	HS	100s	50s
For a winning team	131	43	1830	20.80	52	0	2
For a losing team	140	11	1804	13.98	86	0	4
Drawn or no result	10	1	83	9.22	39*	0	0
Batting day time	250	48	3289	16.28	86	0	6
Batting at night	31	7	428	17.83	43*	0	0
Total	**281**	**55**	**3717**	**16.45**	**86**	**0**	**6**

Bowling summary	Balls	Md	RC	W	Ave	5I	best
In matches at home	3085	29	2241	72	31.13	1	5/15
In matches away	15101	207	9571	430	22.26	5	5/16
Bowling 1st	8694	104	5875	239	24.58	1	5/15
Bowling 2nd	9492	132	5937	263	22.57	5	5/16
For a winning team	9958	154	6149	326	18.86	6	5/15
For a losing team	7845	76	5417	165	32.83	0	4/25
Drawn or no result	383	6	246	11	22.36	0	3/38
Bowling day time	15,774	198	10,285	436	23.59	6	5/15
Bowling at night	2412	38	1527	66	23.14	0	4/25
Total	**18,186**	**236**	**11,812**	**502**	**23.53**	**6**	**5/15**

Best Bowling in an Innings

W	RC	v.	Season	Venue
5	15	Zim	1993-94	Karachi
5	16	RSA	1992-93	East London
5	19	NZ	1992-93	Wellington
5	21	Aus	1984-85	Melbourne
5	28	Nam	2002-03	Kimberley
5	38	WI	1989-90	Sharjah

Results With and Without Wasim Akram in ODIs

	M	W	L	D	T	%W/P	%L/P
Pak without Wasim Akram	122	65	54	3	0	53.28	44.26
With Wasim Akram	356	199	145	6	6	55.90	40.73

Wasim Akram List A Record – Season by Season

Batting

Season	M	Inns	NO	Runs	HS	Ave	100	50	Ct
1984-85	10	4	2	13	0	6.50	0	0	5
1985-86	22	11	3	134	25*	16.75	0	0	5
1986-87	20	13	3	117	48*	11.70	0	0	2
1987	4	3	0	25	13	8.33	0	0	0
1987-88	13	12	0	161	42	23.30	0	0	1
1988	14	12	2	191	29	19.10	0	0	3
1988-89	24	19	3	200	39	12.50	0	0	10
1989	24	21	5	430	56	26.87	0	2	5
1989-90	28	23	5	435	86	24.17	0	1	4
1990	21	14	3	241	50	21.90	0	1	3
1990-91	3	3	0	17	9	5.67	0	0	0
1991	24	19	7	290	45*	24.16	0	0	2
1991-92	25	21	5	182	33	11.38	0	0	6
1992	5	5	1	78	34	19.50	0	0	2
1992-93	31	26	3	385	64	16.74	0	1	6
1993	21	20	5	423	51*	28.20	0	1	4
1993-94	16	12	4	140	33	17.50	0	0	3
1994	16	11	1	146	50	14.60	0	1	2
1994-95	14	10	1	174	50	19.33	0	1	1
1995	24	17	3	248	64	17.71	0	1	6
1995-96	4	4	1	66	36*	22.00	0	0	5
1995-96	10	6	3	106	32*	35.33	0	0	6
1996	9	9	0	162	74	18.00	0	1	5
1996-97	35	32	4	404	66*	14.43	0	2	16
1997	6	5	1	113	52*	28.25	0	1	2
1997-98	16	14	3	213	57	19.36	0	1	3
1998	21	18	5	322	89*	24.76	0	2	7
1998-99	18	14	1	292	79	22.46	0	1	11
1999	12	9	2	148	43	21.14	0	0	6
1999-00	31	29	6	463	42*	20.13	0	0	8
2000	3	1	0	9	9	9.00	0	0	0
2000-01	12	8	0	86	34	10.75	0	0	1
2001	3	3	2	49	28*	49.00	0	0	1
2001-02	17	11	5	145	36*	24.17	0	0	2
2002	13	10	1	122	49*	13.56	0	0	2
2002-03	16	13	5	214	43*	26.75	0	0	2
2003	9	5	2	49	38	16.33	0	0	0
Total	**594**	**467**	**97**	**6993**	**89**	**18.90**	**0**	**17**	**147**

* Not out

Bowling

Season	Balls	Mdns	Runs	Wkts	BB	Ave	5wl	SRate	R/O
1984-85	459	5	275	12	5-21	22.92	1	38.25	3.59
1985-86	891	21	530	28	4-19	18.93	0	31.82	3.57
1986-87	1102	23	653	28	4-40	23.32	0	39.36	3.56
1987	244	5	145	5	2-18	29.00	0	48.80	3.56
1987-88	668	4	493	15	3-25	32.87	0	44.53	4.43
1988	697	6	438	21	4-27	20.85	0	33.19	3.77
1988-89	1247	11	814	38	4-25	21.42	0	32.82	3.92
1989	1179	20	758	43	5-27	17.63	1	27.42	3.86
1989-90	1355	17	827	41	5-38	20.17	1	33.05	3.66
1990	1016	3	727	35	4-19	20.77	0	29.02	4.29
1990-91	168	2	102	6	3-43	17.00	0	28.00	3.64
1991	1214	8	952	28	4-18	34.00	0	43.36	4.71
1991-92	1276	10	858	37	4-32	23.19	0	34.49	4.03
1992	310	3	214	6	2-34	35.66	0	51.66	4.14
1992-93	1659	24	1000	52	5-16	19.23	2	31.90	3.62
1993	996	13	618	36	5-10	17.16	1	27.66	3.72
1993-94	811	10	482	31	5-15	15.55	1	26.16	3.57
1994	810	10	548	28	5-41	19.57	1	28.93	4.06
1994-95	803	7	512	16	2-24	32.00	0	50.19	3.83
1995	1200	17	783	43	4-16	18.20	0	27.90	3.91
1995-96	667	10	365	31	5-16	11.77	2	21.52	3.28
1996	459	9	306	13	4-35	23.54	0	35.31	4.00
1996-97	1811	26	1129	42	4-25	26.88	0	43.12	3.74
1997	306	3	209	11	3-39	19.00	0	27.81	4.09
1997-98	810	6	599	23	4-33	26.04	0	35.22	4.44
1998	915	10	578	26	3-18	22.23	0	35.19	3.79
1998-99	837	5	599	15	3-11	39.93	0	55.80	4.29
1999	664	9	427	18	4-40	23.72	0	36.89	3.86
1999-00	1588	39	972	40	3-10	24.30	0	39.70	3.67
2000	120	0	81	4	2-38	20.25	0	30.00	4.05
2000-01	582	3	465	15	3-40	31.00	0	38.80	4.79
2001	144	2	103	0	-	-			4.29
2001-02	881	18	499	31	4-18	16.10	0	28.42	3.40
2002	641	8	487	22	3-18	22.14	0	29.14	4.56
2002-03	747	10	477	31	5-12	15.39	2	24.10	3.83
2003	442	10	278	10	3-17	27.80	0	44.20	3.77
Total	**29,719**	**387**	**19,303**	**881**	**5-10**	**21.91**	**12**	**33.73**	**3.90**

ACKNOWLEDGEMENTS

There's a reason that *Sultan* is appearing now, more than twenty years after my last Test, which is that I would never have got around to it on my own. The credit goes to my wife Shaniera, whose quiet but constant urging finally convinced me the time was ripe. Her energy and commitment is behind every page, as it has been behind everything else in our lives, including the making of three homes round the world. It was also Shaniera who first sought the help of Gideon Haigh, the ideal co-author, who made what could have been an ordeal into a pleasure.

I have been blessed in my children, Tahmoor, Akbar and Aiyla, who every day make me proud to be their father. I look back with a sense of good fortune on my own childhood, the example of my own late father Chaudhury, the devotion of my mother Begum, the companionship of my brothers Nadeem and Naeem, and my sister Sofia. It says much of our bond that, despite our scattering across the world, I love them still.

A man is lucky if he enjoys one good set of in-laws; I have been hugely fortunate to have two – firstly Huma's parents, Humayun and Katica Mufti; secondly Shaniera's parents, Tony and Greta Thompson. They welcomed me into their hearts and homes with unconditional love. Muhammad Abbas has for decades been an indispensable extension of my family also – trustworthy, tireless and kind. I appreciate this opportunity to express how deeply my boys and I are indebted to him.

My career owes everything to Pakistan's two greatest cricketers: Javed Miandad, who found me, and Imran Khan, who made me. Whatever I achieved is down to their inspiration, as mentors, leaders and teammates. It was an honour to play alongside them; all I really had to do to become a better cricketer was listen. For all our ups and downs along the way, I am proud to have shared a dressing room with Moin Khan, Waqar Younis, Ejaz Ahmed, Saqlain Mushtaq, Mushtaq Ahmed, Inzamam-ul-Haq, Saeed Anwar, Shahid Afridi and Shoaib Akhtar – legends of the game.

I am humbled by those rivals and colleagues who offered kind words for this book: Sachin Tendulkar, Anil Kumble, Ravi Shastri, Rahul David, Allan Border, Steve Waugh, Justin Langer, Mitchell Starc, Pat Cummins, Nasser Hussain, Viv Richards, Alan Wilkins, Mike Atherton, Neil Fairbrother and David Lloyd. Mike and Neil doubled as teammates at Lancashire, where I made other friends for life like Mike Watkinson, David Hughes, Ian Austin, Warren Hegg, Peter Martin, Glen Chapple, Gehan Mendis, Jack Simmons, Gary Yates, Andrew Flintoff, Graeme Fowler and Graham Lloyd.

Then there were those in England who made me feel right at home, notably Ahsan Chishty, Saj Shafiq and Maqsood Khan, my Birmingham A-Team, with whom I have shared so many laughs and memories. Thanks also to Naynesh Desai, Naeem Qayyum, and the Davis family, our beloved neighbours. They have helped me to go on cherishing the memory of Huma, while also appreciating my present good fortune.

When the going has got tough in Pakistan, I have always been able to depend on Arsalan Haider, Fareed Bajwa, Zahid Ibrahim and Ramzan Sheikh. In the US, nothing has ever been too much trouble for Nabil Ahmed.

Thank you to the team at Hardie Grant, notably Sandy Grant and Pam Brewster, for helping to turn our vision into a reality, as well as our invaluable partners at HarperCollins India, including Arcopol Chaudhuri.

My greatest thanks of all, of course, are to those fans whose love kept me going for decades, who refused to abandon me, and whose support I still feel. I hope they enjoy *Sultan*.

INDEX